Right Answers for Wrong Beliefs

*A Collection of Outlines,
Charts, Helps and Notes on a
Selection of Major Cults
and How to Witness to Them*

Matthew J. Slick M.Div

Sovereign World

Sovereign World Ltd
PO Box 777
Tonbridge
Kent
TN11 0ZS
England

ISBN 1 85240 279 2

The publishers aim to produce books which will help to extend and build up the Kingdom of God. We do not necessarily agree with every view expressed by the author, or with every interpretation of Scripture expressed. We expect each reader to make his/her judgement in the light of their own understanding of God's Word and in an attitude of Christian love and fellowship.

Typeset by CRB Associates, Reepham, Norfolk.
Printed in the United States of America

Contents

PART 4
Various Minor Cults and Groups

PART 5
Principles of Effective Evangelism and Witnessing to Cults

Introduction

Have you ever wanted a quick and easy resource of Christian doctrine, information, outlines, and documented refutations of various cults? Would you like to find a good source of information without having to read through pages and pages of material just to get some facts? If so, then *Right Answers for Wrong Beliefs* is for you. This is not a typical book. It is a collection of helps and tools on a variety of subjects related to Christian doctrine and cults. It is designed to make gathering information quick and easy.

Right Answers for Wrong Beliefs is meant to strengthen your faith as well as give you the tools you need to refute the error of the cults. As society becomes more and more liberal and pluralistic, and as cults increasingly make their way into mainstream society, being able to defend your faith is even more important.

This book begins with some basics of Christian doctrine – in outline form. This is so you can have a good foundation in the truth. Then it deals with the relationship between God and the human race as revealed in the examination of the Law and Gospel. What follows is an examination of major and minor cults. These groups are examined and their errors exposed by comparing their teachings to God's Word. Next is a section on evangelism so you can learn how to be more effective in presenting what you have learned. Finally, in the Appendix, is a dictionary of useful theological terms with quick and easy explanations.

In short, the book is a great reference that can help you know and defend your faith better. It is full of information waiting to be absorbed by a willing and able servant of God. May the Lord bless you as you read it.

Matthew J. Slick
www.carm.org

PART 1

*Essential Truths of
the Christian Faith and
the Nature of God*

The Bible – the Living Word of God

The Bible is the handbook of Christian life. It is 'the maker's instruction manual' containing vital information – without which it is impossible for a person to function properly. The Bible reveals the character and nature of God, and sets out His will and purposes for humankind. One of the most prevalent themes of the Bible is the revelation of Christ. Compared to other works of antiquity, such as Homer's *Iliad* for example, the manuscripts that form the basis of our modern Bibles are unsurpassed in their reliability and consistency. Christians also believe that the Bible is inspired Word of God and that all Scripture is inspired by the Holy Spirit.

It is because the Bible is so important and central to the Christian faith that its truths are so often subject to the attack of the enemy. One of Satan's key strategies is to lead people into error by spreading 'distortions' of the Bible's truths. These distortions take the form of what we refer to as 'cults.' A fuller definition will be given later in the book, but for now we can summarize by saying that cultic doctrine is a twisted version of truth. It contains enough of a fragment to entice people to believe in it. But teaching that strays from true biblical doctrine is no longer the truth, it is a lie.

Those who wish to deny the authenticity of the Bible tend to focus on so-called 'inconsistencies' in its text. However, research has shown that the Bible is eminently more reliable than the majority of historic documents passed down to us over the centuries – compared, say, to the writings of Plato or Aristotle.

I list below just a few facts about the Bible as a background to our study. Later we will look at the distinctives of some of the world's major cults. This first section, however, will focus on what the Bible has to say about some key areas of biblical truth, including the deity of Christ and the doctrine of the Trinity. I chose to focus on these aspects because they are issues of vital importance to true Christianity, and it is these doctrines which are most abused by the cults.

The authenticity of the Bible

The Bible consists of sixty-six books: thirty-nine in the Old Testament and twenty-seven in the New Testament, and it is estimated that it took some 1600 years to write. It was written in three languages (Hebrew, Aramaic, and Greek) by about forty authors and is internally consistent throughout. It was written on three continents – Africa, Asia, and Europe – by a variety of people: prophets, priests, cup-bearers, fishermen, etc.

The first English translation of the Bible was begun by John Wycliffe and completed by John Purvey in AD 1388. The first American edition of the Bible was published some time before AD 1752.

Reliability of the biblical documents

- The Bible is $98\frac{1}{2}$ per cent textually pure. This means that through all the copying of the manuscripts of the entire Bible throughout history, only $1\frac{1}{2}$ per cent has any question about it. Nothing in all of the ancient writings of the entire world even approaches the accuracy of transmission found in the biblical documents.

- The $1\frac{1}{2}$ per cent that is in question does not affect doctrine. These 'errors' are called 'variants' and consist mainly of variations of wording and spelling.

- The Old Testament does not have as many supporting manuscripts as the New Testament but it is, nevertheless, remarkably reliable.

- The Septuagint (known by the letters LXX), a Greek translation of the Hebrew Old Testament completed around 250 BC, attests to the reliability and consistency of the Old Testament when it is compared to existing Hebrew manuscripts.

- The Dead Sea Scrolls, discovered in 1947, also verify the reliability of the Old Testament manuscripts. These ancient documents, which were hidden in a cave in Israel about 2000 years ago, contained many Old Testament books, including Isaiah.

- Prior to the discovery of the Dead Sea Scrolls, the earliest existing manuscript of the Old Testament, called the Masoretic Text, was dated around 900 AD. The Old Testament documents found among the Scrolls originate a 1000 years earlier. A comparison between the manuscripts revealed an incredible accuracy of the copies, so much so that critics were silenced.

- The New Testament has over 5,000 supporting Greek manu-scripts existing today with another 20,000 manuscripts in other languages. Some of the manuscript evidence dates to within 100 years of the original writing. There is less than a 1 per cent textual variation in the New Testament manu-scripts.

Inspiration and inerrancy

The Bible is inspired by God. Inspiration means that God, through the Holy Spirit, caused the writers of the Bible to write the accurate and authoritative self-revelation of God. It is God breathed (2 Timothy 3:16) through the instrumentation of the apostles and prophets (2 Peter 1:21).

What the Bible is all about

The Bible is essentially about Jesus. In the Gospels Christ is the prophet to His people; in Acts and the Epistles He is the priest over His people; in the book of Revelation He is King of His people. In the New Testament Jesus often made mention of references to Himself in the Scriptures, and explained how His coming – the Word became flesh – was the fulfillment of God's Word.

> *'Do not think that I have come to abolish the Law or the Prophets; I have not come to abolish them but to fulfill them.'*
> (Matthew 5:17)

> *'And beginning with Moses and all the Prophets, he explained to them what was said in all the Scriptures concerning himself.'*
> (Luke 24:27)

> *'...Everything must be fulfilled that is written about Me in the Law of Moses, the Prophets and the Psalms.'*   (Luke 24:44)

> *'You search the Scriptures ... it is these that bear witness of Me.'*
> (John 5:39 NASB)

> *'Behold, I have come – In the volume of the book it is written of Me...'*   (Hebrews 10:7 NKJV)

Both the Old and the New Testaments speak of Jesus

Old Testament	New Testament
Anticipation of Jesus	Realization of Jesus
Pictures of Jesus	Person of Jesus is presented
Filled with typologies	Truth of Jesus is recorded
Jesus is coming	Jesus has arrived
Jesus is prophesied	Jesus is present
Jesus is concealed	Jesus is revealed

The New Testament revelation of Jesus can be viewed as follows:

- *The Gospels: the manifestation of Jesus*

Matthew	– King to the Jews. Jesus in His Lordship
Mark	– The Servant to the Romans. Jesus in His ministry
Luke	– The Perfect Man to the Greeks. Jesus in His perfect humanity, a servant
John	– The Son of God to the world. Jesus in His full deity
Acts	– The establishment of the church and evangelism by Christians

- *The Epistles: the interpretation and application of Jesus*

Romans	– Justification and redemption in Christ
1 Corinthians	– Sanctification in Christ
2 Corinthians	– Jubilation in Christ
Galatians	– Freedom in Christ
Ephesians	– Exaltation in Christ
Philippians	– Joy in Christ
Colossians	– Completion in Christ
1 Thessalonians	– Expectation in Christ
2 Thessalonians	– Glorification in Christ
1 Timothy	– Pastoral care in Christ
2 Timothy	– A soldier in Christ
Titus	– Sound doctrine in Christ
Philemon	– Mercy and forgiveness in Christ
Hebrews	– High Priest in Christ
James	– Doing right in Christ
1 Peter	– Holiness in Christ
2 Peter	– Our growth and hope in Christ

1, 2 & 3 John	– Our fellowship, our love, and our abiding in Christ
Jude	– Steadfastness in Christ
Revelation	– The Alpha and the Omega, the consummation of all things in Jesus Christ

Three essential doctrines of Christianity

The Bible itself reveals those doctrines that are essential to the Christian faith. They are:

1. the deity of Christ,

2. salvation by grace through faith alone, and

3. the resurrection of Christ.

These are key truths that are persistently abused and distorted by cults. Though there are many other important doctrines, these three are declared by Scripture to be essential to faith. The truly regenerate may be ignorant to some extent of one or more of them at the beginning of their new life in Christ, but will come to a proper understanding of these three issues as they study the Word of God. A non-regenerate person, or a cultist, will always deny the efficacy of one or more of these essentials. Below are the 'headlines' of the scriptures you should study regarding these three areas.

The deity of Christ

- **Jesus is God in flesh** (compare the 'I AM' statements of John 8:58 and Exodus 3:14). *See also* John 1:1, 14; 8:24; 10:30–33.

- **Jesus said 'I am.'** *'I said, therefore, to you that you will die in your sins. For if you do not believe that I am He, you will die in your sins'* (John 8:24). Those who do not believe that Jesus is 'I am' will die in their sins. (The Greek *ego eimi*, meaning 'I am', are the same words used in John 8:58 where Jesus says *'... before Abraham was, I am.'* He was claiming the divine title by quoting Exodus 3:14 in the Greek Septuagint.)

- *'This is how you can recognize the Spirit of God: Every spirit that acknowledges that Jesus Christ has come in the flesh is from God, but every spirit that does not acknowledge Jesus is not from God. This is the spirit of the antichrist, which you have heard is coming and even now is already in the world'* (1 John 4:2–3). This verse is saying that if you deny that Jesus is God in flesh then you are of the spirit of antichrist. The above verse needs to be cross-referenced with John 1:1, 14 (also written by John) where the apostle states that the Word was God and the Word became flesh.

- **Jesus is the proper object of faith**. It is not simply enough to have faith. You must put your faith in the proper object. Cults have false objects of faith; therefore, no matter how sincere they are, their faith is useless. If you put your faith in a vacuum cleaner, then you will be in a lot of trouble on the Day of Judgement! You might have great faith, but so what? The object of your faith is something that can't save you.

- **The doctrine of the deity of Christ includes**:

    (a) *The Trinity* – the biblical teaching that there is one God who exists in three persons: the Father, the Son, and the Holy Spirit. They are all co-eternal, and of the same nature.

    (b) *Monotheism* – the belief that there is only one God in all existence (Isaiah 43:10; 44:6, 8; 45:5).

    (c) *The Hypostatic Union* – the truth that Jesus is both God and man.

    (d) *The sufficiency of the sacrifice of Christ*. The sacrifice of Christ is completely sufficient to pay for the sins of the world:

    - **As God** – Jesus must be God to be able to offer a sacrifice of value greater than that of a mere man. He had to die for the sins of the world (1 John 2:2). Only God could do that.

    - **As man** – Jesus must be a man to be able to be a sacrifice for the human race. As a man He can be the mediator between God and human beings (1 Timothy 2:5).

Salvation by grace

Key scriptures:

- *'For it is by grace you have been saved, through faith – and this not from yourselves, it is the gift of God – not by works, so that no one can boast'* (Ephesians 2:8–9).

- *'You who are trying to be justified by law have been alienated from Christ; you have fallen away from grace'* (Galatians 5:4).
  - ▶ This verse and its context plainly teach that if you believe that you are saved by faith **and** works then you are not saved at all. (Read Romans 3–5 and Galatians 3–5.)
  - ▶ You cannot add to the work of God. Galatians 2:21 says, *'I do not set aside the grace of God, for if righteousness could be gained through the law, Christ died for nothing!'*

- *'Therefore no one will be declared righteous in his sight by observing the law; rather, through the law we become conscious of sin'* (Romans 3:20).

- *'However, to the man who does not work but trusts God who justifies the wicked, his faith is credited as righteousness'* (Romans 4:5).

- *'Is the law, therefore, opposed to the promises of God? Absolutely not! For if a law had been given that could impart life, then righteousness would certainly have come by the law'* (Galatians 3:21).

The resurrection of Christ

- *'And if Christ has not been raised, our preaching is useless and so is your faith.'* (1 Corinthians 15:14)

- *'And if Christ has not been raised, your faith is futile; you are still in your sins'* (1 Corinthians 15:17). To deny the physical resurrection is to deny Jesus' work, sacrifice, and our resurrection. These verses clearly state that if you say that Jesus did not rise from the dead (in the same body in which He died – John 2:19–21), then your faith is useless.

A comment on Galatians 1

'But even if we or an angel from heaven should preach a gospel other than the one we preached to you, let him be eternally

condemned! As we have already said, so now I say again: If anybody is preaching to you a gospel other than what you accepted, let him be eternally condemned!'   (Galatians 1:8–9)

These two verses in Galatians could be considered a fourth self-declarative statement of the essentials. But Galatians 1:8, 9 is simply stating the necessity of believing the gospel message which, in its entirety, is that Jesus is God in flesh, who died for our sins, rose from the dead, and freely gives the gift of eternal life to those who believe.

* 1 Corinthians 15:1–4 defines what the gospel is:

    'Now, brothers, I want to remind you of the gospel I preached to you, which you received and on which you have taken your stand. By this gospel you are saved, if you hold firmly to the word I preached to you. Otherwise, you have believed in vain. For what I received I passed on to you as of first importance: that Christ died for our sins according to the Scriptures, that he was buried, that he was raised on the third day according to the Scriptures . . . '

Jesus' two natures

Jesus is God in human flesh (John 1:1, 14; Colossians 2:9; Philippians 2:5–8). He is not half-God and half-man; He is fully God and fully man. At the incarnation He **added** to His divine nature the nature of man. Thus He has two natures: divine and human. He is both God and man at the same time. He is not merely a man who 'had God within him' nor is he a man who 'manifested the God principle'. He **is God**, the second person of the Trinity:

*'The Son is the radiance of God's glory and the **exact representation** of his being, sustaining all things by his powerful word.'*
(Hebrews 1:3)

Jesus' two natures are not 'mixed together', nor are they combined into a new God-man nature. They are separate yet act as a unit. This is called the **Hypostatic Union**.

The following chart should help you see the two natures of Jesus 'in action':

Jesus as God	Jesus as a man
He is worshiped (Matthew 2:2, 11; 14:33; 28:9).	He worshiped the Father (John 17).
He is prayed to (Acts 7:59).	He prayed to the Father (John 17:1).
He was called God (John 20:28; Hebrews 1:8).	He was called man (Mark 15:39; John 19:5).
He was called Son of God (Mark 1:1).	He was called Son of Man (John 9:35–37).
He is sinless (1 Peter 2:22; Hebrews 4:15).	He was tempted (Matthew 4:1).
He knew all things (John 21:17).	He grew in wisdom (Luke 2:52).
He gives eternal life (John 10:28).	He died (Romans 5:8).
The fullness of deity dwells in Him (Colossians 2:9).	He has a body of flesh and bones (Luke 24:39).

One of the most common errors that non-Christian cults make is not understanding the two natures of Christ. For example, the Jehovah's Witnesses focus on Jesus' humanity and ignore His divinity. The Christian Scientists, on the other hand, focus on the divine nature and ignore the human. For a proper understanding of Jesus and, therefore, all other doctrines that relate to Him, His two natures must be properly understood and defined.

The Bible is about Jesus (John 5:39). The prophets prophesied about Him (Acts 10:43). The Father bore witness of Him (John 5:37; 8:18). The Holy Spirit bore witness of Him (John 15:26). The works that Jesus did bore witness of Him (John 5:36; 10:25). The multitudes bore witness of Him (John 12:17). And Jesus bore witness of Himself (John 14:6; 18:6).

Other verses to consider when examining His deity are: John 1:1, 14; 5:18; 20:28; Romans 9:5; Philippians 2:5–8; Titus 2:13; Hebrews 1:6–8; and 2 Peter 1:1.

In 1 Timothy 2:5 we read,

> 'For there is one God, and one mediator also between God and men, the man Christ Jesus . . . '

Right now, there is a man in heaven on the throne of God. He is our advocate with the Father (1 John 2:1). He is our Savior (Titus 2:13). He is our Lord (Romans 10:9–10). He is Jesus.

Jesus is God

The following table illustrates that Jesus is a perfect reflection of the Father. Scripture points out to us that Jesus **is God** – as Colossians states, *'the exact representation'* (Hebrews 1:3).

Jesus	*Is*	*God ('Yahweh')*
'Through him all things were made; without him nothing was made that has been made.' (John 1:3) *'For by him all things were created: things in heaven and on earth, visible and invisible, whether thrones or powers or rulers or authorities; all things were created by him and for him. He is before all things, and in him all things hold together.'* (Colossians 1:16–17)	**Creator**	*'The Spirit of God has made me; the breath of the Almighty gives me life.'* (Job 33:4) *'Do you not know? Have you not heard? The Lord is the everlasting God, the Creator of the ends of the earth. He will not grow tired or weary, and his understanding no one can fathom.'* (Isaiah 40:28)
'When I saw him, I fell at his feet as though dead. Then he placed his right hand on me and said: "Do not be afraid. I am the First and the Last."' (Revelation 1:17) *'To the angel of the church in Smyrna write: These are the words of him who is the First and the Last, who died and came to life again.'* (Revelation 2:8) *'I am the Alpha and the Omega, the First and the Last, the Beginning and the End.'* (Revelation 22:13)	**First and Last**	*'Who has done this and carried it through, calling forth the generations from the beginning? I, the Lord – with the first of them and with the last – I am he.'* (Isaiah 41:4) *'This is what the Lord says – Israel's King and Redeemer, the Lord Almighty: I am the first and I am the last; apart from me there is no God.'* (Isaiah 44:6) *'Listen to me, O Jacob, Israel, whom I have called: I am he; I am the first and I am the last.'* (Isaiah 48:12)

Jesus	Is	God ('Yahweh')
'Therefore I said to you that you will die in your sins; for if you do not believe that I am He, you will die in your sins.' (John 8:24 NKJV) *'"I tell you the truth," Jesus answered, "before Abraham was born, I am!"'* (John 8:58) *'I am telling you now before it happens, so that when it does happen you will believe that I am He.'* (John 13:19)	**I AM** *ego* *eimi*	*'God said to Moses, "I AM WHO I AM. This is what you are to say to the Israelites: I AM has sent me to you."'* (Exodus 3:14) *'"You are my witnesses," declares the LORD, "and my servant whom I have chosen, so that you may know and believe me and understand that I am he. Before me no god was formed, nor will there be one after me."'* (Isaiah 43:10) *See also* Deuteronomy 32:39.
'In the presence of God and of Christ Jesus, who will judge the living and the dead, and in view of his appearing and his kingdom, I give you this charge . . . ' (2 Timothy 4:1) *'For we must all appear before the judgment seat of Christ, that each one may receive what is due him for the things done while in the body, whether good or bad.'* (2 Corinthians 5:10)	**Judge**	*'Let the nations be roused; let them advance into the Valley of Jehoshaphat, for there I will sit to judge all the nations on every side.'* (Joel 3:12) *'You, then, why do you judge your brother? Or why do you look down on your brother? For we will all stand before God's judgment seat.'* (Romans 14:10)
'. . . Where is the one who has been born king of the Jews? We saw his star in the east and have come to worship him.' (Matthew 2:2) *'So Pilate asked Jesus, "Are you the king of the Jews?" "Yes, it is as you say," Jesus replied.'* (Luke 23:3) *See also* John 19:21.	**King**	*'But the LORD is the true God; he is the living God, the eternal King. When he is angry, the earth trembles; the nations cannot endure his wrath.'* (Jeremiah 10:10) *'This is what the LORD says – Israel's King and Redeemer, the LORD Almighty: I am the first and I am the last; apart from me there is no God.'* (Isaiah 44:6) *See also* Psalm 47.

Jesus	*Is*	*God ('Yahweh')*
'When Jesus spoke again to the people, he said, "I am the light of the world. Whoever follows me will never walk in darkness, but will have the light of life."' (John 8:12) 'a light for revelation to the Gentiles and for glory to your people Israel.' (Luke 2:32) See also John 1:7–9.	**Light**	'The LORD is my light and my salvation – whom shall I fear?' (Psalm 27:1) 'Your sun will never set again, and your moon will wane no more; the LORD will be your everlasting light, and your days of sorrow will end.' (Isaiah 60:20) 'God is light; in him there is no darkness at all.' (1 John 1:5)
'. . . for they drank from the spiritual rock that accompanied them, and that rock was Christ.' (1 Corinthians 10:4) See also 1 Peter 2:6–8.	**Rock**	'He is the Rock, his works are perfect, and all his ways are just. A faithful God who does no wrong, upright and just is he.' (Deuteronomy 32:4) See also 2 Samuel 22:32 and Isaiah 17:10.
'They said to the woman, "We no longer believe just because of what you said; now we have heard for ourselves, and we know that this man really is the Savior of the world."' (John 4:42) 'And we have seen and testify that the Father has sent his Son to be the Savior of the world.' (1 John 4:14)	**Savior**	'For I am the LORD, your God, the Holy One of Israel, your Savior . . . ' (Isaiah 43:3) '. . . And there is no God apart from me, a righteous God and a Savior; there is none but me.' (Isaiah 45:21)
'I am the good shepherd. The good shepherd lays down his life for the sheep.' (John 10:11) 'May the God of peace, who through the blood of the eternal covenant brought back from the dead our Lord Jesus, that great Shepherd of the sheep . . . ' (Hebrews 13:20) See also John 10:14, 16; 1 Peter 2:25.	**Shepherd**	'A psalm of David. The LORD is my shepherd, I shall not be in want.' (Psalm 23:1) 'He tends his flock like a shepherd: He gathers the lambs in his arms and carries them close to his heart; he gently leads those that have young.' (Isaiah 40:11)

Prophecy, the Bible and Jesus

How do you respond to someone's claim that the Bible is not inspired? Is there a way to prove inspiration or, at least, intelligently present evidence for its inspiration? The answer is 'Yes!' One of the best ways to prove inspiration is by examining prophecy. There are many religious books in the world that have many good things to say, but only the Bible has fulfilled prophecies – with more fulfillments to come. The Bible has never been wrong in the past, and it won't be wrong in the future. It claims inspiration from God (2 Timothy 3:16). Since God is the creator of all things (Isaiah 44:24), then He is also the creator of time. It is under His control. Only God, then, would always be right about what is in the future, our future.

Fulfilled prophecy is strong evidence that God is the author of the Bible because when you look at the mathematical odds of prophecy being fulfilled, you quickly see a design, a purpose, and a guiding hand behind the Bible. If just one prophecy failed then we would know that God is not the true God, because the creator of all things, which includes time, would not be wrong about predicting the future. Deuteronomy 18:22 says,

> *'If what a prophet proclaims in the name of the* Lord *does not take place or come true, that is a message the* Lord *has not spoken. That prophet has spoken presumptuously.'*

Isaiah 46:9–10 says,

> *'Remember the former things, those of long ago; I am God, and there is no other; I am God, and there is none like me. I make known the end from the beginning, from ancient times, what is still to come. I say: My purpose will stand, and I will do all that I please.'*

One approach to use with an unbeliever is to turn to Psalm 22 and read verses 12–18. This is a detailed description of the crucifixion – one thousand years before Jesus was born. After you read the section ask the person what it was about. He or she will say, 'The crucifixion of Jesus,' at which point you can respond with something like, 'You're right. This is about the crucifixion. But it was written one thousand years before Jesus was born, and on top of that, crucifixion hadn't even been invented yet. How do you think something like this could happen?' After a brief discussion, you could point out a few other prophecies, such as the birthplace of Jesus being prophesied (Micah 5:2), that He would be born of a virgin (Isaiah 7:14), that His side would be pierced (Zechariah 12:10), etc.

Below is a chart of prophecies about Jesus, showing their fulfillment at a later date:

Prophecy	Fulfillment
Born of the seed of the woman	
'And I will put enmity between you and the woman, and between your seed and her Seed; He shall bruise your head, and you shall bruise His heel.' (Genesis 3:15 NKJV)	*'But while he thought about these things, behold, an angel of the Lord appeared to him in a dream, saying, "Joseph, son of David, do not be afraid to take to you Mary your wife: for that which is conceived in her is of the Holy Spirit."'* (Matthew 1:20 NKJV)
Born of a virgin	
'Therefore the Lord Himself will give you a sign: Behold, the virgin shall conceive, and bear a Son, and shall call his name Immanuel.' (Isaiah 7:14 NKJV)	*'Now the birth of Jesus Christ was as follows: After his mother Mary was betrothed to Joseph, before they came together, she was found with child of the Holy Spirit . . . and* [Joseph] *did not know her till she had brought forth her firstborn son: and he called His name Jesus.'* (Matthew 1:18, 25 NKJV)
Son of God	
'I will declare the decree: the Lord *has said to Me, "You* **are** *my Son, today I have begotten You."'* (Psalm 2:7 NKJV)	*'And suddenly a voice came from heaven, saying, "This is My beloved Son, in whom I am well pleased."'* (Matthew 3:17 NKJV)
Seed of Abraham	
'In your seed all the nations of the earth shall be blessed, because you have obeyed My voice.' (Genesis 22:18 NKJV)	*'The book of the genealogy of Jesus Christ, the son of David, the son of Abraham . . . '* (Matthew 1:1 NKJV)

Prophecy	Fulfillment

Son of Isaac

'But God said to Abraham, "Do not let it be displeasing in your sight because of the lad, or because of your bondwoman. Whatever Sarah has said to you, listen to her voice; for in Isaac your seed shall be called." ' (Genesis 21:12 NKJV)

'Now Jesus Himself began His ministry at about thirty years of age, being (as was supposed) the son of Joseph, *the son* of Heli ... *the son* of Jacob, *the son* of Isaac, *the son* of Abraham, *the son* of Terah, *the son* of Nachor... ' (Luke 3:23, 34 NKJV)

House of David

' "Behold, the days are coming," says the Lord, "that I will raise to David a Branch of righteousness, a King shall reign and prosper, and execute judgment and righteousness in the earth." '
(Jeremiah 23:5 NKJV)

'Now Jesus Himself began His ministry at about thirty years of age, being (as was supposed) the son of Joseph, *the son* of Heli ... *the son* of Melea, the son of Menan, *the son* of Mattathah, *the son* of Nathan, *the son* of David... '
(Luke 3:23, 31 NKJV)

Born at Bethlehem

'But you, Bethlehem Ephrathah, *though* you are little among the thousands of Judah, yet out of You shall come forth to Me the One to be ruler in Israel; whose goings forth *have been* from of old, from everlasting.' (Micah 5:2 NKJV)

'Now after Jesus was born in Bethlehem of Judea in the days of Herod the king, behold, wise men from the east came to Jerusalem... '
(Matthew 2:1 NKJV)

He shall be a Prophet

'[The Lord] will raise up for them a Prophet like you from among their brethren, and will put My words in His mouth; and He shall speak to them all that I command Him.'
(Deuteronomy 18:18 NKJV)

'So the multitudes said, "This is Jesus, the prophet from Nazareth of Galilee." ' (Matthew 21:11 NKJV)

He shall be a Priest

'The Lord has sworn, and will not relent, "You *are* a priest forever according to the order of Melchizedek." '
(Psalm 110:4 NKJV)

'Therefore, holy brethren, partakers of the heavenly calling, consider the Apostle and High Priest of our confession, Christ Jesus... '
(Hebrews 3:1 NKJV)

Prophecy	Fulfillment

He shall be a Priest (*cont.*)

	'So also Christ did not glorify Himself to become High Priest; but it was He who said to Him: "You are My Son, today I have begotten You." As He also says in another place: "You are a priest forever according to the order of Melchizedek."' (Hebrews 5:5–6 NKJV)

He shall be a King

'Yet I have set My King on My holy hill of Zion.' (Psalm 2:6 NKJV)	*'And they put up over his head the accusation written against Him: "THIS IS JESUS THE KING OF THE JEWS."'* (Matthew 27:37 NKJV)

He shall judge

'For the LORD is our Judge, the LORD is our Lawgiver, the LORD is our King; He will save us.' (Isaiah 33:22 NKJV)	*'I can of Myself do nothing. As I hear, I judge; and My judgment is righteous; because I do not seek My own will, but the will of the Father who sent Me.'* (John 5:30 NKJV)

He would be preceded by a messenger

'The voice of one crying in the wilderness: "Prepare the way of the LORD, make straight in the desert a highway for our God."' (Isaiah 40:3 NKJV)	*'In those days John the Baptist came, preaching in the wilderness of Judea, and saying, "Repent, for the kingdom of heaven is at hand."'* (Matthew 3:1–2 NKJV)

Crucifixion

*'To the Chief Musician.
Set to "The Deer of the Dawn."
A Psalm of David.*

1 *My God, My God, why have You forsaken Me?
Why are You so far from helping Me, and from the words of My groaning? . . .*

Prophecy	Fulfillment

Crucifixion (cont.)

11 *Be not far from Me; for trouble is near; for there is none to help.*
12 *Many bulls have surrounded Me; strong bulls of Bashan have encircled Me.*
13 *They gape at Me with their mouths, as a raging and roaring lion.*
14 *I am poured out like water, and all My bones are out of joint: My heart is like wax; it has melted within Me.*
15 *My strength is dried up like a potsherd; and My tongue clings to My jaws; You have brought Me to the dust of death.*
16 *For dogs have surrounded Me: the assembly of the wicked has enclosed Me: they pierced my hands and my feet;*
17 *I can count all My bones. They look and stare at me.*
18 *They divide My garments among them, and for My clothing they cast lots.'*
(Psalm 22:1, 11–18 NKJV)

'But when they came to Jesus, and saw that he was already dead, they did not break his legs.'
(John 19:33 NKJV)

'Then the soldiers, when they had crucified Jesus, took His garments, and made four parts, to each soldier a part; and also the tunic. Now the tunic was without seam, woven from the top in one piece. They said therefore among themselves, "Let us not tear it, but cast lots for it, whose it shall be," that the Scripture might be fulfilled, which says, "They divided My garments among them, and for my clothing they cast lots." Therefore the soldiers did these things.'
(John 19:23–24 NKJV)

'When they had come to the place called Calvary, there they crucified Him, and the criminals, one on the right hand, and the other on the left.'
(Luke 23:33 NKJV)

Rejected by His own people

'He is despised and rejected by men, a Man of sorrows, and acquainted with grief. And we hid, as it were, our faces from Him; He was despised, and we did not esteem Him.'
(Isaiah 53:3)

'For even His brothers did not believe in Him.'
(John 7:5 NKJV)

'Have any of the rulers or the Pharisees believed in Him?'
(John 7:48 NKJV)

Prophecy	Fulfillment
His side pierced	
'And I will pour out on the house of David and on the inhabitants of Jerusalem, the Spirit of grace and supplication; then they will look on Me whom they have pierced; they will mourn for Him, as one mourns for his only son, and grieve for Him as one grieves for a firstborn.' (Zechariah 12:10 NKJV)	*'But one of the soldiers pierced His side with a spear, and immediately blood and water came out.'* (John 19:34 NKJV)

The mathematical odds of Jesus fulfilling prophecy

The following probabilities are taken from Peter Stoner in *Science Speaks* (Moody Press, 1963) to show that coincidence is ruled out by the science of probability. Stoner says that by using the modern science of probability in reference to eight prophecies, 'we find that the chance that any man might have lived down to the present time and fulfilled all eight prophecies is 1 in 10^{17}.' That would be 1 in 100,000,000,000,000,000. In order to help us comprehend this staggering probability, Stoner illustrates it by supposing that 'we take 10^{17} silver dollars and lay them on the face of Texas. They will cover all of the state two feet deep. Now mark one of these silver dollars and stir the whole mass thoroughly, all over the state. Blindfold a man and tell him that he can travel as far as he wishes, but he must pick up one silver dollar and say that this is the right one. What chance would he have of getting the right one? Just the same chance that the prophets would have had of writing these eight prophecies and having them all come true in any one man.'

Stoner considers forty-eight prophecies and says,

'we find the chance that any one man fulfilled all 48 prophecies to be 1 in 10^{157}, or 1 in
100,000,000,000,000,000,000,000,000,000,000,000,000,
000,000,000,000,000,000,000,000,000,000,000,000,000,
000,000,000,000,000,000,000,000,000,000,000,000,000,
000,000, 000, 000,000,000,000,000,000,000,000.'

The estimated number of electrons in the universe is around 10^{79}. It should be quite evident that Jesus did not fulfill the prophecies by accident. This information was taken from the book *Evidence that Demands a Verdict* by Josh McDowell (publisher).

100 truths about Jesus

1. Jesus claimed to be God (John 8:24; 8:56–59 *see* Exodus 3:14; 10:30–33)
2. Jesus created all things (John 1:3; Colossians 1:15–17)
3. Jesus is before all things (Colossians 1:17)
4. Jesus is eternal (John 1:1, 14; 8:58)
5. Jesus is honored in the same way as the Father (John 5:23)
6. Jesus is prayed to (Acts 7:54–60)
7. Jesus is worshiped (Matthew 2:2, 8, 11; 14:33; 28:9, 17; John 9:35–37)
8. Jesus is called God (John 1:1, 14; 20:28; Colossians 2:9; Titus 2:13)
9. Jesus is omnipresent (Matthew 28:20)
10. Jesus is with us always (Matthew 28:20)
11. Jesus is our only mediator between God and ourselves (1 Timothy 2:5)
12. Jesus is the guarantee of a better covenant (Hebrews 7:22; 8:6)
13. Jesus said, *'I AM the Bread of Life'* (John 6:35, 41, 48, 51)
14. Jesus said, *'I AM the Door'* (John 10:7, 9)
15. Jesus said, *'I AM the Good Shepherd'* (John 10:11, 14)
16. Jesus said, *'I AM the Way, the Truth and the Life'* (John 14:6)
17. Jesus said, *'I AM the Light of the world'* (John 8:12; 9:5;12:46; Luke 2:32)
18. Jesus said, *'I AM the True Vine'* (John 15:1, 5)
19. Jesus said, *'I AM the Resurrection and the Life'* (John 11:25)
20. Jesus said, *'I AM the First and the Last'* (Revelation 1:17; 2:8; 22:13)
21. Jesus always lives to make intercession for us (Hebrews 7:25)
22. Jesus cleanses from sin (1 John 1:9)
23. Jesus discloses Himself to us (John 14:21)

24. Jesus draws all men to Himself (John 12:32)
25. Jesus forgives sins (Matthew 9:1–7; Luke 5:20; 7:48)
26. Jesus gives eternal life (John 10:28; 5:40)
27. Jesus gives joy (John 15:11)
28. Jesus gives peace (John 14:27)
29. Jesus has authority (Matthew 28:18; John 5:26–27; 17:2; 3:35)
30. Jesus judges (John 5:22, 27)
31. Jesus knows all men (John 16:30)
32. Jesus opens the mind to understand scripture (Luke 24:45)
33. Jesus received honor and glory from the Father (2 Peter 1:17)
34. Jesus resurrects (John 5:39; 11:25–26; 6:40, 44, 54)
35. Jesus reveals grace and truth (John 1:17 see John 6:45)
36. Jesus reveals the Father (Matthew 11:27; Luke 10:22)
37. Jesus saves forever (Matthew 18:11; John 10:28; Hebrews 7:25)
38. Jesus bears witness of Himself (John 8:18; 14:6)
39. Jesus' works bear witness of Himself (John 5:36; 10:25)
40. The Father bears witness of Jesus (John 5:37; 8:18; 1 John 5:9)
41. The Holy Spirit bears witness of Jesus (John 15:26)
42. The multitudes bear witness of Jesus (John 12:17)
43. The prophets bear witness of Jesus (Acts 10:43)
44. The Scriptures bear witness of Jesus (John 5:39)
45. The Father will honor us if we serve Jesus (John 12:26 *see* Colossians 3:24)
46. The Father wants us to fellowship with Jesus (1 Corinthians 1:9)
47. The Father tells us to listen to Jesus (Luke 9:35; Matthew 17:5)
48. The Father tells us to come to Jesus (John 6:45)
49. The Father draws us to Jesus (John 6:44)
50. Everyone who's heard and learned from the Father comes to Jesus (John 6:45)
51. The Law leads us to Christ (Galatians 3:24)
52. Jesus is the Rock (1 Corinthians 10:4)
53. Jesus is the Savior (John 4:42; 1 John 4:14)
54. Jesus is King (Matthew 2:1–6; Luke 23:3)

55. In Jesus are the treasures of wisdom and knowledge (Colossians 2:2–3)
56. In Jesus we have been made complete (Colossians 2:10)
57. Jesus indwells us (Colossians 1:27)
58. Jesus sanctifies (Hebrews 2:11)
59. Jesus loves (Ephesians 5:25)
60. We come to Jesus (John 5:40; 7:37; 6:35, 37, 45, 65)
61. We sin against Jesus (1 Corinthians 8:12)
62. We receive Jesus (John 1:12; Colossians 2:6)
63. Jesus makes many righteous (Romans 5:19)
64. Jesus is the image of the invisible God (Hebrews 1:3)
65. Jesus sends the Holy Spirit (John 15:26)
66. Jesus abides forever (Hebrews 7:24)
67. Jesus offered up Himself (Hebrews 7:27; 9:14)
68. Jesus offered one sacrifice for sins for all time (Hebrews 10:12)
69. The Son of God has given us understanding (1 John 5:20)
70. Jesus is the author and perfecter of our faith (Hebrews 12:2)
71. Jesus is the Apostle and High Priest of our confession (Hebrews 3:1)
72. Jesus is preparing a place for us in heaven (John 14:1–4)
73. Jesus cleanses us from our sins by His blood (Revelation 1:5; Romans 5:9)
74. Jesus is the Light of the world (John 9:5)
75. Jesus has made the Father known to us (John 1:18)
76. Jesus was crucified in weakness (2 Corinthians 13:4)
77. Jesus has overcome the world (John 16:33)
78. Truth is in Jesus (Ephesians 4:21)
79. The fruit of righteousness comes through Jesus Christ (Philippians 1:11)
80. Jesus delivers us from the wrath to come (1 Thessalonians 1:10)
81. Disciples bear witness of Jesus Christ (John 15:27)
82. Jesus died and rose again (1 Thessalonians 4:14)
83. The Christian dead have fallen asleep in Jesus (1 Thessalonians 4:15)
84. Jesus died for us (1 Thessalonians 5:10)
85. Jesus tasted death for everyone (Hebrews 2:9)
86. Jesus rendered the devil powerless (Hebrews 2:14)
87. Jesus is able to save completely (Hebrews 7:25)

88. Jesus came to be a ransom for many and to serve (Matthew 20:28)
89. Jesus came to be a high priest (Hebrews 2:17)
90. Jesus came to save (John 3:17; Luke 19:10)
91. Jesus came to preach the kingdom of God (Luke 4:43)
92. Jesus came to bring division (Luke 12:51)
93. Jesus came to do the will of the Father (John 6:38)
94. Jesus came to give the Father's words (John 17:8)
95. Jesus came to testify to the truth (John 18:37)
96. Jesus came to die and destroy Satan's power (Hebrews 2:14)
97. Jesus came to fulfill the Law and the Prophets (Matthew 5:17)
98. Jesus came to give life (John 10:10, 28)
99. Jesus came to taste death for everyone (Hebrews 2:9)
100. Jesus came to proclaim freedom for believers (Luke 4:18)

The Trinity

God is a trinity of persons: the Father, the Son, and the Holy Spirit. The Father is not the same person as the Son; the Son is not the same person as the Holy Spirit; and the Holy Spirit is not the same person as the Father. They are separate persons, yet they are all the one God. They are in absolute, perfect harmony consisting of one substance. They are co-eternal and co-powerful. If any one of the three were removed, there would be no God.

There is, though, an apparent separation of some functions among the members of the Godhead. For example, the Father chooses who will be saved (Ephesians 1:4), the Son redeems them (Ephesians 1:7), and the Holy Spirit seals them (Ephesians 1:13).

God is **not** one person known as the Father, with Jesus as a created being and the Holy Spirit as a force (which the Jehovah's Witnesses believe). Neither is He one person who took three consecutive forms – the Father became the Son, who became the Holy Spirit. Nor is God the divine nature of the Son – a belief that states Jesus had a human nature perceived as the Son, and a divine nature perceived as the Father (United Pentecostal). Nor is the Trinity an office held by three separate Gods (a Mormon doctrine). Three separate Gods would be a triad, not a trinity which is one God.

The chart below should help you to see how the doctrine of the Trinity is derived from Scripture. The list is not exhaustive, only illustrative.

The first step is to establish how many Gods exist: **One!**

'I am the LORD, *and there is no other; apart from me there is no God.'*
(Isaiah 45:5; *see also* Isaiah 43:10; 44:6; 45:14, 18, 21, 22; 46:5, 9)

	The Trinity		
	Father	*Son*	*Holy Spirit*
Called God	Philippians 1:2	John 1:1, 14; Colossians 2:9	Acts 5:3, 4
Creator	Isaiah 64:8; 44:24	John 1:3; Colossians 1:15–17	Job 33:4; 26:13
Resurrects	1 Thessalonians 1:10	John 2:19; 10:17	Romans 8:11
Indwells	2 Corinthians 6:16	Colossians 1:27	John 14:17
Everywhere	1 Kings 8:27	Matthew 28:20	Psalm 139:7–10
All knowing	1 John 3:20	John 16:30; 21:17	1 Corinthians 2:10–11
Sanctifies	1 Thessalonians 5:23	Hebrews 2:11	1 Peter 1:2
Life giver	Genesis 2:7; John 5:21	John 1:3; 5:21	2 Corinthians 3:6, 8
Fellowship	1 John 1:3	1 Corinthians 1:9	2 Corinthians 13:13; Philippians 2:1
Eternal	Psalm 90:2	Micah 5:2	Romans 8:11; Hebrews 9:14
A Will	Luke 22:42	Luke 22:42	1 Corinthians 12:11
Speaks	Matthew 3:17; Luke 9:35	Luke 5:20; 7:48	Acts 8:29; 11:12; 13:2
Loves	John 3:16	Ephesians 5:25	Romans 15:30
Searches the heart	Jeremiah 17:10	Revelation 2:23	1 Corinthians 2:10
We belong to	John 17:9	John 17:6	
Savior	1 Timothy 1:1; 2:3; 4:10	2 Timothy 1:10; Titus 1:4; 3:6	
We serve	Matthew 4:10	Colossians 3:24	
Believe in	John 14:1	John 14:1	
Gives joy		John 15:11	Romans 14:17
Judges	John 8:50	John 5:22, 30	

Another look at the Trinity

The Trinity can be a difficult concept to understand. Some think it is a logical contradiction while others call it a mystery. Does the Bible teach it? Yes, it does. But that doesn't automatically make it easier to comprehend.

The Trinity is defined as one God who exists in three eternal, simultaneous, and distinct persons known as the Father, the Son, and the Holy Spirit. Such a definition may suffice for some, but for others this explanation is insufficient.

Therefore, to help us understand the Trinity better, I offer the following analogy that, I think, is hinted at in Romans 1:20:

> 'For since the creation of the world His invisible qualities, His eternal power and divine nature, have been clearly seen, being understood through what has been made...'   (NASB)

Notice that this verse says God's attributes, power, and nature can be clearly seen in creation. What does that mean? Should we be able to learn about God's attributes, power, and nature by looking at what He has made? Apparently, according to the Bible, this is possible.

When a painter paints a picture, what is in him is reflected in the painting he produces. When a sculptor creates a work of art, it is in her heart and mind that the sculpture has its source. The work is shaped by her creative ability. The creators of art leave their marks, something that is their own, something that reflects who they are. Is this the same with God? Has God left His fingerprints on creation? Of course He has.

Creation

Basically, the universe consists of three elements: time, space, and matter. Each of these is comprised of three 'components'.

Time	Past	Present	Future
Space	Height	Width	Depth
Matter	Solid	Liquid	Gas

As the doctrine of the Trinity maintains, each of the persons of the Godhead is distinct, yet each is, by nature, God.

The same attribute is evident in time: the past is distinct from the present, which is distinct from the future. Each is simultaneous, yet they are not 'three times' but one – that is they all share the same nature: time.

With space, height is distinct from width, width is distinct from depth, and depth is distinct from height. Yet, they are not three 'spaces' but one – that is, they all share the same nature: space.

With matter, solid is not the same as liquid, liquid is not the same as gas, and gas is not the same as solid. Yet, they are not three 'matters' but one – that is, they all share the same nature: matter.

Note that there are three sets of threes. In other words, there is a trinity of trinities. As we look at the universe and notice these qualities within it, is it fair to say that these are the fingerprints of God upon His creation? I think so. Not only is this simply an observation, but it also provides a helpful analogy of the Trinity.

Some critics say that the doctrine of the Trinity is really teaching that there are three gods, not one. They say that the identification of God the Father, God the Son, and God the Holy Spirit means there are three gods – one plus one plus one equals three! [1] But this is not a logical necessity. Instead of adding, why not multiply? One times one times one equals one! Rather, the doctrine should stand or fall based upon biblical revelation, not human logic. Is the 'past' plus the 'present' plus the 'future' a total of three times? Not at all. It is simply a representation of three distinct aspects of the nature of time: past, present, and future. Likewise, the Father and the Son and Holy Spirit are not three **separate beings** or entities, but three **distinct persons** in the one nature of the Godhead.

Jesus is God

One more comment about Jesus. All cults deny that Jesus is God, the creator of the universe, in flesh. Various objections are raised saying that Jesus could not be God, otherwise He would be praying to Himself, etc. Let's work with this proposition and continue with 'time' as our illustration.

Let's stretch our thinking a little here and imagine that the dimension of time called 'present' could be embodied in human form. 'Present', then, would have two natures: time and human. If 'present' were truly human then he would be able to communicate with us, and we would be able to see and touch him. But, because he is also 'time' by nature, he would be able to tell us about aspects of time as he manifested the 'time' nature within him. If 'present' then communicated with the past and the future, it would not mean he was communicating with himself, but with the distinctions known as past and future.

I don't want to stretch such an analogy too far, but I think it helps us begin to understand this vital facet of God's nature as expressed by the Trinity.

Early Trinitarian quotes

There are cult groups (Jehovah's Witnesses, The Way International, Christadelphians, etc.) who deny the Trinity, stating that the doctrine was not mentioned until the fourth century, after the time of the Council of Nicea (325). This Council 'was called by Emperor Constantine to deal with the error of Aryanism which was threatening the unity of the Christian Church.'[2] However, the following quotes show that the doctrine of the Trinity was indeed alive-and-well before the Council of Nicea.

- **Polycarp** (70–c. 155/160 AD). Bishop of Smyrna; disciple of John the Apostle.

  'O Lord God almighty ... I bless you and glorify you through the eternal and heavenly high priest Jesus Christ, your beloved Son, through whom be glory to you, with Him and the Holy Spirit, both now and forever.'

  (n. 14, ed. Funk; P.G. 5.1040)

- **Justin Martyr** (c. 100–c. 165 AD). Christian apologist and martyr.

  'For, in the name of God, the Father and Lord of the universe, and of our Savior Jesus Christ, and of the Holy Spirit, they then receive the washing with water.'

  (First Apol., LXI)

- **Ignatius of Antioch** (d. *c.* 98/117 AD). Bishop of Antioch. He wrote much in defense of Christianity.

  'In Christ Jesus our Lord, by whom and with whom be glory and power to the Father with the Holy Spirit for ever.'

  (n. 7; P.G. 5.988)

  'We have also as a Physician the Lord our God Jesus the Christ the only-begotten Son and Word, before time began, but who afterwards became also man, of Mary the virgin. For "the Word was made flesh." Being incorporeal, He was in the body; being impassible, He was in a passable body; being immortal, He was in a mortal body; being life, He became subject to corruption, that He might free our souls from death and corruption, and heal them, and might restore them to health, when they were diseased with ungodliness and wicked lusts.'

  (Alexander Roberts and James Donaldson (eds.),
  The Ante-Nicene Fathers, Grand Rapids: Eerdmans,
  1975 reprinted, vol. 1, p. 52, Ephesians 7)

- **Irenaeus** (115–190 AD). As a boy he listened to Polycarp, the disciple of John; he became Bishop of Lyons.

  'The Church, though dispersed throughout the whole world, even to the ends of the earth, has received from the apostles and their disciples this faith: ... one God, the Father Almighty, Maker of heaven, and earth, and the sea, and all things that are in them; and in one Christ Jesus, the Son of God, who became incarnate for our salvation; and in the Holy Spirit, who proclaimed through the prophets the dispensations of God, and the advents, and the birth from a virgin, and the passion, and the resurrection from the dead, and the ascension into heaven in the flesh of the beloved Christ Jesus, our Lord, and His manifestation from heaven in the glory of the Father "to gather all things in one," and to raise up anew all flesh of the whole human race, in order that to Christ Jesus, our Lord, and God, and Savior, and King, according to the will of the invisible Father, "every knee should bow, of things in heaven, and things in earth, and things under the earth, and that every tongue should confess; to him, and that He should execute just judgment towards all..."'

  (Against Heresies X.l)

- **Tertullian:** (160–215 AD). African apologist and theologian. He wrote much in defense of Christianity.

  'We define that there are two, the Father and the Son, and three with the Holy Spirit, and this number is made by the pattern of salvation ... [which] brings about unity in trinity, interrelating the three, the Father, the Son, and the Holy Spirit. They are three, not in dignity, but in degree, not in substance but in form, not in power but in kind. They are of one substance and power, because there is one God from whom these degrees, forms and kinds devolve in the name of Father, Son and Holy Spirit.'   (Adv. Prax. 23; PL 2.156–7)

- **Origen:** (185–254 AD). Alexandrian theologian. Defended Christianity and wrote much about the faith.

  'If anyone would say that the Word of God or the Wisdom of God had a beginning, let him beware lest he direct his impiety rather against the unbegotten Father, since he denies that he was always Father, and that he has always begotten the Word, and that he always had wisdom in all previous times or ages or whatever can be imagined in priority ... There can be no more ancient title of almighty God than that of Father, and it is through the Son that he is Father.'   (*De Principiis*, 1.2.; P.G. 11.132)

  'For if [the Holy Spirit were not eternally as He is, and had received knowledge at some time and then became the Holy Spirit] this were the case, the Holy Spirit would never be reckoned in the unity of the Trinity, i.e., along with the unchangeable Father and His Son, unless He had always been the Holy Spirit.'
  (Alexander Roberts and James Donaldson (eds.),
  The Ante-Nicene Fathers, Grand Rapids: Eerdmans,
  1975 reprinted., vol. 4, p. 253, *De Principiis*, 1.111.4)

  'Moreover, nothing in the Trinity can be called greater or less, since the fountain of divinity alone contains all things by His word and reason, and by the Spirit of His mouth sanctifies all things which are worthy of sanctification ... '
  (Roberts and Donaldson, *Ante-Nicene Fathers*,
  vol. 4, p. 255, *De Principiis*, I. iii. 7)

If, as the anti-Trinitarians maintain, the Trinity is not a biblical doctrine and was never taught until the council of Nicea in 325, then why do these quotes exist? The answer is simple: the Trinity **is** a biblical doctrine and it **was** taught before the council of Nicea in 325 AD.

Part of the reason that the Trinity doctrine was not 'officially' taught until the time of the Council of Nicea is because Christianity was illegal until shortly before the Council. It wasn't really possible for official Christian groups to meet and discuss doctrine. For the most part, they were fearful of making public pronouncements concerning their faith.

In addition, official doctrines were formulated as a response to pressure from outside. If, for instance, a group had attacked the person of Adam, the early Church would have responded with an official doctrine of who Adam was. As it was, the person of Christ was attacked, and so in defending the deity of Christ, the doctrine of the Trinity was further defined.

The early Church believed in the Trinity, as is evidenced by the quotes above, and had no need to formulate official doctrines. It wasn't until errors started to creep in that it became necessary to meet in councils to discuss the Trinity as well as other doctrines that came under fire.

Who is God?

God does not seek to shroud His being in mystery. He wants us all to know who He is and what He is like. He has communicated what we need to know in His Word. Here is a list of scriptures dealing with God's nature, attributes, and character.

1. God is One (Deuteronomy 6:4; 1 Corinthians 8:4)
2. God is Truth (Psalm 117:2; Jeremiah 10:10)
3. God is Light (1 John 1:5)
4. God is Love (1 John 4:8, 16; John 3:16)
5. God is infinite (Jeremiah 23:24; Psalm 147:5)
6. God is all knowing (1 John 3:20)
7. God is everywhere (Psalm 139:7–12)
8. God is all powerful (Jeremiah 32:17, 27)
9. God is unequaled (Isaiah 40:13–25)
10. God is perfect (1 Kings 8:27; Psalm 139)
11. God is Spirit (John 4:24)
12. God is invisible (1 Timothy 1:17)
13. God does not have a human body (Luke 24:39; Deuteronomy 4:15, 16)
14. God does not change (Numbers 23:19; Malachi 3:6; James 1:17)
15. God is without limit (1 Kings 8:27; Jeremiah 23:23, 24)
16. God is eternal (Psalm 90:2; 1 Timothy 1:17)
17. God is incomprehensible (Romans 11:33; Psalm 145:3)
18. God is the Almighty One (Revelation 1:8, 4:8)
19. God is most wise (Romans 16:27; Jude 25)
20. God is most holy (Isaiah 6:3; Revelation 4:8)
21. God is most free (Psalm 115:3)
22. God is most absolute (Isaiah 44:6; Acts 17:24, 25)
23. God works according to His will (Ephesians 1:11; Romans 8:28)
24. God receives glory (Romans 11:36; Revelation 4:11)
25. God is most loving (1 John 4:8, 10)
26. God is gracious (Exodus 33:19; 1 Peter 2:3)
27. God is merciful (Exodus 34:6; Deuteronomy 4:31; Psalm 67:1; James 5:11)
28. God is longsuffering (Psalm 86:15; 2 Peter 3:15)
29. God abounds in goodness (Psalm 31:19; 52:1; Romans 11:22)
30. God is forgiving (Daniel 9:9; Ephesians 1:7; Psalm 86:5)

31. God rewards those who seek Him (Hebrews 11:6)
32. God is just in all His judgements (Nehemiah 9:32, 33; 2 Thessalonians 1:6)
33. God hates sin (Psalm 5:5, 6; Habakkuk 1:13)
34. God is the Creator (Isaiah 40:12, 22, 26)
35. God is Shepherd (Genesis 49:24)
36. God is Lord (YHWH) (Joshua 22:34; 1 Kings 8:60; 20:28)
37. God cannot lie (Numbers 23:19; Titus 1:2)
38. God is the Judge (Psalm 35:24; 50:6; 75:7)
39. God is righteous (Psalm 7:9; 116:5; Daniel 9:14; Lamentations 1:18; Revelation 16:7)
40. God is in heaven (Deuteronomy 3:24)
41. God is a consuming fire (Deuteronomy 4:24)
42. God is a jealous God (Deuteronomy 6:15)
43. God is your refuge (Deuteronomy 33:27)
44. God is great (Job 36:26)

PART 2

God's Relationship with Us – Law and Covenant

Law and Gospel

The Law sets out the dos and don'ts of moral behavior. God gave the Law so that people would have a guide to live by and a standard by which they might recognize God's purity and their own sinfulness. In the Old Testament there are 613 commandments governing moral, judicial, and religious behavior.

The Law is a reflection of the character of God because it comes out of the very heart of God. The Bible says that *'out of the abundance of the heart the mouth speaks'* (Matthew 12:34 NKJV). When God gave the Law, He was speaking out of the abundance of His heart. He was speaking from what was in Him. Therefore, the Law is good, pure, right, and holy. It is wrong to lie, because it is against God's nature to lie. It is wrong to steal, because it is against God's nature to steal.

This Law, then, by its very nature of coming out of the heart of God and being spoken to human beings, is a standard for human conduct – a perfect standard. However, because it was perfect and we are not, it was an impossible standard for sinful people to keep. For this reason the Law became a stumbling block. It became an obstacle to men and women because it is an unattainable perfect standard. The Law, then, brings about the opposite of what it demands. The Law says, 'Be perfect,' but shows you where you are not. It requires you to be holy, but condemns you when you are not. Since we can never 'earn' a position with God – because there simply isn't any way for us to attain to the standard of God – we need the holiness of God to be given to us. Therefore, *'... the law was put in charge to lead us to Christ that we might be justified by faith'* (Galatians 3:24) – that is, the Law shows us that we can't get to God by what we do. We need the grace of God in Christ Jesus manifested in His sacrifice.

The Law reveals our sinfulness

'Therefore no one will be declared righteous in his sight by observing the law; rather, through the law we become conscious of sin.'
(Romans 3:20)

'What shall we say, then? Is the law sin? Certainly not! Indeed I would not have known what sin was except through the law. For I

would not have known what it was to covet if the law had not said, "Do not covet."'   (Romans 7:7)

The Law is for those who are not under grace

'Now we know that whatever the law says, it says to those who are under the law, so that every mouth may be silenced and the whole world held accountable to God.'   (Romans 3:19)

'For sin shall not be your master, because you are not under law, but under grace.'   (Romans 6:14)

No one is justified by the Law

'Therefore no one will be declared righteous in his sight by observing the law.'   (Romans 3:20)

The Law makes no concessions; it makes demands

'Cursed is every man who does not continue to do everything written in the Book of the Law.'   (Galatians 3:10)

The Law is spiritual: it works on the Spirit, not on the body

'For we know that the law is spiritual; but I am unspiritual, sold as a slave to sin.'   (Romans 7:14)

'Thou shalt not . . . ' applies to the heart, not the body.

We are made righteous in God's eyes by grace apart from the Law of God

'For we maintain that a man is justified by faith apart from observing the law.'   (Romans 3:28)

'Therefore, since we have been justified through faith, we have peace with God through our Lord Jesus Christ.'   (Romans 5:1)

'[We] know that a man is not justified by observing the law, but by faith in Jesus Christ. So we, too, have put our faith in Christ Jesus

that we may be justified by faith in Christ and not by observing the law, because by observing the law no one will be justified.'

(Galatians 2:16)

The Law brings judgement

'...because law brings wrath.' (Romans 4:15)

The Law prepares us for the gospel

The Law shows us that the free gift of the gospel is the only way to attain righteousness.

'...the law was put in charge to lead us to Christ that we might be justified by faith.' (Galatians 3:24)

The concept of being saved by grace through faith (Ephesians 2:8) is only found in the Christian religion. Only Christianity has the message of free, unearned grace.

The Law is for the ungodly

'But we know that the Law is good, if one uses it lawfully, realizing the fact that law is not made for a righteous man, but for those who are lawless and rebellious, for the ungodly and sinners, for the unholy and profane, for those who kill their fathers or mothers, for murderers and immoral men and homosexuals and kidnappers and liars and perjurers, and whatever else is contrary to sound teaching, according to the glorious gospel of the blessed God.'

(1 Timothy 1:8–11 NASB)

The Law differs from the gospel in:

The manner of revelation
* The Law is revealed in the hearts of men and women.

    'For when Gentiles who do not have the Law do instinctively the things of the Law, these, not having the Law, are a law to themselves, in that they show the work of the Law written in their hearts...' (Romans 2:14–15 NASB)

- If the Law had not been written on the hearts of human beings, it would be impossible to convert anyone because the Law reveals sin (Romans 3:20).

- The gospel is given by direct revelation; it is not written on the heart.

    'Now, brothers, I want to remind you of the gospel I preached to you, which you received and on which you have taken your stand.'   (1 Corinthians 15:1 NIV)

Content

- The Law tells people what they are to do (our works). It makes demands (Deuteronomy 27:26).

- The gospel reveals what God is doing (God's work). Therefore, it makes no demands on us except faith (Romans 6:23).

- The Law is a list of dos and don'ts (Exodus 20).

- The gospel is the death, burial, and resurrection of Jesus for sins (1 Corinthians 15:1–4). It contains grace and truth (John 1:17) because the gospel is about Jesus.

Promises

- The Law and the gospel both promise eternal life.

- The Law promises eternal life by complete obedience to all its commands (Leviticus 18:5; Luke 10:26).

- The gospel promises eternal life by grace unconditionally (Romans 3:22–24; Ephesians 2:8–9). It demands nothing, makes no threats. It removes from sinners the desire to sin.

Effects of preaching the Law

- The Law tells us what to do, but does not enable us to do it. This can frustrate us because we cannot keep it!

- Although the Law reveals their sins to human beings it offers them no way out. It hurls them into despair.

    '. . . I would not have known what sin was except through the law. For I would not have known what it was to covet if the law had not said, "Do not covet."'   (Romans 7:7)

- It makes us aware of damnation, hell, and hopelessness.

   'But your iniquities have separated you from your God; and your sins have hidden his face from you, so that He will not hear.'
   (Isaiah 59:2 NKJV)

   'Christ redeemed us from the curse of the law by becoming a curse for us, for it is written: "Cursed is everyone who is hung on a tree."'
   (Galatians 3:13)

Effects of preaching the gospel

- It demands faith **and** gives it to us.

   'Faith comes by hearing and hearing by the word of God.'
   (Romans 10:17 NKJV)

- It does not reprove the sinner.

   'Therefore, there is now no condemnation for those who are in Christ Jesus ... '
   (Romans 8:1)

- It does not require a man or a woman to do anything good – either in heart, mind or body – because it is a free gift.

   'For the wages of sin is death, but the gift of God is eternal life in Christ Jesus our Lord.'
   (Romans 6:23)

Those to whom the Law and the Gospel are preached

- The Law is preached to sinners, those secure in their sin.

   'But we know that the Law is good, if one uses it lawfully, realizing the fact that law is not made for a righteous man, but for those who are lawless and rebellious, for the ungodly and sinners, for the unholy and profane, for those who kill their fathers or mothers, for murderers and immoral men and homosexuals and kidnappers and liars and perjurers, and whatever else is contrary to sound teaching.'   (1 Timothy 1:8–10 NASB)

- The gospel is preached to those who are alarmed, frightened, smitten by the law; to those who are made thirsty for the gospel message.

'. . . through the law we become conscious of sin.'

(Romans 3:20)

'So the law was put in charge to lead us to Christ that we might be justified by faith.'   (Galatians 3:24)

Covenant

A covenant is a contract or agreement between two or more parties. Covenant is how God has chosen to communicate to us, to redeem us, and to guarantee us eternal life in Jesus. These truths, revealed in the Bible, are the basis of Christianity. The Bible is a covenant document. The Old and New Testaments are really Old and New Covenants. The word 'testament' is Latin for 'covenant'.

There is a pattern to the covenants found in the Bible. Basically, it is as follows: the initiating party describes himself and what he has done; then there is a list of obligations between the two (or more) parties, followed by a description of the rewards and punishments that govern the keeping and breaking of the covenant. The Ten Commandments fit this pattern and are a covenant document.[3] 'Covenant' is the method that God has chosen for His dealings with humankind.

Hebrews 13:20 tells us of the Eternal Covenant, forged before the creation of the universe between the Father and Jesus, the Son:

'May the God of peace, who through the blood of the eternal covenant brought back from the dead our Lord Jesus, that great Shepherd of the sheep . . .'   (Hebrews 13:20)

In this covenant God the Father and the Son make an agreement with regard to the elect, in which the Father promises to bring to the Son all whom the Father has given Him (John 6:39; 17:9, 24).[4] The Son would later become a man (Colossians 2:9; 1 Timothy 2:5), become for a while lower than the angels (Hebrews 2:7), and be found under the Law (Galatians 4:4–5). The Son would die for the sins of the world (1 John 2:2; 1 Peter 2:24) and the Father would raise the Son from the dead (Psalm 2).

The Eternal Covenant then leads to the Covenant of Grace. Whereas the Eternal Covenant was made between the Father and the Son, the Covenant of Grace is made between God and the human race. In this latter covenant God promises eternal salvation based upon the sacrifice of Jesus on the cross. The manifestation of that covenant occurs in our world in a sequence of additional covenants that God made with individuals: Adam (Genesis 2:15–17), Noah (Genesis 9:12–16), Abraham (Genesis 17), the Israelites at Mount Sinai (Exodus 34:28), David (2 Samuel 7:12–16), believers in the New Covenant (Jeremiah 31:31–37), etc. I present the view that there are two main covenants. However, there is disagreement as to the number of covenants. Some say there is really only one, the Eternal Covenant, with all others falling under it. Some say two, some say three, and others four, etc. There really is no absolute answer.

Understanding covenant is important for several reasons:

- We learn that God deals with men and women covenantally.

- Since a covenant is an agreement, it is a promise made by God. By virtue of the fact that we can rely on God's word for eternity, we can take great comfort in His covenant promising us eternal life in His Son.

- It helps us to see the Bible as a covenant document. The Old and New Testaments are Old and New Covenants.

- Knowing that 'covenant' was the framework through which the Bible was written, we can better understand it, God's dealings with us through it, and our responsibilities to God as well as His to us.

- We can better understand the symbols used by God in covenant ratification: the Lord's Supper and Baptism, for example.

Requirements and promises in the Eternal Covenant

1. The Father required of the Son that He should atone for the sins of those whom the Father had given Him (1 John 2:2; John 6:39; 10:11, 15), and should do what Adam failed to do by keeping the Law (Galatians 4:4–5; 1 Peter 2:22).

2. This requirement included the following particulars:
   (a) that He should assume human nature (John 1:1, 14; Colossians 2:9);

(b) that He should place Himself under the Law (Galatians 4:4–5);

(c) that, after accomplishing forgiveness of sins and eternal life, He should apply them to the elect (Romans 5:18; 1 Corinthians 15:22; 2 Corinthians 5:14).

The relation of the Eternal Covenant and the Covenant of Grace

The Eternal Covenant is the model for the Covenant of Grace. The former is eternal, that is, from eternity, and the latter temporal in the sense that it is realized in time. The former is a contract between the Father and the Son as a surety and head of the elect, while the latter is a contract between the triune God and the elect sinner.

• Without the Eternal Covenant between the Father and the Son there could be no Covenant of Grace between God and sinful human beings.

• The Holy Spirit, who produces faith in the sinner, was promised to Christ by the Father, and the acceptance of the way of life through faith was guaranteed by Christ.

The Covenant with Adam

(Also known as the Covenant of Works)

1. This was a covenant made between God and Adam in which Adam would have everlasting life based upon obedience to God. This apparently was possible since Adam did not have a sin nature.

   *'And the L*ord* God commanded the man, "You are free to eat from any tree in the garden; but you must not eat from the tree of the knowledge of good and evil, for when you eat of it you will surely die."'*   (Genesis 2:16–17 NIV)

2. God entered into a covenant with Adam.
   The promise connected to that covenant was life. The condition was perfect obedience. Its penalty was death.

The Covenant with Noah

This covenant was God's promise to Noah never again to destroy the world with a flood. God gave the rainbow as a sign.

> ' "I now establish my covenant with you and with your descendants after you and with every living creature that was with you – the birds, the livestock and all the wild animals, all those that came out of the ark with you – every living creature on earth. I establish my covenant with you: Never again will all life be cut off by the waters of a flood; never again will there be a flood to destroy the earth." And God said, "This is the sign of the covenant I am making between me and you and every living creature with you, a covenant for all generations to come: I have set my rainbow in the clouds, and it will be the sign of the covenant between me and the earth. Whenever I bring clouds over the earth and the rainbow appears in the clouds, I will remember my covenant between me and you and all living creatures of every kind. Never again will the waters become a flood to destroy all life. Whenever the rainbow appears in the clouds, I will see it and remember the everlasting covenant between God and all living creatures of every kind on the earth." So God said to Noah, "This is the sign of the covenant I have established between me and all life on the earth." '
>
> (Genesis 9:9–17 NIV)

The Covenant with Abraham

God promised a land and descendants to Abraham, who was commanded to 'keep' the covenant (Genesis 17:9f., 14) and was given circumcision as the sign (Genesis 15:8–18; 17:1–14).

> 'On that day the Lᴏʀᴅ made a covenant with Abram and said, "To your descendants I give this land, from the river of Egypt to the great river, the Euphrates . . . " '
>
> (Genesis 15:18)

The Covenant with Moses

In the giving of the Law, the nation of Israel was constituted a holy nation and given stipulations to follow to ensure fellowship with God. The covenant was ratified by a covenant sacrifice and the sprinkling of blood:

'Moses then wrote down everything the Lord *had said. He got up early the next morning and built an altar at the foot of the mountain and set up twelve stone pillars representing the twelve tribes of Israel. Then he sent young Israelite men, and they offered burnt offerings and sacrificed young bulls as fellowship offerings to the* Lord*. Moses took half of the blood and put it in bowls, and the other half he sprinkled on the altar. Then he took the Book of the Covenant and read it to the people. They responded, "We will do everything the* Lord *has said; we will obey." Moses then took the blood, sprinkled it on the people and said, "This is the blood of the covenant that the* Lord *has made with you in accordance with all these words."'*   (Exodus 24:4–8)

The Covenant with David

God gave a promise to David that his descendants would have an everlasting kingdom and be known as his sons.

'You said, "I have made a covenant with my chosen one, I have sworn to David my servant, I will establish your line for ever and make your throne firm through all generations."'   (Psalm 89:3)

It was through the descendants of David that Jesus was born.

The New Covenant

1. This is the New Covenant of the Messianic age in which the Law of God would be written upon the hearts of men and women.

    '"The time is coming," declares the Lord*, "when I will make a new covenant with the house of Israel and with the house of Judah ... This is the covenant I will make with the house of Israel after that time," declares the* Lord*. "I will put my law in their minds and write it on their hearts. I will be their God, and they will be my people."'*   (Jeremiah 31:31, 33 NIV)

2. It was promised in Eden.

    'And I will put enmity between you and the woman, and between your offspring and hers; he will crush your head, and you will strike his heel.'   (Genesis 3:15 NIV)

3.   It was proclaimed to Abraham.

'I will bless those who bless you, and whoever curses you I will curse; and all peoples on earth will be blessed through you.'

(Genesis 12:3 NIV)

4.   It was fulfilled in Christ.

'Praise be to the Lord, the God of Israel, because he has come and has redeemed his people. He has raised up a horn of salvation for us in the house of his servant David (as he said through his holy prophets of long ago), salvation from our enemies and from the hand of all who hate us – to show mercy to our fathers and to remember his holy covenant, the oath he swore to our father Abraham: to rescue us from the hand of our enemies, and to enable us to serve him without fear in holiness and righteousness before him all our days. And you, my child, will be called a prophet of the Most High; for you will go on before the Lord to prepare the way for him, to give his people the knowledge of salvation through the forgiveness of their sins, because of the tender mercy of our God, by which the rising sun will come to us from heaven to shine on those living in darkness and in the shadow of death, to guide our feet into the path of peace.'

(Luke 1:68–79)

The Covenant of Grace

This may be defined as that gracious agreement between the offended God and the offending sinner, in which God promises salvation through faith in Christ, accepted by the sinner by faith, promising a life of faith and obedience (John 1:12–13; 3:16; Romans 10:9–10).

Comparison of the Covenant of Works (the Adamic Covenant) and the Covenant of Grace

The table on the next page presents a comparison of the Covenant of Works and the Covenant of Grace.

Just as in the Covenant of Works, so in the Covenant of Grace God is the first of the contracting parties; He takes the initiative and determines the relation in which the second party will stand to Him.

Covenant of Works	Covenant of Grace
God is the Creator and Lord. Established because of His love and benevolence.	God is the Redeemer and Father. Established because of His mercy.
Human beings appear simply as God's creatures, rightly related to their God.	Human beings appear as sinners who have perverted their ways, and can only appear in union with Christ and grace.
No Mediator.	Jesus is Mediator.
Righteousness is based upon the obedience of a changeable human being which is uncertain.	Based on the obedience of Christ as Mediator which is absolute and certain.
The way of life is by keeping the Law.	The way of life is by faith in Jesus Christ.
The Covenant is partly known in nature, since the Law of God is written in the heart of humankind.	The Covenant is known exclusively through special revelation: the Bible.

It is not easily determined who the second party is, but in general, it may be said that God naturally established the Covenant of Grace with fallen humanity.

The idea that the Covenant is fully realized only in the elect [5] is a perfectly scriptural idea, as appears, for instance, from Jeremiah 31:21–34; Hebrews 8:8–12. It is also entirely in line with the relation in which the Covenant of Grace stands to the Eternal Covenant.

The path to our salvation

God is holy; we are sinners. He is infinite; we are finite. He is powerful; we are helpless. We have sinned against Him and we need to escape His judgement. Through the Bible, God has revealed just how He is delivering His people.

By following the outline below, point by point, you will see the progression, beginning with God, that leads to our salvation. This will help you to see who God is, who you are, and what your need is before Him, all according to the Bible.

1. **God – is the standard of righteousness**
    (a) Is holy (1 Samuel 2:2; Isaiah 43:3, 14, 15; Revelation 4:8)
    (b) Just (Deuteronomy 32:4; Psalm 89:14; 97:2; 145:17)
    (c) Righteous (Psalm 145:17)
    (d) Judge (Psalm 50:6; 96:10, 13; Isaiah 11:3–4)
    (e) Visits wrath on the ungodly (Romans 1:18)
    (f) Is too pure to look upon evil (Habakkuk 1:13)

2. **The Law – is a reflection of His character**
    (a) Comes from God (Exodus 20:1–26; Isaiah 33:22; James 4:12)
    (b) Is holy (Romans 7:12)
    (c) Covenantal (Deuteronomy 4:13, 23)
    (d) Inaugurated with blood (Hebrews 9:18–23)
    (e) Brings the knowledge of sin (Romans 3:20)
    (f) Is perfect (Psalm 19:7)
    (g) Cannot make men and women perfect (Hebrews 7:19; 10:1)

3. **Human beings – are sinners or law breakers**
    (a) Sin is breaking the Law of God (1 John 3:4)
    (b) Human beings are law breakers (Romans 3:23)
    (c) Because of Original Sin – our inherited sinful nature from Adam (Genesis 3:1–6; Romans 5:12)
    (d) Because of human nature – we are by nature children of wrath because we are sinners (Ephesians 2:3)
        ▶ Our heart is wicked (Jeremiah 17:9; Mark 7:21–23)
        ▶ We are spiritually blind (1 Corinthians 2:14)
        ▶ We do not seek God (Romans 3:11)
        ▶ We are lawless, rebellious, unholy, and profane (1 Timothy 1:9)
        ▶ We suppress the truth of God in unrighteousness (Romans 1:18)
        ▶ We are futile in heart and mind (Romans 1:21)
    (e) Human beings are at enmity with God (Romans 5:10)

4. **Judgement – is God's lawful action upon the sinner**
    (a) God punishes evil (Exodus 20:5; Isaiah 11:4)
    (b) Is according to the Law (Deuteronomy 29:21; Joshua 8:34; Revelation 21:8)
    (c) Results in eternal punishment (Matthew 3:12; Revelation 14:11)
    (d) Results in separation from God (Isaiah 59:2)
    (e) Ignorance is no excuse (Leviticus 5:17)

5. **Reconciliation – our need before God**
    Reconciliation, through Jesus, is the means God has ordained to make peace between Him and ourselves.
    (a) We need our sin removed (Isaiah 59:2; 1 Peter 2:24)
    (b) We need to regain fellowship with God (1 Corinthians 1:9)
    (c) We need to find God's favor
    (d) We need to escape God's lawful judgement

6. **Atonement – the means of reconciliation**
    (a) The nature of the atonement is in the shedding of blood (Leviticus 17:11)
    (b) The requirements of the Law regarding atonement:
        ▶ The sacrifice must be unblemished (Leviticus 22:19)
        ▶ Must be made by appointed priests (1 Samuel 2:28)
        ▶ The high priest must be lawfully clean (Exodus 29:1–9, 19–35)
    (c) Jesus as the Atonement, the Sacrifice
        ▶ Is unblemished (1 Peter 1:19)
        ▶ According to the Law (Hebrews 9:22)
        ▶ As the High Priest (Hebrews 4:14; 6:20)
        ▶ Is substitutionary (1 Peter 2:24; Isaiah 53; Ephesians 5:2)
        ▶ Our propitiation – He removed God's wrathful judgement (1 John 2:2; 4:10)
    (d) Jesus as God and Man (Colossians 2:9; Philippians 2:5–8)
        ▶ Man – to atone for human beings (Hebrews 2:14; 5:1)
        ▶ God – to offer an infinite and satisfactory sacrifice to God (Ephesians 5:2, 10)

7. **Justification – result of the Atonement**
    Because of Jesus' sacrifice
    (a) We are lawfully righteous before God (Romans 3:24–26)

(b) We are clothed in righteousness (Isaiah 61:10)
(c) We have imputed righteousness (Romans 4:6)
  ▶ *Active* – Christ's obedience to the Law and His fulfill-ment of it (Romans 8:3–4)
  ▶ *Passive* – Christ being led to the cross to atone for us (John 19:16–18; 1 Peter 2:24)
(d) We escape the judgement of God (Romans 8:1)
(e) We are restored to fellowship (1 Thessalonians 5:9–10)
(f) We are at peace with God (Romans 5:1)
(g) We are reconciled to God (2 Corinthians 5:19)
(h) We are righteous before God (2 Corinthians 5:21)
(i) We have access to God (Ephesians 2:18)
(j) We have an advocate with the Father (1 John 2:1)

PART 3

Analysis of Major Cults

Cults – What are they?

Cults are a relatively new development on the Christian scene. Though there have been deviations from the truth throughout the centuries, it wasn't until the last two hundred years or so that cults have proliferated. Since the turn of the nineteenth century several thousand cults have arisen in the United States alone. Some of the more prominent are Mormonism, Jehovah's Witnesses, Christian Science, Unity School of Christianity, The Way International, Christadelphians, The Unification Church, Children of God, The Alamo Christian Foundation and The Farm.

Cults deviate from biblical truth so as to lead people further and further from Christ. In addition, in some cults a sort of mind control or brainwashing occurs. For example, Jehovah's Witnesses require their members to attend church three to five times a week. In these meetings they are indoctrinated over and over again to deny the Trinity, the deity of Christ, and the personality of the Holy Spirit.

All cults err in one or more of the following essential doctrines: the deity of Christ (which involves the Trinity), the resurrection, and salvation by grace. Apart from the basic essentials, additional related doctrines are often redefined and altered: the Trinity, the Holy Spirit, the Bible, the Virgin Birth, and more.

Cult groups often add to Christian doctrine and Scripture. Mormons have the *Book of Mormon*, *Doctrine and Covenants*, and *The Pearl of Great Price*. Christian Science has *Science and Health with Key to the Scriptures*. The Jehovah's Witnesses, however, have actually changed text within the Bible to make it fit with what they want (see 'Bad Translations of the Jehovah's Witness Bible,' p. 115). Though the Jehovah's Witnesses don't have additional Scriptures, they do use the *Watchtower* magazine in much the same way. It 'reveals' to them what the Bible really means (see 'Interesting Quotes from the *Watchtower*,' p. 135.

Also, cults place emphasis on 'earning' their salvation through their own efforts, and seek to 'add' their own works of righteousness to the finished work of salvation accomplished by Jesus on the cross. All cults say that Jesus' sacrifice is sufficient, but our works must be 'mixed' with His in order to prove that we are saved and worthy of salvation. In this, they are actually denying the finished work of Jesus' sacrifice.

But what is most common among the cults is their methods for twisting Scripture. Some of the errors they commit in interpreting Scripture are:

- Taking scriptures out of context.

- Reading into scriptures information that is not there.

- Picking and choosing only the scriptures that suit their needs.

- Ignoring other explanations.

- Combining scriptures that don't have anything to do with each other.

- Quoting a verse without giving its location.

- Incorrect definitions of key words.

- Mistranslation.

These are only a few of the many ways cults misuse Scripture.

If you want to be able to witness well to a person in a cult, you need to understand **their** doctrines as well as your own. The section 'Three Essential Doctrines of Christianity' should help you to become better equipped with the truth of the Bible and true Christian doctrine. Through study you will be able to answer questions that often come up in witnessing encounters. Christians should know their doctrine well enough to be able to recognize not only what is true, but also what is false in a religious system (1 Peter 3:15; 2 Timothy 2:15).

Jesus warned us that in the last days false 'Christs' and false prophets would arise and deceive many (Matthew 24:24). The Lord knew that there would be a rise of the spirit of Antichrist (1 John 4:1–3). Its manifestation is here. There are many excellent books on cults and cult evangelism, for example *Kingdom of the Cults* by Walter Martin (Bethany House) and *Larson's Book of Cults* by Bob Larson (Tyndale House Pub., 1982).

An analysis of cult practices and methods

Here is an outline of cult practices, recruitment techniques and warning signs. Not all cults exhibit all of them. Some cults have such a subtle form of brainwashing that it is barely noticeable. Others are openly evangelistic and seek to be recognized as a denomination (Mormonism). Some are aggressive and retaliatory (Scientology). Others simply hide themselves from public examination; in fact, some survivalist groups operate using cult principles. But all are harmful; all lead away from the truth of Jesus, His redemption, and His message.

What is a cult?

Generally, it is a group that is unorthodox, esoteric, and has a devotion to a person, object, or a set of new ideals. Characteristics will include some or all of the following:

- *New teaching* – has a new theology and doctrine.

- *Only true teaching* – often considers traditional religious systems to be apostate and believes it alone possesses the complete truth.

- *Strong leadership* – is often led by an individual or small but powerful leadership group, who exert control over the group's teaching and practices.

- *Asset acquirement* – often demands more than simply tithing, requiring major financial input and even the transfer of property to the group.

- *Isolationist* – seeks to facilitate control over the members physically, intellectually, financially, and emotionally.

- *Controlling* – readily exercises its control over the members. Sometimes this is through fear, threatening loss of salvation if you leave the group. Sometimes it is through indoctrination.

- *Indoctrination* – the cult's beliefs and standards are continually reinforced in members and opposing views are ridiculed and often misrepresented.

- *Apocalyptic* – warns of the imminent 'end of the world' in order to give the members a future focus and philosophical purpose in avoiding the apocalypse or being delivered through it.

- *Experience* – seeks to bring members to a place of emotional dependency on the group through experiences. Various practices, including meditation, repetition of words and/or phrases, and 'spiritual enlightenment' with God, are used as confirmation of their truth.

- *Deprivation* – sleep and food deprivation are techniques that weaken the will of the subject. This is uncommon, though practiced by more extreme cults.

- *Persecution* – cult leaders make claims that any views opposing the cult's beliefs are a form of persecution.

Many cults have non-verifiable belief systems

- Philosophies based on reincarnation, alien communications, or a humanistic 'create your own reality' mindset.

- Belief that God, an alien, or an angel appeared solely to the leader and gave him/her a revelation.

- Belief that the members are seeded angels from another world, etc.

Often, the philosophy makes sense only if you adopt the full set of values and definitions that it teaches. With this kind of belief, truth becomes unverifiable, internalized, and easily manipulated through the philosophical systems of its inventor.

The leader of a cult

Cult leaders are often charismatic and considered special for varying reasons:

- The leader is thought to have received special revelation from God.

- The leader claims to be the incarnation of a deity, angel, or special messenger.

- The leader claims to be 'appointed' by God, an alien, or a spirit, for a specific mission on earth.

- The leader claims to have special abilities – maybe visions, insights, etc.

- The leader is often above reproach and is not to be denied or contradicted.

Cult ethos

- Cults usually seek to do some good works, otherwise no one would join them.
- They are usually moral and possess a good standard of ethical teaching.
- Many times the Bible is used or additional 'scriptures' are penned.
- When they use the Bible, cults always distort it and deviate from standard interpretations.
- Many cults claim Jesus as one of their own and redefine Him accordingly.

Cult groups vary greatly

- From the aesthetic to the promiscuous.
- From esoteric knowledge to very simple teachings.
- From the rich and powerful to the poor and weak.

Who is vulnerable to joining a cult?

- *Everyone is vulnerable* – rich, poor, educated, non-educated, old, young, previously religious, atheistic, etc. Often those most vulnerable are in emotional, spiritual, or financial need.
- *Those curious about spiritual things* – UFOs, the occult, religion, etc.
- *The intellectually confused* – perhaps over religious and/or philosophical issues.

General profile of potential cult member

(Some or all of the following)

- Disenchanted with conventional religious establishments.
- Sometimes disenchanted with society as a whole.
- Has a need for encouragement and support.
- Emotionally needful.

- Lacks a sense of purpose.
- Financially needful.

Recruitment techniques

- *Focusing on needs* – cult 'recruiters' tend to identify a need in a potential member and then fill it. They do this by asking questions, being curious about the person, and befriending him/her.
- *'Love Bombing'* – constant positive affection in word and deed is used to engender emotional dependency. Sometimes there is a great deal of physical contact like hugging, pats on the back, and touching. There is usually also lots of affirmation, compliments, making members the center of attention, giving support and encouragement. Cult group members will lend emotional support to someone in need.
- *Practical help* – cult members may help a potential member in a variety of ways. The person then becomes indebted to the cult.
- *Scripture twisting* – many cults use the influence of the Bible and/or mention Jesus as being one of their own, thereby adding validity to their system. Those that use the Bible take verses out of context, then mix their misinterpreted verses with their aberrant philosophy.
- *Evangelism* – cults also have their own missionaries, and use the media – TV, radio, newspapers, special conferences, literature, magazines, the Internet, etc. – to promote their 'cause'.

Why would someone join?

The cult satisfies various needs:

- *Psychological* – it attracts people who may have a weak personality, or are easily led.
- *Emotional* – it could be a support to someone who has recently suffered an emotional trauma. The cult gives them approval, acceptance, purpose, and a sense of belonging.
- *Intellectual* – it may appear to be answering questions that a person has.

- *Financial security* – it may share resources among members and increase the sense of dependence and indebtedness to the group.

- *Spiritual* – it could be appealing for reasons of moral rigidity and purity, promises of exaltation, redemption, a higher consciousness, or a host of other rewards that membership in the group brings.

How are people kept in?

- *Dependence* – people often want to stay because the cult meets their needs: psychological, intellectual, financial, and/or spiritual.

- *Isolation* – outside contacts are reduced and more and more of the life of the member is built around the cult. It then becomes very easy to control and shape the member.

- *Brainwashing* – thinking processes and belief systems are slowly altered through repeated teaching. People usually accept cult doctrines one point at a time. New beliefs are reinforced by other cult members. Critical thinking is discouraged. Once the person is indoctrinated, their thinking processes are reconstructed to be consistent with the cult and to be submissive to its leaders. This facilitates control by the cult leader(s).

- *Mind control* – meditation, chanting, and repetitive activities are often employed to 'stop the mind' from thinking. Sleep and/or food deprivation coupled with indoctrination and sensory overload break down the subject's will and thinking processes, leaving little time for critical examination.

- *Substitution* – the cult and its leaders often take the place of normal relationships – mother, father, pastor, teacher, doctor, etc. – especially in those who have suffered a bereavement.

- *Indebtedness* – cult members are usually 'indebted' in some way to the group: emotionally, financially, etc.

- *Guilt* – cult members are told that to leave the group is to betray the leader, God, the rest of the group, etc., or told that to leave would mean to reject the love and help the group has given.

- *Threat* – the threat of destruction by God for turning from the truth is often used. Sometimes physical threats are also made, though not often. The threat of missing the apocalypse, or being judged on judgement day, etc., is also used.
- *Identification* – dressing alike, talking alike, thinking alike, and defending the group energetically is a technique also used to create solidarity.

Cult member behavior

People who become entangled in cults often exhibit many behavioral changes. Some or all of the following might occur as their free will is subjected to the cult and/or cult leader:

- *Loss of humor.*
- *'Snapping'* – a sudden change in behavior and thinking processes due to a complete acceptance of the cult philosophy.
- *Childlike behavior* – often the member takes on the characteristics of a dependent child seeking to win the approval of the leader and/or group.
- *Indecisiveness* – sometimes the person cannot make decisions without consulting the group or its leadership.
- *Tunnel vision* – cult members can become one-sided in their opinions and tend to avoid or ignore harmful evidence concerning their cult.
- *Inability to reason* – members may also suffer a loss of critical thinking processes when dealing with evidence about the cult. Most cults place emphasis on inner light, testimony, feelings, etc., to validate their beliefs. This is non-verifiable evidence which is a sign that the person is not dealing with facts in the real world.

How do you get a person out?

Prevention is always better than cure. The best thing is to prevent people from becoming trapped in the first place. However, if you are a Christian you can pray for anyone you know who is involved in a cult. But, getting a person out of a cult takes time, energy, and support. You can:

- Offer the cult member a true replacement for his or her aberrant belief system.
- Study the group and learn its history seeking clues and information.
- Show the individual the cult group's philosophical inconsistencies.
- Try to get the person physically away from the cult group in order to reason with him or her.
- Give the individual the emotional support he or she needs.
- Alleviate the threat that if the individual leaves the group he or she is doomed or in danger.
- Generally, don't seek to attack or criticize the leader of the group. Converts usually feel a strong loyalty and respect for the founder of the group. This issue needs to be confronted later on.
- As a last resort it may even be necessary to enlist the help of a deprogrammer.

Hopefully, this basic outline has given you an insight into how cult systems work. If you know someone who is lost in a cult, you need to pray and ask the Lord to remove him or her and give you the insight and tools needed. It can be a long and arduous task and very often ends in failure. This is not an easy ministry.

Comparison between Christianity and the major cults

The chart on the next two pages presents a comparison between Christianity and the major cults under various headings.

Cult comparison chart

Group name	Founder	The gospel	The church	God	Jesus	Salvation	Writings
Christianity	Jesus Christ	Jesus saves from sin	Those who are saved	Trinity: 3 Persons in one God	God in flesh	By grace	*The Bible* alone
Christa-delphianism	John Thomas (1805–1871), founded 1848	Faith, Christ and baptism	Members of their church	One Person	A man with a sin nature	Baptism is required	*Elpis Israel, Eureka*
Christian Science	Mary Baker Eddy (1821–1910)	Religious beliefs of Jesus' teachings, not the atonement	A collection of spiritual ideas	Impersonal Universal Presence	A man in tune with the Divine Consciousness, not the Christ	Correct thinking	*Science and Health with Key to the Scriptures, Miscellany*
Jehovah's Witnesses	Charles T. Russell (1852–1916), founded 1879	Jesus opened the door for us to earn our salvation	Members of their church	One Person	Michael the archangel who became a man	Keeping the commandments; being in their organization	*Studies in the Scriptures*, presently the *Watchtower* and *Awake* magazines
Mormonism	Joseph Smith (1805–1844), founded 1830	The Laws and ordinances of the gospel	Members of their church	Triad – 3 gods	The brother of the devil and of all people	Resurrected by grace, saved by doing works	*Book of Mormon, Doctrine and Covenants, Pearl of Great Price*

Group name	Founder	The gospel	The church	God	Jesus	Salvation	Writings
Theosophy	Madame Helena Blavatsky (1831–1891), founded 1875	n/a	n/a	God is a principle	A great teacher	No	*The Secret Doctrine*, *Isis Unveiled*, *The Key to Theosophy*, and *The Voice of the Silence*
Unity	Charles Fillmore (1854–1948), founded 1889	The overall principles of Unity	A collection of spiritual ideas	Impersonal Universal Power	A man, not the Christ	Adopting the correct Unity thought principles	*Unity* magazine, *Metaphysical Bible Dictionary*
Way International	Victor Paul Weirwell (1917–1985)	Earned	Members of their church	One Person	A man, not God in flesh	By works	*Jesus Christ is Not God*, *Power for Abundant Living*

List of cults

There are an estimated 2500 cults in America. Many use the Bible to add validity to their theologies, but many do not. It doesn't matter which group a cult belongs to because they are always harmful; they lead to hell. The only sure way to be immune from them is to be well grounded in God's Word. Keep your eyes on Jesus and you will be safe.

Aetherius Society
Alamo Christian Foundation
Anthroposophical Society
Astara
Children of God
Christadelphianism
Christian Science
Church of Armageddon
Church of the Living Word
Church Universal and Triumphant
Divine Light Mission
Eckankar
Est
Farm, The
Foundation of Human Understanding (Roy Masters)
Holy Order of Mans
Jehovah's Witnesses
Krishna
Life Spring
Local Church
Mormonism
Rosicrucianism
Scientology
Self Realization Fellowship
Silva Mind Control
Swedenborgianism
Theosophy
Transcendental Meditation
Two by Twos
Unification Church, The
Unitarian Universalist Association
Unity School of Christianity
Urantia
Way International, The

Mormonism: its history

Mormonism was begun by Joseph Smith Jr who was born in Vermont on 23 December 1805 as the fourth child of Lucy and Joseph Smith. Joseph senior, who searched for buried treasure, particularly that of Captain Kid, was known as a money digger. His mother was a highly superstitious person.

Joseph Smith Jr was disturbed by all the different denominations of Christianity and wondered which was true. In 1820, at the age of fourteen, having gone into the woods to pray concerning this, he claimed to have had an experience in which God the Father and Jesus appeared to him and told him not to join any of the denominational churches. [6]

Three years later, on 21 September 1823, when he was seventeen years old, an angel called Moroni (supposedly the son of Mormon, the leader of the people called the Nephites who had lived in the Americas), allegedly appeared to him and told him that he had been chosen to translate the book of Mormon which was written by Moroni over a thousand years earlier. The book was written on golden plates which were hidden near where Joseph was then living in Palmyra, New York. Joseph Smith said that on 22 September 1827 he received the plates and the angel Moroni instructed him to begin the translation process. The translation was finally published in 1830 as the *Book of Mormon*. Joseph claimed that, during this translation process, John the Baptist appeared to him and ordained him to accomplish the divine work of restoring the true Church by preaching the true gospel which, allegedly, had been lost from the earth. He maintained that, after the translation was complete, the golden plates were taken away again by the angel.

The *Book of Mormon,* which covers the period of about 600 BC to 400 AD, is supposedly the account of a people, the Jeredites, who migrated from the Tower of Babel in the Middle East to Central America, where they perished because of their own immorality. It also describes some Jews who, led by a man called Nephi, fled to America as a result of persecution in Jerusalem. The Jews divided into two groups known as the Nephites and Lamanites and these two groups fought each other. Having defeated the Nephites in 428 AD, the Lamanites lived on and are known as the American Indians. The *Book of Mormon* is the account of the Nephite leader,

Mormon, concerning their culture, civilization, and appearance of Jesus to the Americas.

After the publication of the *Book of Mormon*, Mormonism began to grow. Because their religion was so deviant from Christianity, i.e., plurality of gods, polygamy (Joseph is said to have had twenty-seven wives), etc., persecution soon forced them to move from New York to Ohio, then to Missouri, and finally to Nauvoo, Illinois. After breaking some laws in Nauvoo, Joseph and his brother Hyrum ended up in jail. A mob later broke into the jail and killed Joseph and his brother. [7]

After the shooting, the Church divided into two groups: one led by his widow which went back to Independence, Missouri. They are known as the Reorganized Church of Jesus Christ of Latter-day Saints. They maintain that they are the true Church and lay claim to the legal succession of the church presidency which was bestowed upon Joseph's son by Joseph Smith himself. [8] The other group, which was led by Brigham Young, went to Utah, eventually ending up in Salt Lake in 1847 and founding Salt Lake City. Brigham had twenty-five wives and accumulated much wealth.

Mormonism in a nutshell

Mormonism teaches that God used to be a man on another planet and that he became a god by following the laws and ordinances of his god on his home planet. In his present god-state he rules our world. He has a body of flesh and bones and, according to Mormonism, he has a goddess wife. Since they are both 'exalted' [9] persons, they each possess physical bodies. In their exalted state as deities, they have sexual relations and produce spirit children that grow and mature in the spiritual realm. The first spirit child born was Jesus, and afterwards came the devil and all other spirit creatures. After the spirit children are born to god and his goddess wife in heaven, they come down and enter into the bodies of babies that are being born on earth. During this 'compression' into the infant state, the memories of their pre-existence are erased. All people were, according to Mormonism, born in heaven first and then on earth where they are to grow, learn, and return to god.

God the father, whom the Mormons call Elohim,[10] needed a plan for the future salvation of the people on earth. In the heavenly realm, both Jesus and Lucifer offered a plan. When Elohim accepted Jesus' plan and rejected Lucifer's, Lucifer became jealous and rebelled. In his rebellion he convinced a third of the spirits existing in heaven to side with him and oppose God. God, being more powerful than they, cursed these rebellious spirits to become demons.

Of the remaining spirits, one third sided with Jesus. Since they chose the better way, when it comes time for them to live on earth, they have the privilege of being born into white-skinned families. The final third of the spirits that didn't choose a side were cursed to be born into black-skinned families.

In the Mormon plan of salvation there needed to be a savior: Jesus. But Jesus was a spirit in heaven. For him to be born on earth, Brigham Young, the second prophet of the Mormon Church, said that instead of letting any other man do it, God the Father conceived him with Mary. He said that the birth of our savior was as natural as the birth of our parents. Essentially, Young was proposing that God the Father came down and had sexual relations with Mary, his spirit daughter, to produce the body of Jesus. Jesus was then born, got married, and had children. He died on the cross and paid for sins. However, Mormonism teaches that the atonement began in the Garden of Gethsemane **before** Jesus went to the cross.

Mormon men and women have the potential of becoming gods. A famous Mormon saying is: 'As god once was, man is. As God is, man may become.' In order to reach this exalted state a person must first become a good Mormon and pay a full ten per cent tithe to the church. Afterwards, he or she can enter the temple [11] and go through secret rituals: baptism for the dead, celestial marriage, and various oaths. Additionally, four secret handshakes along with four secret hugs are taught so the believing Mormon, upon entering the third level of Mormon heaven, can shake hands and hug God in a certain way. This celestial ritual is for the purpose of permitting entrance into that level of heaven.

For those who achieve this highest of heavens, exaltation to godhood awaits them. Then, he or she will be permitted to have his or her own planet and be the gods of their own worlds.

Key elements of Mormon doctrine

The teachings of Mormonism have grown stranger as the movement has developed. Presently, Mormon doctrines are as follows:

1. The true gospel was lost from the earth. Mormonism is its restoration (*Mormon Doctrine* by Bruce R. McConkie (pub), p. 635). They teach there was an apostasy and the true Church ceased to exist on earth.

2. We need prophets today, like those in the Old Testament (*ibid.*, p. 606).

3. The *Book of Mormon* is more correct than the Bible (*History of the Church*, 4:461).

4. If it had not been for Joseph Smith and the restoration, there would be no salvation. There is no salvation (the context is the full gospel including exaltation to god-hood) outside the Church of Jesus Christ of Latter Day Saints (*Mormon Doctrine*, p. 670).

5. There are many gods (*ibid.*, p. 163).

6. There is a mother god (*Articles of Faith* by James Talmage, p. 443).

7. God used to be a man on another planet (*Mormon Doctrine*, p. 321; *Times and Seasons* by Joseph Smith, vol. 5, pp. 613–614; *Journal of Discourses* by Orson Pratt, vol. 2, p. 345; *Journal of Discourses* by Brigham Young, vol. 7, p. 333).

8. A person who becomes a good Mormon has the potential of becoming a god (*Teachings of the Prophet Joseph Smith*, pp. 345–347, 354).

9. God the Father had a father (Orson Pratt in *The Seer*, p. 132; one of the purposes of the Seer was 'to elucidate' Mormon doctrine, *ibid.*, 1854, p. 1).

10. God the Father has a body of flesh and bones (*Doctrine and Covenants*, 130:22).

11. God is in the form of a man (*Journal of Discourses* by Joseph Smith, vol. 6, p. 3).

12. God is married to his goddess wife and has spirit babies (*Mormon Doctrine*, p. 516).

13. We were first begotten as spirit babies in heaven and then born naturally on earth (*Journal of Discourse*, vol. 4, p. 218).

14. The first spirit to be born in heaven was Jesus (*Mormon Doctrine*, p. 129).

15. The devil was born as a spirit after Jesus 'in the morning of pre-existence' (*ibid.*, p. 192).

16. Jesus and Satan are spirit brothers (*ibid.*, p. 163).

17. A plan of salvation was needed for the people of earth so Jesus offered a plan to the Father and Satan offered a plan to the Father, but Jesus' plan was accepted (*ibid.*, p. 193; *Journal of Discourses*, vol. 6, p. 8).

18. God had sexual relations with Mary to make the body of Jesus (*ibid.*, vol. 4, 1857, p. 218).

19. Jesus' sacrifice was not able to cleanse us from all our sins (*ibid.*, vol. 3, 1856, p. 247).

20. Good works are necessary for salvation (*Articles of Faith*, p. 92).

21. There is no salvation without accepting Joseph Smith as a prophet of God (*Doctrines of Salvation*, vol. 1, p. 188).

22. Baptism for the dead (*ibid.*, vol. 2, p. 141). This is the practice of baptizing each other in place of non-Mormons who are now dead. Their belief is that in the afterlife the 'newly baptized' person will be able to enter into a higher level of Mormon heaven.

23. There are three levels of heaven: telestial, terrestrial, and celestial (*Mormon Doctrine*, p. 348).

A comparison between Christian and Mormon teachings

'Take up the Bible, compare the religion of the Latter-day Saints with it and see if it will stand the test.'

(Brigham Young, 18 May 1873, *Journal of Discourses*, vol. 16, p. 46)

The following table presents a comparison between Christian and Mormon doctrine. It is clear that Mormonism does not agree with the Bible. In fact, Mormonism has simply used the same words found in Christianity and redefined them. But with a proper understanding of what Mormonism really teaches, you will be able to see past those definitions into the real differences between Christianity and Mormonism. It is the difference between eternal life and damnation.

Topic	Christian	Mormon
GOD	There is only one God (Isaiah 43:11; 44:6, 8; 45:5).	'And they (the Gods) said: Let there be light: and there was light.' (*Book of Abraham* 4:3)
	God has always been God (Psalm 90:2; Isaiah 57:15).	'God himself was once as we are now, and is an exalted man, and sits enthroned in yonder heavens!!! ... We have imagined that God was God from all eternity. I will refute that idea and take away the veil, so that you may see.' (*Teachings of the Prophet Joseph Smith*, p. 345)
	God is a spirit without flesh and bones (John 4:24; Luke 24:39).	'The Father has a body of flesh and bones as tangible as man's.' (*Doctrine and Covenants* 130:22; cf. *Almas* 18:26–27; 22:9–10)
		'Therefore we know that both the Father and the Son are in form and stature perfect men; each of them possesses a tangible body ... of flesh and bones.' (James Talmage, *Articles of Faith*, p. 38)

Topic	Christian	Mormon
TRINITY	The Trinity is the doctrine that there is only **one** God, not three, in all the universe and that He exists in three, eternal, simultaneous persons: the Father, the Son, and the Holy Spirit.	The trinity is three separate Gods: the Father, the Son, and the Holy Ghost. 'That these three are separate individuals, physically distinct from each other, is demonstrated by the accepted records of divine dealings with man.' (Talmage, *Articles of Faith*, p. 35)
JESUS	Jesus was born of the virgin Mary (Isaiah 9:6; Matthew 1:23).	'The birth of the Savior was as natural as are the births of our children; it was the result of natural action. He partook of flesh and blood – was begotten of his Father, as we were of our fathers.' (*Journal of Discourses*, vol. 8, p. 115) 'Christ was begotten by an Immortal Father in the same way that mortal men are begotten by mortal fathers.' (Bruce McConkie, *Mormon Doctrine*, p. 547)
	Jesus is the eternal Son. He is second person of the Trinity. He has two natures. He is God in flesh and man (John 1:1, 14; Colossians 2:9) and the creator of all things (Colossians 1:15–17).	Jesus is the literal spirit-brother of Lucifer, a creation. (*Gospel Through the Ages*, p. 15)
THE HOLY SPIRIT	The Holy Spirit is the third person of the Trinity. He is not a force. He is a person (Acts 5:3–4; 13:2).	Mormonism distinguishes between the Holy Spirit (God's presence via an essence) and the Holy Ghost (the third god in the Mormon doctrine of the trinity). 'He [the Holy Ghost] is a being endowed with the attributes and powers of Deity, and not a mere force, or essence.' (Talmage, *Articles of Faith*, p. 144)

Topic	Christian	Mormon
SALVATION	Salvation is the forgiveness of sin and deliverance of the sinner from damnation. It is a free gift received by God's grace (Ephesians 2:8; Romans 6:23) and cannot be earned (Romans 11:6).	Salvation has a double meaning in Mormonism: universal resurrection and 'The first effect [of the atonement] is to secure to all mankind alike, exemption from the penalty of the fall, thus providing a plan of General Salvation. The second effect is to open a way for Individual Salvation whereby mankind may secure remission of personal sins.' (Talmage, *Articles of Faith*, pp. 78–79)
	Salvation (forgiveness of sins) is not by works (Ephesians 2:8; Romans 4:5; Galatians 2:21).	'As these sins are the result of individual acts it is just that forgiveness for them should be conditioned on individual compliance with prescribed requirements – "obedience to the laws and ordinances of the Gospel." ' (Talmage, *Articles of Faith*, p. 79)
BIBLE	The inspired inerrant Word of God (2 Timothy 3:16). It is authoritative in all subjects it addresses.	'We believe the Bible to be the word of God as far as it is translated correctly . . . ' (8th Article of Faith of the Mormon Church)

This is only a sample of the many differences between Christianity and Mormonism. As you can see, they are quite different doctrines. God cannot be uncreated and created at the same time. There cannot be only one God and many gods at the same time. The Trinity cannot be one God in three persons and three gods in an office known as the Trinity, etc. These teachings are mutually exclusive. This is important because faith is only as good as the object in which it is placed. Is the Mormon god the real one? Or, is the God of historic and biblical Christianity the real one? Mormonism is obviously not a biblical version of Christianity. Mormons do not serve the Living God of the Christians.

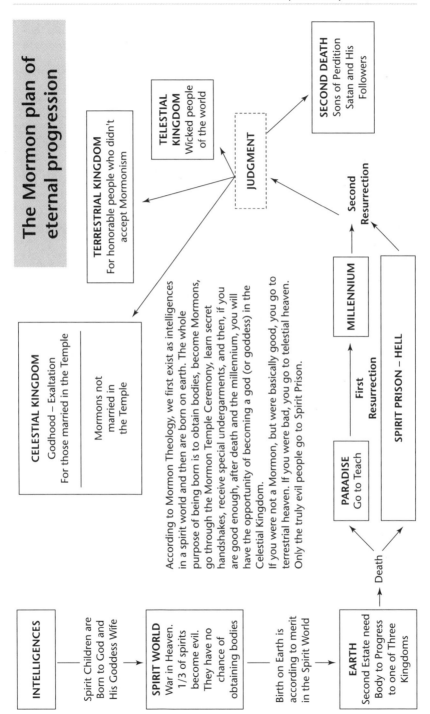

The Mormon plan of eternal progression

CELESTIAL KINGDOM
Godhood – Exaltation
For those married in the Temple

Mormons not
married in
the Temple

TERRESTRIAL KINGDOM
For honorable people who didn't
accept Mormonism

TELESTIAL KINGDOM
Wicked people
of the world

JUDGMENT

SECOND DEATH
Sons of Perdition
Satan and His
Followers

INTELLIGENCES

Spirit Children are
Born to God and
His Goddess Wife

SPIRIT WORLD
War in Heaven.
1/3 of spirits
become evil.
They have no
chance of
obtaining bodies

Birth on Earth is
according to merit
in the Spirit World

EARTH
Second Estate need
Body to Progress
to one of Three
Kingdoms

Death

PARADISE
Go to Teach

First
Resurrection

MILLENNIUM

Second
Resurrection

SPIRIT PRISON – HELL

According to Mormon Theology, we first exist as intelligences
in a spirit world and then are born on earth. The whole
purpose of being born is to obtain bodies, become Mormons,
go through the Mormon Temple Ceremony, learn secret
handshakes, receive special undergarments, and then, if you
are good enough, after death and the millennium, you will
have the opportunity of becoming a god (or goddess) in the
Celestial Kingdom.
If you were not a Mormon, but were basically good, you go to
terrestrial heaven. If you were bad, you go to telestial heaven.
Only the truly evil people go to Spirit Prison.

The *Book of Mormon*

According to Joseph Smith, the *Book of Mormon* is more correct than the Bible (*History of the Church*, vol. 4, p. 461) and contains the truths of Mormonism. However, if that is true, then why does the *Book of Mormon* contradict Mormon theology? Compare the section on Mormon doctrine with this list of references found in the *Book of Mormon*.

I recommend that you get a copy of the *Book of Mormon*, put tabs against the following references, and use it as a witnessing tool to the Mormons.

You might wonder why the *Book of Mormon* says things which are contrary to Mormon theology. This is because the theology of Joseph Smith didn't really start to go astray until after the *Book of Mormon* was printed. To harmonize their changing theology with their written scripture, the Mormons gradually redefined common Christian words. That is why the definitions of Mormon words are different from those of Christianity.

- **One God** (Mosiah 15:1, 5; Alma 11:28; 2 Nephi 31:21)
- **Trinity** (Alma 11:44; Mosiah 15:5; 2 Nephi 31:21)
- **God is unchanging** (Mormon 9:9, 19; Moroni 8:18; Alma 41:8; 3 Nephi 24:6)
- **God is spirit** (Alma 18:24, 28; 22:9, 11)
- **God cannot lie** (Ether 3:12; Enos 6)
- **Polygamy condemned** (Jacob 1:15; 2:23, 24, 27, 31; 3:5; Mosiah 11:2, 4; Ether 10:5, 7)
- **Eternal hell** (Jacob 3:11; 6:10; 2 Nephi 19:16; 28:21–23)
- **God the Father**
  - ▶ Redeemed man (Mosiah 13:32)
  - ▶ Created all (Jacob 4:9)
- **Jesus Christ**
  - ▶ Is God (2 Nephi 10:3; Mosiah 16:15)
  - ▶ Was virgin born (Alma 7:10)
  - ▶ Created all (3 Nephi 9:15)
  - ▶ Is prayed to (3 Nephi 19:18)
  - ▶ Is called God (3 Nephi 19:18)

- **Holy Spirit**
  - ▶ Dwells in man (Alma 18:35)
  - ▶ Is God (Alma 18:28)
  - ▶ Created all (Alma 22:9, 11)
- **Redemption for mankind is through**
  - ▶ The Lord (Alma 1:4)
  - ▶ Christ (Alma 22:13)
  - ▶ Jesus Christ (Mormon 9:12)
  - ▶ God (Mosiah 13:32)
  - ▶ Creator (2 Nephi 9:5)

Twelve essential Mormon doctrines not found in the Book of Mormon

If the *Book of Mormon* is the 'most correct book of any on earth' then why does it not contain essential Mormon doctrines such as:

1. Church organization
2. The Aaronic priesthood
3. Plurality of gods
4. God is an exalted man
5. Men may become gods
6. Three degrees of glory
7. Plurality of wives' doctrine
8. Celestial marriage
9. Baptism for the dead
10. Word of Wisdom
11. Pre-existence doctrine
12. Eternal progression

Interesting quotes from the *Book of Mormon*

Joseph Smith said that the *Book of Mormon* was 'the most correct of any book on earth' (*History of the Church*, vol. 4, p. 461).

According to Mormonism, and contrary to what the Bible says in Matthew 16:18, the true Church was lost from the earth. There was, then, a need for a restoration. But if that is true, why does the *Book of Mormon* say concerning the Apostle John, ' . . . ye have desired the thing which John, my beloved, who was with me in my ministry, before that I was lifted up by the Jews, desired of me. Therefore, more blessed are ye, for ye shall never taste of death ... until all things be fulfilled according to the will of the Father, when I shall come in my glory with the powers of heaven' (3 Nephi 28:6, 7)?

> 'And it came to pass that as my father arose in the morning, and went forth to the tent door, to his great astonishment he beheld upon the ground a round ball of curious workmanship; and it was of fine brass. And within the ball were two spindles; and the one pointed the way whither we should go into the wilderness ... And it came to pass that I, Nephi, beheld the pointers which were in the ball, that they did work according to the faith and diligence and heed which we did give unto them.'   (1 Nephi 16:10, 28)

Notice how they are putting faith in something other than God.

Mormonism has its own account of an ark-type voyage, only it wasn't one ark, it was several barges. It was allegedly in these barges that a lost tribe of Israel traveled to the Americas as is described in the book of Ether in the *Book of Mormon*. At any rate,

> 'God caused that there should be a furious wind blow upon the waters, towards the promised land; and thus they were tossed upon the waves of the sea before the wind ... And it came to pass that the wind did never cease to blow towards the promised land while they were upon the waters ... And thus they were driven forth, three hundred and forty and four days upon the water.'   (Ether 6:5, 8, 11)

Apart from anything else, there is a problem in the math here. A furious wind could be, let us say, as low as forty miles per hour and as high as eighty – but let's stay with the low end, forty miles per hour. A barge that is floating on the water blown by a forty mile an hour wind could easily travel three miles in an hour. Three miles per hour times 24 hours times 344 days equals 24,768 miles! Even at two miles per hour the distance covered would be 16,512 miles! Both of these are far greater than the distance of the Atlantic Ocean which is about 3000 miles across and the Mediterranean which is about 2500 miles. Combined the two are 5,500 miles across. Oooops! Sounds like the story was made up.

Interesting quotes from Joseph Smith

Joseph Smith boasted that he did more than Jesus to keep a church together

> 'God is in the still small voice. In all these affidavits, indictments, it is all of the devil – all corruption. Come on! ye prosecutors! ye false swearers! All hell, boil over! Ye burning mountains, roll down your lava! For I will come out on the top at last. I have more to boast of than ever any man had. I am the only man that has ever been able to keep a whole church together since the days of Adam. A large majority of the whole have stood by me. Neither Paul, John, Peter, nor Jesus ever did it. I boast that no man ever did such a work as I. The followers of Jesus ran away from Him; but the Latter-day Saints never ran away from me yet . . . '
>
> (*History of the Church*, vol. 6, pp. 408–409)

Joseph Smith made a false prophecy (one of several)

> ' . . . I prophesy in the name of the Lord God of Israel, unless the United States redress the wrongs committed upon the Saints in the state of Missouri and punish the crimes committed by her officers that in a few years the government will be utterly overthrown and wasted, and there will not be so much as a potsherd left . . . '   (*History of the Church*, vol. 2, p. 182)

Joseph Smith said mothers have babies in eternity and some are on thrones

> 'A question may be asked, "Will mothers have their children in eternity?" Yes! Yes! Mothers, you shall have your children.'
>
> (*Journal of Discourses*, vol. 6, p. 10)

> 'Eternity is full of thrones, upon which dwell thousands of children reigning on thrones of glory, with not one cubit added to their stature.'   (*Journal of Discourses*, vol. 6, p. 10)

Joseph Smith said there were many gods

> 'Hence, the doctrine of a plurality of Gods is as prominent in the Bible as any other doctrine. It is all over the face of the Bible . . . Paul says there are Gods many and Lords many [12] . . .

but to us there is but one God – that is pertaining to us; and he is in all and through all.'

(History of the Church, vol. 6, p. 474)

'In the beginning, the head of the Gods called a council of the Gods; and they came together and concocted a plan to create the world and people it.'   (*Journal of Discourses*, vol. 6, p. 5)

Joseph Smith said the Trinity is three gods

'I have always declared God to be a distinct personage, Jesus Christ a separate and distinct personage from God the Father, and the Holy Ghost was a distinct personage and a Spirit: and these three constitute three distinct personages and three Gods.'   (*Teachings of Prophet Joseph Smith*, p. 370)

Joseph Smith said God was once a man

'God himself was once as we are now, and is an exalted Man, and sits enthroned in yonder heavens.'

(Journal of Discourses, vol. 6, p. 3)

Interesting quotes from Brigham Young

Brigham Young said your own blood must atone for some sins

'There is not a man or woman, who violates the covenants made with their God, that will not be required to pay the debt. The blood of Christ will never wipe that out, your own blood must atone for it . . . '   (*Journal of Discourses*, vol. 3, p. 247; see also vol. 4, pp. 53–54, 219–220)

Brigham Young said you must confess Joseph Smith as a prophet of God in order to be saved

' . . . and he that confesseth not that Jesus has come in the flesh and sent Joseph Smith with the fullness of the Gospel to this generation, is not of God, but is antichrist.'

(Journal of Discourses, vol. 9, p. 312)

Brigham Young said his discourses are as good as Scripture

'I say now, when they [his discourses] are copied and approved by me they are as good Scripture as is couched in this Bible...'
                                        (*Journal of Discourses*, vol. 13, p. 264; *see also* p. 95)

Brigham Young said you are damned if you deny polygamy

'Now if any of you will deny the plurality of wives, and continue to do so, I promise that you will be damned.'
                                        (*Journal of Discourses*, vol. 3, p. 266)

Brigham Young said you can't get to the highest heaven without Joseph Smith's consent

'...no man or woman in this dispensation will ever enter into the celestial kingdom of God without the consent of Joseph Smith.'   (*Journal of Discourses*, vol. 7, p. 289)

Brigham Young said Jesus' birth was as natural as ours

'The birth of the Savior was as natural as the births of our children; it was the result of natural action. He partook of flesh and blood – was begotten of his Father, as we were of our fathers.'   (*Journal of Discourses*, vol. 8, p. 115)

Brigham Young said God was progressing in knowledge

'God himself is increasing and progressing in knowledge, power, and dominion, and will do so, worlds without end.'
                                        (*Journal of Discourses*, vol. 6, p. 120)

Brigham Young boasted of his own wisdom

'What man or woman on earth, what spirit in the spirit-world can say truthfully that I ever gave a wrong word of counsel, or a word of advice that could not be sanctioned by the heavens? The success which has attended me in my presidency is owing to the blessings and mercy of the Almighty...'
                                        (*Journal of Discourses*, vol. 12, p. 127)

Brigham Young said that we are obligated to keep all the laws and ordinances of God

'Some of you may ask, "Is there a single ordinance to be dispensed with? Is there one of the commandments that God has enjoined upon the people, that he will excuse them from obeying?" Not one, no matter how trifling or small in our own estimation. No matter if we esteem them non-essential, or least or last of all the commandments of the house of God, we are under obligation to observe them.'

(*Journal of Discourses*, vol. 8, p. 339)

Interesting quotes from *Articles of Faith*

On the jacket cover of James Talmage's book it says, 'For clarity, brevity, and forthrightness, there is no finer summary statement of the basic beliefs of Latter-day Saints than the *Articles of Faith*, which were written by the Prophet Joseph Smith ... For more than eighty years this book has been a standard text for gospel students and teachers alike. The publication of the work preceded Elder Talmage's call to the apostleship' (Salt Lake City, Utah: Deseret Book Company, 1984).

The Publisher's Preface in the book says, 'Articles of Faith is considered one of the classics in Latter-day Saint literature. It is the outgrowth of a series of lectures in theology give by Dr. James E. Talmage, commencing in October of 1893. At that time Dr. Talmage was serving as the president of the LDS College in Salt Lake City. The First Presidency of the Church invited Dr. Talmage to prepare a text for use in Church schools and religion classes ... ' On 7 December 1911 he was called as a member of the Quorum of the Twelve Apostles, where he served faithfully until his death on 27 July 1933.

Here are some quotes from *Articles of Faith*:

'Therefore we know that both the Father and the Son are in form and stature perfect men; each of them possesses a tangible body, infinitely pure and perfect and attended by transcendent glory, nevertheless a body of flesh and bones.'

(p. 38)

'The twofold effect of the atonement is implied in the article of our faith now under consideration. The first effect is to secure to all mankind alike, exemption from the penalty of the fall, thus providing a plan of general Salvation. The second effect is to open a way for Individual Salvation whereby mankind may secure remission of personal sins. As these sins are the result of individual acts it is just that forgiveness for them should be conditioned on individual compliance with prescribed requirements – "obedience to the laws and ordinances of the Gospel."'   (pp. 78–79)

'Hence the justice of the scriptural doctrine that salvation comes to the individual only through obedience.'   (p. 81)

'There are some who have striven to obey all the divine commandments, who have accepted the testimony of Christ, obeyed "the laws and ordinances of the Gospel", and received the Holy Spirit; these are they who have overcome evil by godly works and who are therefore entitled to the highest glory.'   (p. 83)

'The sectarian dogma of justification by faith alone has exercised an influence for evil. The idea upon which this pernicious doctrine was founded was at first associated with that of an absolute predestination, by which man was fore-doomed to destruction, or to an undeserved salvation.'   (p. 432)

'...the spirits of mankind passed through a stage of existence prior to their earthly probation. This antemortal period is oftentimes spoken of as the stage of primeval childhood or first estate.'   (p. 174)

'The Church of Jesus Christ of Latter-day Saints proclaims against the incomprehensible God, devoid of "body, parts, or passions", as a thing impossible of existence...'   (p. 44)

'The opportunity of winning the victor's reward by overcoming evil was explained to our parents, and they rejoiced. Adam said: "Blessed be the name of God, for because of my transgression my eyes are opened, and in this life I shall have joy, and again in the flesh I shall see God." Eve was glad and declared: "Were it not for our transgression we never should have had seed, and never should have known good and evil, and the joy of our redemption, and the eternal life which God giveth unto all the obedient."'   (p. 62)

'The redemption of the dead will be effected in accordance with the law of God, which is written in justice and framed in mercy. It is alike impossible for any spirit, in the flesh or disembodied, to obtain promise of eternal glory except on condition of obedience to the laws and ordinances of the Gospel. And, as baptism is essential to the salvation of the living, it is likewise indispensable to the dead.'   (pp. 134–135)

'Temples or other sacred places are required for the administration of the ordinances pertaining to the salvation of the dead, and in certain ordinances for the living.'   (p. 138)

'The preexistent condition is not characteristic of human souls alone; all things of earth have a spiritual being of which the temporal structure forms but the counterpart.'   (p. 442)

Does Mormonism attack Christianity?

Mormons claim they are Christian and do not go around condemning other religions as 'anti-Mormons' do. They say they are forgiving, tolerant, good Christian people who don't have anything against anyone. They maintain they are being more Christ-like than those who oppose Mormonism.

Their desire for a good image is understandable. But the question remains: Does the Mormon Church condemn other religious systems? The answer is definitely 'Yes.' Let's look at some Mormon writers and see what they have said.

Joseph Smith

(Regarding Joseph Smith's alleged first vision when he saw celestial personages appear to him)

'My object in going to inquire of the Lord was to know which of all the sects was right, that I might know which to join. No sooner, therefore, did I get possession of myself, so as to be able to speak, than I asked the personages who stood above me in the light, which of all the sects was right – and which I should join. I was answered that I must join none of them, for they were all wrong, and the personage who addressed me said that all their creeds were an abomination in his sight: that those professors were all corrupt...'

(History of the Church, vol. 1, pp. 5–6)

'What is it that inspires professors of Christianity generally with a hope of salvation? It is that smooth, sophisticated influence of the devil, by which he deceives the whole world.'

(Teachings of the Prophet Joseph Smith,
compiled by Joseph Fielding Smith, p. 270)

(In questions directed to Joseph Smith, the founder of Mormonism...)

First: 'Do you believe the Bible?'
Smith: 'If we do, we are the only people under heaven that does, for there are none of the religious sects of the day that do.'
Third: 'Will everybody be damned but Mormons?'
Smith: 'Yes, and a great portion of them, unless they repent, and work righteousness.' *(ibid.*, p. 119)

Brigham Young

'But He did send His angel to this same obscure person, Joseph Smith ... who afterwards became a Prophet, Seer, and Revelator, and informed him that he should not join any of the religious sects of the day, for they were all wrong.'

(Journal of Discourses, vol. 2, 1855, p. 171)

John Taylor

'We talk about Christianity, but it is a perfect pack of nonsense ... myself and hundreds of the Elders around me have seen its pomp, parade, and glory; and what is it? It is a sounding brass and a tinkling symbol; it is as corrupt as hell; and the Devil could not invent a better engine to spread his work than the Christianity of the nineteenth century.'

(ibid., vol. 6, 1858, p. 167)

'Where shall we look for the true order or authority of God? It cannot be found in any nation of Christendom.'

(ibid., vol. 10, 1863, p. 127)

James Talmage

'A self-suggesting interpretation of history indicates that there has been a great departure from the way of salvation as laid down by the Savior, a universal apostasy from the Church of Christ.'   (*Articles of Faith*, Salt Lake City, Utah: Deseret Book Company, p. 182)

Bruce McConkie

'With the loss of the gospel, the nations of the earth went into a moral eclipse called the Dark Ages.'   (*Mormon Doctrine*, Salt Lake City, Utah: Bookcraft, p. 44)

Joseph Fielding Smith

'Again, following the death of his apostles, apostasy once more set in, and again the saving principles and ordinances of the gospel were changed to suit the conveniences and notions of the people. Doctrines were corrupted, authority lost, and a false order of religion took the place of the gospel of Jesus Christ, just as it had been the case in former dispensations, and the people were left in spiritual darkness.'   (*Doctrines of Salvation*, p. 266)

Book of Mormon

'And he said unto me: Behold there are save two churches only; the one is the church of the Lamb of God, and the other is the church of the devil; wherefore, whoso belongeth not to the church of the Lamb of God belongeth to that great church which is the mother of abominations; and she is the whore of all the earth.'   (1 Nephi 14:10)

'And when the day cometh that the wrath of God is poured out upon the mother of harlots, which is the great and abominable church of all the earth, whose foundation is the devil, then, at that day, the work of the Father shall commence...'   (1 Nephi 14:17)

Doctrine and Covenants

'Verily, verily, I say unto you, darkness covereth the earth, and gross darkness the minds of the people, and all flesh has become corrupt before my face.'   (*Doctrine and Covenants*, 112:23)

When the Mormon missionaries come to the door and do their 'gospel' presentation, they mention an apostasy and the need for a prophet (their prophet) to restore the true teachings of Jesus. Of course, these 'restored' teachings are completely false. Nevertheless, the Mormon Church clearly condemns other religious systems. Those Mormons who complain about poor treatment should familiarize themselves with their teachers' words.

The Book of Abraham papyri problem

There are many proofs that Joseph Smith was a false prophet, but Mormons typically will not accept them. From the biblical evidence that contradicts Mormon theology, to the contradictions within its own history and doctrine, proofs abound. But Mormons, completely dedicated to their religion and their testimony, cannot and will not see the evidence. They rely not on biblical evidence, not on historical evidence, but rather trust a 'testimony' that Mormonism is the restored Church and Joseph Smith its true prophet.

One of the tests of whether or not a belief is grounded in reality is whether it can be proven to be true or false. If someone says, 'I don't care what evidence you show me, I will always believe,' then that person's faith is not rooted in reality. And since Christianity is a religion of historical fact – crucifixion, resurrection, an empty tomb, etc. – it is a religion rooted in reality. If it could be proven beyond doubt that Jesus did not rise from the dead, then Christianity would be a false religion. Likewise, if it can be proven that Joseph Smith was a false prophet, then Mormonism is a false religion. It just so happens that there is such a proof.

The Book of Abraham

Joseph Smith claimed that an angel appeared to him and revealed the location of some golden plates on which was written the account of the ancient people of the Americas. Joseph Smith maintained that he later translated those plates into what is now known as the *Book of Mormon*. He claimed this translation was done by the power of God through special means. Joseph Smith, being the Lord's chosen instrument, became the prophet of the Mormon Church, and held the office of Seer. A Seer, according to the *Book of Mormon* in Mosiah 8:13, can translate records that are otherwise untranslatable. Hence, Joseph Smith was able to translate the golden plates into the *Book of Mormon*. But his Seer abilities did not stop there.

In July of 1835, an Irishman named Michael Chandler brought an exhibit of four Egyptian mummies and papyri to Kirtland Ohio, then the home of the Mormons. The papyri contained Egyptian hieroglyphics which at that time were unreadable.

As Prophet and Seer of the Church, Joseph Smith was given permission to look at the papyri scrolls in the exhibit and, to everyone's shock, revealed that 'one of the rolls contained the writings of Abraham, another the writings of Joseph of Egypt' (*History of the Church*, vol. 2, p. 236, July 1835). The Church bought the exhibit for $2400. Joseph finished the translation of the Book of Abraham some time later, but the Book of Joseph was never translated. The papyri were lost soon afterwards and thought to have been destroyed in a fire in Chicago in 1871. There was, therefore, no way to validate Smith's translation. If the papyri were rediscovered and translated it would either prove or disprove the abilities of Joseph as a prophet of God. After all, he was supposed to be a prophet and have the abilities of a Seer as the *Book of Mormon* and the Book of Abraham supposedly proved.

In October of 1880 *The Pearl of Great Price*, a collection of writings, which contained the Book of Abraham, was recognized as scripture by the Mormon Church.

The papyri are found

To everyone's surprise, in 1966 the papyri were rediscovered in one of the vault rooms of New York's Metropolitan Museum of Art. The *Deseret News* of Salt Lake City on 27 November 1967 acknowledged the rediscovery of the papyri. On the back of the papyri were 'drawings of a temple and maps of the Kirtland, Ohio area.'[13] There could be no doubt that this was the original document from which Joseph Smith translated the Book of Abraham.

With the papyri rediscovered and Egyptian hieroglyphics decipherable since the late 1800s, it would then be an easy task to translate the papyri and prove once and for all that Joseph Smith was a prophet with the gift of 'Seer' as he and the Mormon Church have claimed. This would prove the truth of the *Book of Mormon* and the Book of Abraham and would validate Smith as a true prophet of God.

What do the experts say?

Joseph Smith copied three drawings from the scrolls, labeled them Facsimile No. 1, No. 2, and No. 3, and incorporated them into the Book of Abraham with his explanations of what they were. Egyptologists have viewed the drawings and found Joseph Smith's interpretations of them to be wrong. But the Mormons, in defense of the sacred book, maintained that the Facsimiles alone were not sufficient proof that Joseph Smith had erred in his translating abilities. Following the rediscovery of the papyri, it was clear that these were the same drawings as those in the scrolls, and so was the text from which Joseph Smith had made his translation. It was now possible to determine absolutely the accuracy of Smith's translating abilities and claims.

Joseph Smith said that Facsimile No. 1, which was of a bird, represented the 'Angel of the Lord' with 'Abraham fastened upon an altar' being offered up as a sacrifice by a false priest. The pots

Facsimile No. 1

Figure A

under the altar were various gods 'Elkenah, Libnah, Mahmackrah, Korash, Pharaoh', etc. In reality, this is 'an embalming scene showing the deceased lying on a lion-couch.'[14]

In the original papyri, this drawing is attached to the hieroglyphics (see Figure A) from which Joseph derived the beginning of the Book of Abraham, which opens with the words, 'In the Land of the Chaldeans, at the residence of my father, I, Abraham, saw that it was needful for me to obtain another place of residence' (1:1). In reality, the hieroglyphics translate as,

> 'Osiris shall be conveyed into the Great Pool of Khons – and likewise Osiris Hor, justified, born to Tikhebyt, justified – after his arms have been placed on his heart and the Breathing permit (which [Isis] made and has writing on its inside and outside) has been wrapped in royal linen and placed under his left arm near his heart; the rest of the mummy-bandages should be wrapped over it. The man for whom this book was copied will breathe forever and ever as the bas of the gods do.'[15]

'It is the opening portion of an Egyptian *Shait en Sensen*, or *Book of Breathings* ... a late funerary text that grew out of the earlier and more complex *Book of the Dead*.' This particular scroll was prepared (as determined by handwriting, spelling, content, etc.) some time during the late Ptolemaic or early Roman period (*c.* 50 BC to 50 AD).[16]

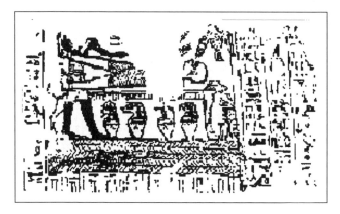

Figure B

Figure A is a professional reconstruction of the original (Figure B). Note the hieroglyphics on the right side from which Joseph Smith began his translation of the Book of Abraham.

In actuality, it 'depicts the mythical embalming and resurrection of Osiris, Egyptian god of the underworld. Osiris was slain by his jealous brother Set, who cut up his body into 16 pieces and scattered them ... The jackal-headed god Anubis is shown embalming the body of Osiris on the traditional lion-headed couch so that he might come back to life ...'[17]

Figure B shows a reprint of the actual papyrus used by Joseph Smith. Note the areas where the papyrus has been lost. These are the sections of the drawing which Joseph Smith 'finished,' resulting in Facsimile No. 1. His restoration, according to Egyptologists, reveals a complete lack of understanding of Egyptian practice and theology.

As is explained by Joseph Smith and included in *The Pearl of Great Price*, the second drawing (Facsimile No. 2) contains different scenes which Joseph Smith interpreted. They vary: 'Kolob, signifying the first creation, nearest to the celestial, or the residence of God'; 'Stands next to Kolob, called by the Egyptians Oliblish, which is the next grand governing creation near to the celestial or the place where God resides'; 'God, sitting upon his throne, clothed with power and authority'; '... this is one of the governing planets also, and is said by the Egyptians to be the Sun, and to borrow its light from Kolob through the medium of Kae-e-vanrash, which is the grand Key ...'

Facsimile No. 2

But again scholarship disagrees with Smith's rendition. 'It is actually a rather common funerary amulet termed a *hypocephalus*, so-called because it was placed under (*hypo*) a mummy's head (*cephalus*). Its purpose was to magically keep the deceased warm and to protect the body from desecration by grave robbers.' [18]

According to Smith, this drawing shows 'Abraham sitting upon Pharaoh's throne, by the politeness of the king, with a crown upon his head, representing the Priesthood ... King Pharaoh, whose name is given in the characters above his head ... Signifies

Facsimile No. 3

Abraham in Egypt ... Olimlah, a slave belonging to the prince...'
But this is not what the Egyptologists say is the meaning of
Facsimile No. 3. In reality it shows 'the deceased being led before
Osiris, god of the dead, and behind the enthroned Osiris stands his
wife Isis.'[19] 'The explanations are completely wrong insofar as any
interpretation of the Egyptian original is concerned.'[20]

Conclusion

It should be quite obvious that present scholarship has revealed
that Joseph Smith did not translate the Book of Abraham by the
power of God as he had claimed. It follows that if he did not
translate the Book of Abraham by the power of God, then neither
did he the *Book of Mormon.*

When Joseph first gave his translation, hieroglyphics were
undecipherable. Today they are. He was safe in saying anything
he wanted to without the possibility of anyone proving him wrong.
But the re-emergence of the same papyri he used for his Book of
Abraham translation and clear evidence of the fact that his interpretation was wrong, should be proof enough that Joseph Smith
lied about his abilities from God. He has been shown to be a false
prophet.

Witnessing to Mormons

Witnessing to a Mormon is like trying to climb a sheer cliff-face: it's
hard to get a foothold. But if you know what Mormonism teaches
then you are well on your way. The following basic approaches
should aid you in witnessing to a Mormon. Though none of these
is foolproof, they will provide you with the basic framework you
need. It will be up to you to use what you have learned, develop
more skill in witnessing, and perfect your method as you go.
Remember, the best way to learn to witness is *to witness!*

There are three important things to know before you begin
evangelizing Mormons. Firstly, you need to understand their
definitions of the same biblical words that you use: Trinity, Jesus,
salvation, heaven, etc. Secondly, you must be able to show them
that they believe in a wrong Jesus. This is important because only

the true Jesus gives eternal life (John 10:28), reveals the Father (Matthew 11:27), and sends the Holy Spirit (John 15:26). The Mormons have a false understanding of Jesus and, therefore, a useless faith. Thirdly, you must show them that salvation (forgiveness of sins) is completely by grace. For the first part you really need to study the section below on the 'Terminology' of Mormons and Jehovah's Witnesses. Once you understand what it is that they are saying, you will be more equipped to witness. For the second part, it would be a very good idea to become familiar with the section 'An Easy and Powerful Way of Witnessing to the Cults.' To witness means you must teach. To teach means you must understand. To understand means you must know not only what you believe, but also what they believe.

1. Terminology

When Mormons say they believe in the Trinity they do not mean the historical orthodox Trinity of one God who exists in three persons. To Mormons, the Trinity is an office held by three separate gods: the Father, the Son, and the Holy Ghost. Remember, the correct doctrine of the Trinity is that there is only one God who has existed for eternity. This one God exists in three persons: the Father, the Son, and the Holy Spirit. They are not three separate gods, but only **one God**.

When Mormons say they believe in God they do not mean in the one true God, the creator of all things, the One who has always existed from all time. They mean they believe in a god who used to be a man on another planet, following the laws and ordinances of 'another' god who ruled that planet. They believe that this 'man' became exalted to god-hood himself, and, to top it all off, he has a wife who is a goddess.

2. They have a testimony

Mormons will bear testimony of their faith and tell you that they know the Mormon Church is true and that Joseph Smith was a true prophet of God.

If you ask how they received their testimony, Mormons will usually say that they prayed and God bore witness to them by the Holy Spirit that the *Book of Mormon* was true, that Joseph Smith was a true prophet, and that the Church of Jesus Christ of Latter-day Saints is the true Church. All this, they will say, was revealed by the Holy Spirit. In response to the question 'Who bears witness of the truth?', they will reaffirm that the Holy Spirit does. Gently correct the person to whom you are witnessing by showing that the Holy Spirit bears witness to Jesus (John 15:26) and the truth, and that Jesus sends the Holy Spirit (John 15:26). Once you've shown that the Holy Spirit is sent from Jesus, ask if a false Jesus would send the true Spirit of God. The answer, of course, is no. The point is that only the Jesus of the Bible will send the Holy Spirit. If Mormons don't have the right Jesus they can't have the true Holy Spirit, and their testimony is invalid.

3. *Praying about the* Book of Mormon

Members of the Church of Jesus Christ of Latter-day Saints believe that if you read the *Book of Mormon* and then pray and ask God whether or not it is true, you will receive a testimony from the Holy Spirit verifying its truth. If it is true, then Joseph Smith is true and so is Mormonism. Many Mormons claim to have this testimony.

This claim can be contradicted in three ways. First of all, God never tells us to pray about truth. He tells us to search the Scriptures to find truth (Acts 17:11; 2 Timothy 3:16). So, what Mormons are doing is unbiblical. Secondly, it doesn't matter what you **feel**. If what you feel contradicts the Bible, then what you feel is wrong. Thirdly, ask if they ever had to pray about the Bible to see if it was true. Of course they haven't, so why should praying about the *Book of Mormon* be any guide to its veracity?

The response to this argument will typically be that 'The *Book of Mormon* **says** to pray about it.' In the *Book of Mormon*, Moroni 10:4, it says, '... I would exhort you that ye would ask God, the Eternal Father, in the name of Christ, if these things are not true, and if you ask with a sincere heart, with real intent, having faith in Christ, he will manifest the truth of it unto you, by the power of the Holy Ghost.' The Mormons are actually missing what the text plainly says: '... that ye would ask God ... if these things are **not** true ... ' Ask if the person has prayed to see if the *Book of Mormon* is **not** true. The Moroni passage is really a false test. There is no room for doubting it. If you don't believe, it is because you aren't sincere.

Only sincere people believe. There is no room for sincere people finding out that it is false.

A common verse that Mormons use to support their belief that you can pray about the *Book of Mormon* is found in James 1:5: *'If any of you lacks wisdom, he should ask God, who gives generously to all without finding fault, and it will be given to him.'* They say that, because they are sincere, God will answer them. The first problem with this argument is that it promotes 'works righteousness.' The person is in effect saying, 'Because of my sincerity, God will listen to me' – i.e., God will look favorably upon them because of what is in their heart. God never works like this. He already knows that there is no real 'good' to be found in any person (Romans 3:10–12; Ephesians 2:3). Furthermore, God does not show partiality (Romans 2:11).

Secondly, this verse in James was specifically written to those who were already believers. James' epistle opens with the greeting,

> *'James, a servant of God and of the Lord Jesus Christ, to the twelve tribes scattered among the nations: Greetings.'*   (James 1:1)

The recipients of his letter were believers who already had the truth.

Thirdly, James is referring to gaining wisdom from God. He is not speaking about the context of testing the probity of 'religious' documents, e.g., the *Book of Mormon*. Wisdom is the proper use of knowledge, not the acquisition of knowledge. You acquire true spiritual knowledge from the Bible, not your heart. It is a redundant exercise to pray about the *Book of Mormon*. You can only pray about the truth you've learned from the Bible and ask God to teach you more, and show you how to apply properly what He's already revealed to you.

4. What is the gospel?

The following approach is a direct and hard-hitting way of witnessing to a Mormon. Sometimes it is necessary to be blunt in order to get a person's attention. Ask the question, 'What is the gospel?' In reply a Mormon will usually say something like, 'The gospel is the laws and the ordinances of the Mormon Church.' Ask the same question again, listening closely for any hint of the free forgiveness of sins through the sacrifice of Jesus on the cross. You usually receive an answer dealing with works, obedience, doing things for God, etc.

After the person has answered, explain that, according to the Bible, the gospel is what saves us, what cleanses us from our sins, and enables us to stand in the presence of God the Father. Explain that the Bible specifically defines the gospel and that the gospel is what makes you a Christian. Then ask again, 'What is the gospel?'

After you've heard a works-righteousness-type answer, turn in your Bible to 1 Corinthians 15:1–4 and read:

> *'Now, brothers, I want to remind you of the gospel I preached to you, which you received and on which you have taken your stand. By this gospel you are saved, if you hold firmly to the word I preached to you. Otherwise, you have believed in vain. For what I received I passed on to you as of first importance: that Christ died for our sins according to the Scriptures, that he was buried, that he was raised on the third day according to the Scriptures.'*

Explain that the gospel is the death, burial, and resurrection of Jesus ... for the remission of our sins! Then turn to 2 Corinthians 4:3–4 and read again:

> *'And even if our gospel is veiled, it is veiled to those who are perishing. The god of this age has blinded the minds of unbelievers, so that they cannot see the light of the gospel of the glory of Christ, who is the image of God.'*

Say something like, 'You clearly did not understand the gospel message of Jesus the Savior, and the Bible clearly shows you why. It is because your mind has been blinded. Apparently, you are not a Christian.'

5. The Apostasy

- Mormonism maintains that the true gospel message was lost from the earth shortly after the apostles died. The Mormon Apostle Orson Prat said, 'Jesus ... established his kingdom on earth ... the kingdoms of this world made war against the kingdom of God, established eighteen centuries ago, and they prevailed against it, and the kingdom ceased to exist' (*Journal of Discourses*, vol. 13, p. 125).

But Jesus said,

> *'And I also say to you, that you are Peter, and on this rock I will build My church; and the gates of Hades shall not prevail against it.'*   (Matthew 16:18 NKJV)

As you can see, Mormonism contradicts what Jesus said.

- Mormonism claims to be the restoration of the New Testament Church. This means that Mormonism is saying that all religions except their own are false.

- Mormons often use 2 Thessalonians 2:1–3, where it speaks of an apostasy, as proof for their position. But taken in context the apostasy is concomitant with the arrival of the antichrist. This hasn't happened yet.

6. Authority and the Mormon priesthoods

- Since Mormonism claims to be the restoration of the gospel, it also claims to have the authority to perform priestly duties and, therefore, properly represent God here on earth.

- All offices of the Mormon Church grow out of the priesthoods of:

    (a) *Melchizedek* – this is the greater priesthood of the Mormon Church consisting of several offices:
    (i) elder, seven, high priest, patriarch or evangelist, and apostle;
    (ii) deacon, teacher, priest, and bishop.
    (b) *Aaron* – called the lesser priesthood. It is
    (i) synonymous with the Levitical priesthood (D. & C. 107:1, 6, 10), and
    (ii) performs the administration of the ordinances (D. & C. 107:13–14).

- Quite simply, the Bible contradicts what Mormonism teaches concerning the priesthood.

    (a) Jesus is the only high priest after the order of Melchizedek (Hebrews 3:1; 5:6, 10; 6:20; 7:11, 15, 17, 21, 24, 26; 8:1; 9:11).

    > *'...where Jesus, who went before us, has entered on our behalf. He has become a high priest forever, in the order of Melchizedek.'*   (Hebrews 6:20)

> *'And what we have said is even more clear if another priest like Melchizedek appears, one who has become a priest not on the basis of a regulation as to his ancestry but on the basis of the power of an indestructible life.'*
>
> (Hebrews 7:15–16)

(b) The Melchizedek priesthood is unchangeable and untransferable:

> *'... but because Jesus lives for ever, he has a permanent priesthood.'*   (Hebrews 7:24)

7. Many Gods

- One of the truly dividing lines between Christianity and Mormonism is the latter's doctrine of the plurality of gods.

(a) Mormonism teaches that there are many gods (Bruce McConkie, *Mormon Doctrine*, p. 163; *Teachings*, pp. 348–349).

(b) In their desire for legitimacy they will even quote 1 Corinthians 8:5 to assert that the Bible also teaches many gods. 1

> *'For even if there are so-called gods, whether in heaven or on earth (as indeed there are many "gods" and many "lords").'*
>
> (1 Corinthians 8:5)

You can respond to this by saying, 'It says there are many that are **called** gods. It doesn't say they really are gods. The Bible recognizes that there are false gods.' (*See also* Galatians 4:8.)

(c) You can say that the Bible flatly denies the existence of any other gods:

> *' "You are my witnesses," declares the* LORD, *" ... Before me no god was formed, nor will there be one after me." '*
>
> (Isaiah 43:10)

> *'This is what the* LORD *says ... "I am the first and I am the last; apart from me there is no God ... Is there any God besides me? No, there is no other Rock; I know not one." '*
>
> (Isaiah 44:6, 8)

> *'I am the* LORD, *and there is no other; apart from me there is no God.'*   (Isaiah 45:5)

At this point Mormons will often say that these verses really mean 'of this world.' In other words, they are trying to twist the meaning of these scriptures to say that there are many gods, but only one of **this** world. I usually respond to this by saying, 'Really? That isn't what the text says. Why are you adding to it?'

Additionally, they might say that the context is referring to idols and false gods, that God was saying He was the only true God among **them** and that the verses still do not exclude the possibility of other gods. My response is, 'If the context is about idols and God says there are no other gods besides Him, then is He saying there are no other idols besides Him ... or any other false gods besides Him? No, He is saying that they are false and that He alone is God.'

8. Errors in the Book of Mormon

There are of course many inconsistencies in the *Book of Mormon*. Here are just a few to use during witnessing:

- Saved by grace after all you can do? (2 Nephi 25:23).

- How could Moroni have 'read' Hebrews 13:7 and James 1:17 when the New Testament apparently never reached America? (Mormon 9:9).

- Helaman 12:25–26, written 6 BC says, 'we read' (quoting 2 Thessalonians 1:9 and John 5:29) ninety years too early.

- Jesus, a son of God (Alma 36:1).

- Mosiah 21:28 says King Mosiah had a gift from God, but the original *Book of Mormon* manuscript reads 'King Benjamin.'

- Jacob 7:27 has the French word 'adieu' used by people speaking 'reformed Egyptian' around 500 BC. But the French language did not exist until about AD 700. Mormons argue that Joseph Smith was simply translating this into common terms. However, since he was translating allegedly by the power of God, was there then French writing on the golden tablets?

- 2 Nephi 3:11–16 predicts the coming of Joseph Smith from the loins of Joseph, son of Lehi. Yet, Lehi's descendants were wiped out (Mormon 6:11, 8:2–3), while Joseph Smith's ancestors came from England.

- Jesus was born in Bethlehem (Micah 5:1–2; Matthew 2:1). In the *Book of Mormon* (Alma 7:9, 10), it says He was born in Jerusalem.

What is the Baptism for the Dead mentioned in 1 Corinthians 15:29?

'Otherwise, what will those do who are baptized for the dead? If the dead are not raised at all, why then are they baptized for them?'
(1 Corinthians 15:29 NASB)

Numerous explanations have been offered for this verse ranging from the sophisticated to the inane. Mormonism, in particular, has claimed that this verse supports their view of baptism for the dead. In their practice, individuals go to their local Mormon temple, where they representatively adopt the name of a person who has died, and, dressed appropriately, are baptized in water for that deceased person. They maintain that, in this way, the dead person has fulfilled the requirements of salvation in the afterworld and can enjoy further spiritual benefits in the spiritual realm.

But, the Mormons are incorrect; they have taken this verse out of context. In verses 1–19, the fact of Christ's resurrection is expounded by Paul. He then speaks about the order of the resurrection: first Christ – in a glorified body – and then at His return those who are His (vv. 20–23). Next, he speaks about Christ's reign and the abolition of death (vv. 24–29). It is in this context that the controversial verse 29 occurs.

Just north of Corinth, a city named Eleusis was the location of a pagan religion which practiced baptism in the sea to guarantee a good afterlife. This religion was mentioned by Homer in *Hymn to Demeter* 478–79.[21] The Corinthians were known to be heavily influenced by other customs – after all, they were in a large economic area frequented by a great many people of different cultures – and it is probable that the Corinthians were being influenced by this pagan practice. Paul is using this example from the pagans to make his point. He says, *'... if the dead are not raised,* *then why are **they** baptized for the dead?'* He does not say '**we**.' This is significant because the Christian Church was not practicing baptism for the dead – the pagans were. Paul's point is simple: the resurrection is a reality. It is going to happen when Jesus returns. Even the pagans believe in the resurrection, otherwise, why would **they** baptize for the dead?

Therefore, this verse does not support the Mormon belief that people should be baptized for the dead so they can ascend to higher levels of heaven in the Mormon afterlife.

History of the Jehovah's Witnesses

The Jehovah's Witness organization was begun by Charles Taze Russell in 1872. He was born on 16 February 1852, the son of Joseph L. and Anna Eliza Russell. Russell had great difficulty in dealing with the doctrine of eternal hell fire and came to deny not only eternal punishment, but also the Trinity, the deity of Christ and the Holy Spirit. 'In 1870, at the age of 18, Russell organized a Bible class in Pittsburgh.'[22] In 1879 he sought to popularize his aberrant ideas on doctrine, co-publishing *The Herald of the Morning* magazine with its founder, N.H. Barbour. By 1884 Russell controlled the publication and renamed it *The Watchtower Announcing Jehovah's Kingdom*, also founding Zion's Watch Tower Tract Society (now known as the Watchtower Bible and Tract Society). In its first editions of *The Watchtower* only 6,000 copies of the magazine were produced each month but by 1982 the Witnesses' publishing complex in Brooklyn, New York, was producing over 100,000 books and 800,000 copies of its two magazines – daily![23]

Russell claimed that the Bible could be only understood according to his interpretations. This was a dangerous arrangement since he controlled what was written in the *Watchtower* magazine.

After the death of Russell on 31 October 1916, a Missouri lawyer named Joseph Franklin Rutherford took over the presidency of the Watchtower Society which was then known as the Dawn Bible Students Association. In 1931 he changed the name of the organization to 'The Jehovah's Witnesses.'

After Rutherford's death, Nathan Knorr took over. After Knorr, Frederick William Franz became president.

Today the Society is led by Mr Henschel and has over four million members worldwide. The Watchtower Society statistics indicate that 740 house calls are required to recruit each of the nearly 200,000 new members who join every year.

The JWs have several 'book studies' each week. The members are not required to attend, but there is a level of expectation that gently urges converts to participate. It is during these 'book studies' that the JW is consistently exposed to counter-Christian teachings. The average JW, with his constant *Watchtower* indoctrination, could easily pummel the average Christian when it comes to defending his beliefs.

The JWs vehemently state that the doctrine of the Trinity is pagan in origin and that Christendom, as a whole, has bought the lie of the devil. Along with denying the Trinity there is an equally strong denial of the deity of Christ, the deity of the Holy Spirit, the belief in hell, and eternal punishment.

Doctrine of the Jehovah's Witnesses

1. There is one God in one person (*Make Sure of All Things*, p. 188).
2. There is no Trinity (*Let God be True*, pp. 100–101; *Make Sure of All Things*, p. 386).
3. The Holy Spirit is a force, not alive (*Reasoning from the Scriptures*, 1985, pp. 406–407).
4. The Holy Spirit is God's impersonal active force (*The Watchtower*, 1 June, 1952), p. 24.
5. Jehovah's first creation was his 'only-begotten Son' who 'was used by Jehovah in creating all other things', (*Aid to Bible Understanding*, pp. 390–391).
6. Jesus was Michael the archangel who became a man (*The Watchtower*, 15 May 1963, p. 307; *The New World*, 284).
7. Jesus was only a perfect man, not God in flesh (*Reasoning from the Scriptures*, 1985, p. 306).
8. Jesus did not rise from the dead in his physical body (*Awake!* 22 July 1973, p. 4).
9. Jesus was raised 'not a human creature, but a spirit' (*Let God be True*, p. 276).
10. Jesus did not die on a cross but on a stake (*Reasoning from the Scriptures*, 1985, pp. 89–90).
11. Jesus returned to earth, invisibly, in 1914 (*The Truth Shall Make You Free*, p. 300).
12. Jesus' ransom sacrifice did not include Adam (*Let God be True*, p. 119).
13. Their Church is the self-proclaimed prophet of God (*The Watchtower*, 1 April 1972, p. 197).

14. They claim to be the only channel of God's truth (*The Watchtower*, 15 February 1981, p. 19).

15. Only their church members will be saved (*The Watchtower*, 15 February 1979, p. 30).

16. Good works are necessary for salvation (*Studies in the Scriptures*, vol. 1, pp. 150, 152).

17. The soul ceases to exist after death (*Let God be True*, pp. 59, 60, 67).

18. There is no hell fire where the wicked are punished (*Let God be True*, pp. 79, 80).

19. Only 144,000 Jehovah's Witnesses go to heaven (*Reasoning from the Scriptures*, 1985, pp. 166–167, 361; *Let God be True*, p. 121).

20. Blood transfusions are a sin (*Reasoning from the Scriptures*, 1985, pp. 72–73).

21. The cross is a pagan symbol and should not be used (*Reasoning from the Scriptures*, 1985, pp. 90–92).

22. Salvation is by faith and what you do (*Studies in the Scriptures*, vol. 1, pp. 150, 152).

23. It is possible to lose your salvation (*Reasoning from the Scriptures*, 1985, pp. 358–359).

24. The universe is billions of years old (*Your Will Be Done on Earth*, p. 43).

25. Each of the six creative days of God in Genesis 1 was 7000 years long. Therefore, the human race was created toward the end of 42,000 years of earth's preparation (*Let God be True*, p. 168).

26. They also refuse to vote, salute the flag, sing the 'Star Spangled Banner,' or celebrate Christmas or birthdays. They are not allowed to serve in the armed forces.

How to respond to JWs using the Bible

Their attacks on the deity of Jesus

1. JWs say that Jesus wasn't God, but was only a man.

2. Therefore, they might ask, 'If Jesus were God, then . . . '
    (a) Why did Jesus pray to the Father (John 17)?
        (i) Because as a man He needed to pray to the Father.
        (ii) Because He was both God and man (Colossians 2:9; John 8:58 with Exodus 3:14).
            ► Remember, Jesus has two natures. This is called the Hypostatic Union. It is because of these two natures of Christ that we have two types of scriptures concerning Jesus: those that seem to focus on His divine side, and those that seem to focus on His human side. The JWs are simply ignoring, or changing, the divine-side scriptures and concentrating on those that describe His human side.
        (iii) Was Jesus praying to Himself?
            ► Jesus is not the same person as the Father. He was praying to the Father.
            ► At this point it is necessary to explain again what the doctrine of the Trinity is.
    (b) Why did He say the Father was greater than He (John 14:28 John)?
        ► This is because His **position** was different from that of God, not His nature. It says in Hebrews 2:9 that Jesus was made for a little while lower than the angels – that is, when He became a man. The Father sent the Son (1 John 4:10).
    (c) Why did He say, *'Why do you call me good? . . . No one is good – except God alone'* (Luke 18:19)?
        ► Jesus was confirming His own deity because what He was doing **was** good.
        ► Jesus was not saying He wasn't God, but was asking the inquirer to think about what He was saying.
        ► He didn't say, 'Don't call me good.'
        ► Ask them, 'Was Jesus good?'

(d) Why did Jesus say that He could only do those things that He saw the Father do (John 5:19)?

  (i) This is an interesting verse and it is one that proves the divinity of Christ, rather than disproving it.

  (ii) Ask the JW who could do the same things that God the Father can do? Could an angel? Could a man? Of course not. Jesus, however, said He **could** do whatever He saw the Father do.

> *'I tell you the truth, the Son can do nothing by himself; he can do only what he sees his Father doing, because whatever the Father does the Son also does.'*
>
> (John 5:19)

    ▶ The answer to this verse and others like it is that Jesus has two natures. Jesus was fully man as well as fully God and so there will be verses that show His humanity. (*See* 'Hypostatic Union', p. 00, where the two natures of Christ are discussed.)

Bad translations in the Jehovah's Witness Bible, the New World Translation (NWT)

1. Colossians 1:15–17: the word 'other' is inserted four times. It is not in the original Greek, nor is it implied. In this passage Jesus is described as being the creator of all things. Since the JW organization believes that Jesus is created, they have inserted the word 'other' to show that Jesus was before all 'other' things, implying that He is created.

2. Zechariah 12:10: God is speaking:

> *'And I will pour out on the house of David and the inhabitants of Jerusalem a spirit of grace and supplication. They will look on me, the one they have pierced, and they will mourn for him as one mourns for an only child, and grieve bitterly for him as one grieves for a firstborn son.'*

  (a) The JWs change the word 'me' to 'the one' so that it says in their Bible, '... they will look upon the one whom they have pierced ...'

    ▶ There is a very minor manuscript variation with the word 'one'. But it is not preferred.

(b) Since the JWs deny that Jesus is God in flesh, then Zechariah 12:10 would present obvious problems – so they changed the Bible.

3. John 1:1: they mistranslate the verse to say 'a god.' Again it is because they deny who Jesus is and must change the Bible to make it agree with their theology. The JW version is: 'In the beginning was the Word, and the Word was with God, and the Word was a god.'

4. Hebrews 1:6: in this verse they translate the Greek word for 'worship', *proskuneo*, as 'obeisance.' Obeisance is a word that means to honor, show respect, even bow down before someone. Since Jesus, to them, is created, then he cannot be worshiped. They have also done this in other verses concerning Jesus, i.e., Matthew 2:2, 11; 14:33; 28:9.

    Nevertheless, note what the organization used to teach about Jesus being worshiped:

    (a) In the *Watchtower*, 15 July 1898, it says, 'The fact that our Lord received worship is claimed by some to be an evidence that while on earth he was God the Father disguised in a body of flesh and not really a man. Was he *really* worshiped, or is the translation faulty? Yes we believe our Lord Jesus while on earth was really worshiped, and properly so. While he was not *the* God, Jehovah, he was *a* God' (p. 216).

    (b) In the book, *New Heavens and a New Earth*, published in 1953, it says: 'For example, to which one of the angels did he ever say: "You are my Son; today I have become your Father"? And again: "I shall be a Father to him, and he will be a Son to me"? But when he again brings his Firstborn into the inhabited earth, he says: "And let all God's angels worship him"' (pp. 27–28).

5. Hebrews 1:8: in this verse God the Father is calling Jesus God:

    'But about the Son he says, "Your throne, O God, will last for ever and ever, and righteousness will be the scepter of your kingdom."'

Since the JWs don't agree with that they have changed the Bible, yet again, to agree with their theology. They have translated the verse as '...God is your throne...' The problem with the JW translation is that this verse is a quote from Psalm 45:6 which from the Hebrew is best translated as:

> '... *Your throne, O God, will last for ever and ever; a scepter of justice will be the scepter of your kingdom.'*

In order to justify their New Testament translation they have also changed the Old Testament verse to agree with their theology!

▶ Note: There are various Bible translations that translate the verse in the same way as the NWT, but it is not the preferred translation.

Witnessing approaches using the Bible

1. John 1:1: translated as, 'In the beginning was the word and the word was with God and the word was **a** god.'

    (a) If Jesus is a god, then doesn't that mean there are two gods? They often answer, 'Yes. But Jesus is not the *Almighty* God, He is only the *mighty* god. And besides, there are those in the Bible who are called gods but really aren't' (Psalm 82:6, for example).

    (b) The problem with this is that every God besides Jehovah is a false god. God tells us to have no other gods before Him (Exodus 20:3) because they are not by nature gods (Galatians 4:8).

2. Colossians 1:15: used by the JWs to say that Jesus is the first created thing. This verse says,

    > 'He [Jesus] *is the image of the invisible God, the firstborn over all creation.'*

    (a) The JWs maintain that 'firstborn' means 'first created.' This is incorrect because

        (i) There is a Greek word for 'first created' and it is not used here.

            ▶ There is no word used in the NT for 'first created.' However, if there were, the construction would be *proto*, 'first,' with *ktizo*, 'to create,' forming *proto-ktisis*, which is not the construction used in Colossians 1:15.

▸ In Greek, 'first born' – *proto*, 'first,' with *tikto* 'to bring forth, bear, produce' – would produce the Greek word *prototokos*.

(ii) 'Firstborn' can certainly mean the first one born in a family. However, it can also mean preeminence and was a title that was transferable. For example:

▸ In Genesis 41:51–52, the firstborn title is assigned to Manasseh:

> *'Joseph named his firstborn Manasseh and said, "It is because God has made me forget all my trouble, and all my father's household." The second son he named Ephraim...'*

▸ In Jeremiah 31:9, the firstborn title is attributed to one of the tribes of northern Israel and calls Ephraim the firstborn:

> *'They will come with weeping; they will pray as I bring them back. I will lead them beside streams of water on a level path where they will not stumble, because I am Israel's father, and Ephraim is my firstborn son.'*

(iii) Understanding biblical culture is important when interpreting Scripture. Firstborn was a title, not only of the firstborn male, but also of preeminence which is precisely what is occurring when it is said that Jesus is the firstborn.

3. Colossians 1:15–17: in the JW Bible with the addition of four words. Their version reads,

> 'He is the image of the invisible God, the firstborn of all creation; because by means of him all [other] things were created in the heavens and upon the earth, the things visible and the things invisible, no matter whether they are thrones or lordships or governments or authorities. All [other] things have been created through him and for him. Also, he is before all [other] things and by means of him all [other] things were made to exist...'

(Their insertion of the word '[other]' is in their Bible *with* the brackets. They maintain that they know it isn't in the original Greek Scriptures but the word is implied and should be there.)

(a) Instead of refuting the bad translation, simply ask them if this means that Jesus created everything. They will say yes. Review this, getting them to admit very clearly that it was Jesus who created everything. Then turn to Isaiah 44:24:

> 'This is what the LORD says – your Redeemer, who formed you in the womb: I am the LORD, who has made all things, who alone stretched out the heavens, who spread out the earth by myself...'

> ▶ If Jesus created everything, then why does it say that the Lord (Jehovah in the Hebrew) did it by Himself?
> ▶ The only answer is that Jehovah is not simply the name of the Father, but that it is the name of God the Trinity. Therefore, since Jesus is God in flesh, it could be said that Jesus created all things and that Jehovah did it alone.

(b) You can also ask them to try to read the section of verses omitting the word 'other.' You will find it to be an interesting experience.

4. John 8:58: in the JW Bible, '... Before Abraham came into existence, **I have been.**'

(a) They have translated the present tense *ego eimi*, in the Greek, into the English perfect tense, 'I have been.' Though this can be done on rare occasions in the New Testament, it is not correct here because Jesus was quoting Exodus 3:14 in the Old Testament where *'God said to Moses, "I am who I am. This is what you are to say to the Israelites: 'I AM has sent me to you.'"'* Jesus was purposely using the divine title 'I AM.'

(i) The JW won't agree. So ask him why, if Jesus was saying that He 'had been' before Abraham, it says in the next verse that the Jews picked up stones to kill him?

> ▶ They may respond that it was because Jesus had insulted and upset the Jews in John 8 and they snapped when Jesus said, '... I have been.'
> ▶ Then draw the connection with John 10:30–34 below where the Jews again tried to kill Jesus.

(ii) Additionally, about 250 years BC the Jews translated the Hebrew Scriptures into Greek. It is called the Septuagint, also known as LXX. In the Septuagint Exodus 3:14 is translated in the Greek in a present tense, i.e., I AM ... The correct translation is, therefore, *'Before Abraham was, I AM.'*

(b) Jesus also said 'I am' in John 8:24 and 8:32.

▶ Why does the NWT not translate it as 'I was' or 'I have been?' The third time Jesus said it, they tried to kill Him.

▶ Notice that 8:24 and 8:32 both speak of Christ's death. Go to Zechariah 12:10.

(c) It wasn't 'I have been' in English that made them mad; it was *ego eimi* in the Greek that was the last straw.

(d) If this verse should really be translated as 'I have been' then why did the Jews want to kill Jesus? The answer is simple: they knew He was claiming to be God.

5. John 10:30–34: a passage in which the Pharisees accuse Jesus of making Himself out to be God (v. 33).

'"I and the Father are one." Again the Jews picked up stones to stone him, but Jesus said to them, "I have shown you many great miracles from the Father. For which of these do you stone me?" "We are not stoning you for any of these," replied the Jews, "but for blasphemy, because you, a mere man, claim to be God."'

(a) You can say, 'See, even the Jews knew He was claiming to be God.' The JW (if he's quick enough) will say something like, 'Jesus wasn't God, the Jews only **thought** that Jesus was claiming to be God.' Then you can say, 'Oh, I see. Then let me get this right. You agree with the Pharisees that Jesus wasn't God? Is that correct?' The JW will not like to be found agreeing with a Pharisee.

(b) What was it that Jesus said that caused the Jews to want to kill him here? They believed he was claiming to be God.

6. The following group of scriptures strongly suggests a plurality within the Godhead. These verses are translated correctly in the JW Bible so you can encourage them to use it. The NIV is not as literal in its translation in the Amos verses, so I recommend using either the New King James Version or the New American Standard Bible when making your own study.

(a) Genesis 1:26:

> 'Then God said, "Let us make man in our image, in our likeness..."'

> ▶ JWs will say that angels are the ones who helped God make human beings. However, there is no scriptural evidence for that. God is the only creator.
> ▶ You can also take the JW to Colossians 1:15–17 where it says that Jesus is the creator of all things – including human beings.

(b) Genesis 19:24:

> 'Then the LORD [24] rained down burning sulphur on Sodom and Gomorrah – from the LORD out of the heavens.'

> ▶ Is this saying there are two Lords, two Jehovahs?

(c) Amos 4:10–11:

> '"I sent among you a plague after the manner of Egypt; your young men I killed with a sword along with your captive horses; I made the stench of your camps come up into your nostrils; yet you have not returned to Me," says the LORD. "I overthrew some of you as God overthrew Sodom and Gomorrah..."'   (NKJV)

> ▶ Jehovah is the one talking. He says, 'I overthrew some of you as God overthrew Sodom and Gomorrah...' Very interesting.

(d) Isaiah 44:6:

> 'Thus says the LORD, the King of Israel and his Redeemer, the LORD of hosts: "I am the First and I am the Last, besides me there is no God..."'

> ▶ See also Isaiah 48:16.

If you are reading these verses to a JW he might say something like, 'Are you trying to show me the Trinity from these verses?' You can then say, 'You got the Trinity out of these verses? That's very interesting.'

> ▶ (These verses and others are more fully developed in 'The Plurality Study' which is a powerful tool for witnessing to JWs.)

7.   John 20:25 says:

> *'The other disciples therefore were saying to him, "We have seen the Lord!" But he said to them, "Unless I shall see in His hands the imprint of the nails, and put my finger into the place of the nails, and put my hand into His side, I will not believe."'*   (NASB)

> ▶ The JWs deny that Jesus was crucified on a cross. They say He was put to death on a torture stake where His wrists were forced together over His head and a single nail put through them both. If that is true, then why does Thomas say, *'Unless I shall see in His hands the imprint of the nails...'* In the Greek the word used here for 'nails,' *helos*, is in the plural. Therefore, more than one nail must have pierced the hands of Christ at the crucifixion.

8.   How many firsts and lasts are there? In the Bible God is called the First and Last and so is Jesus. The fact that God says there is no God apart from Him, and Jesus and God are both addressed by the same title, poses a problem for JWs.

(a)   Isaiah 44:6:

> *'This is what the LORD says – Israel's King and Redeemer, the LORD Almighty: I am the first and I am the last; apart from me there is no God.'*

(b)   Revelation 1:8:

> *'"I am the Alpha and the Omega," says the Lord God, "who is, and who was, and who is to come, the Almighty."'*

(c)   Revelation 1:17–18:

> *'When I saw him, I fell at his feet as though dead. Then he placed his right hand on me and said: "Do not be afraid. I am the First and the Last. I am the Living One; I was dead, and behold I am alive for ever and ever! And I hold the keys of death and Hades."'*

> ▶ Obviously, Revelation 1:17–18 can only refer to Jesus.

(d)   Revelation 22:12–13:

> *'Behold, I am coming soon! My reward is with me, and I will give to everyone according to what he has done. I am the Alpha and the Omega, the First and the Last, the Beginning and the End.'*

> ▶ Here, both the 'Alpha and the Omega' and the 'First and the Last' are said to be one and the same.
>
> ▶ Also, at this point go to Titus 2:13 where it says that Jesus is the one who is coming soon, therefore, Jesus and Jehovah are the same.

The Holy Spirit

1. JWs teach that the Holy Spirit is an active force like radar. They deny that He is alive, that He is a person. This is because they deny the Trinity. Yet, if the Holy Spirit is simply a force then...

   > ▶ Why is He called God (Acts 5:3–5)?
   > ▶ How is it that He can teach (John 14:26)?
   > ▶ How can He be blasphemed (Matthew 12:31, 32)?
   > ▶ How can He be the one who comforts (Acts 9:31)?
   > ▶ How is it possible for Him to speak (Acts 28:25)?
   > ▶ How then can He be resisted (Acts 7:51)?
   > ▶ How can He be grieved (Ephesians 4:30)?
   > ▶ How can He help us in our weaknesses (Romans 8:26)?

2. If the Holy Spirit is a force, then how is it possible for the above-mentioned phenomena to be attributed to Him? A force doesn't speak, teach, comfort, etc. Nor can you blaspheme against a force. (*See* 'Trinity', p. 00.)

3. They will say that the Holy Spirit cannot be a person because it is poured out (Acts 2:33; 10:45).

   > ▶ Yet, in a prophecy about His crucifixion, Jesus is also described as being poured out: '*I am poured out like water*' (Psalm 22:14).

The resurrection of Jesus

1. The Jehovah's Witnesses deny the physical resurrection of Jesus. They say that, in order for the sacrifice of Jesus to be real, the body had to stay in the grave. They maintain that He rose in a spirit body. The manifestation of this body was similar to the way angels revealed themselves in the Old Testament.

   > ▶ The problem with their view is that the angels were not incarnated. Jesus became a man by birth, and, therefore, He

had a real, physical body – a permanent body. In fact, right now, Jesus is in heaven in the form of a man. He still has two natures, God and man, and will have them eternally.

2. For scriptural proof of Jesus being raised in the same body in which He died, consider the following verses:

    (a) Luke 24:39:

    > *'...a spirit does not have flesh and bones as you see I have.'*
    > (NKJV)

    ▶ Jesus said that He had 'flesh and bones' not 'flesh and blood.' This is important because flesh and blood cannot inherit the kingdom of God (1 Corinthians 15:50). The blood of Jesus was the sacrifice for sin (Romans 5:9). It is the blood that cleanses us of our sin (Hebrews 9:22).

    (b) John 20:27 (to Thomas):

    > *'...Reach out your hand and put it into my side...'*

    ▶ If Jesus were not raised from the dead, then why did He have a physical body?
    ▶ They will reply that it was a temporary body materialized so the apostles would believe that He was raised. Yet...

    (c) In John 2:19–22 John before the crucifixion Jesus asserted:

    > *'Destroy this temple and I will raise it again in three days ... But the temple he had spoken of was his body.'*

    ▶ Since Jesus said He would raise the same body in which He died, then it must be true.
    ▶ This last verse is worth focusing on. Remember, Jesus said **He** would be the one to raise His body. So, it must be true.

3. They will say that Jesus was raised a life-giving spirit (1 Corinthians 15:451).

    ▶ There is much figurative language within this verse. Jesus is a life-giving spirit in the sense that He gives eternal life. Combine this with John 2:19 above and you will see that Jesus rose from the dead in His glorified body and, as such, is a life-giving spirit.

Similarities between the Jehovah's Witnesses and the Pharisees

1. Both deny the Trinity and the deity of Christ.
2. Both deny the physical resurrection of Christ and salvation by grace alone.
3. Both believe the wicked are annihilated. [25]

When witnessing to Jehovah's Witnesses, you should check every Bible reference they quote to you. Ask them to read the verse and then look at the context to see if what they are saying is true. Be patient with them.

Likewise, you will need to show them the verses you are using to explain the truth from your Bible. It can be a time-consuming effort, but you will learn a great deal from the experience.

'I AM,' (John 8:58 and 10:30–33)

In John 8:58 Jesus said, *'Before Abraham was, I am.'* This is a very important verse to Trinitarians because it can be used to show that Jesus is God. We maintain that Jesus attributed the divine name of God ('I AM' from Exodus 3:14), to Himself.

This section will not attempt to analyze the Greek translation principles that have led various Bibles to render John 8:58 as 'I have been,' or 'I was in existence,' etc. Suffice it to say that the best recognized translations which have sought literal renderings of the text, have translated the verse as 'I AM': NASB, NIV, KJV, RSV, etc.

The Jehovah's Witness Watchtower organization claims that the best translation of John 8:58 is 'Before Abraham was, **I have been.**' Notice that it does not say, 'I AM.' Is it legitimate for the Watchtower organization to **insist** that John 8:58 is best translated as 'I have been'? No, it isn't.

Ego eimi means 'I am'

In Greek, the words recorded in John 8:58 are *'prin abraam genesthai ego eimi.'* Literally, this translates as: *'Before Abraham was existing, I am.' Ego eimi* is literally *'I am.'* It is the present tense. The rendition 'I have been' uses the perfect tense. There is a perfect tense in Greek, but Jesus did not use it here.

There are places, however, in the New Testament where the Greek present tense of *ego eimi*, *'I am,'* can be translated into the English perfect tense, *'I have been.'* An example of this is John 14:9 where Jesus says, *'Have I been with you so long, and yet you have not known Me . . . '* (NKJV). In this verse, *'Have I been'* is being used to translate the Greek present tense, *ego eimi.* But here, Jesus was answering the statement in verse 8, *'Lord, show us the Father, and it is sufficient for us.'* Since in English it is awkward to say, *'I am with you so long and you still don't know me . . . ?'*, it has been rendered as, *'Have I been with you so long and yet you have not known me . . . ?'* The translation of the Greek present into the English perfect tense is perfectly justifiable here because the literal translation doesn't make sense in English. But is it the case with John 8:58? Must it be translated as 'I have been?' No. There is no linguistic require-ment to translate it as 'I have been' particularly when you notice that the words provoked such a strong reaction that the Jews wanted to kill Jesus after he said them.

Two views

Some say that the reason the Jews wanted to kill Jesus after He said, *'Before Abraham was, I am'* is because it was the last straw in a series of difficult and insulting things Jesus had been saying to the Jews in John 8. Others say that the Jews wanted to kill Jesus for saying, *'Before Abraham was, I am,'* because *'I am'* is close to God saying *'I am that I am'* in Exodus 3:14. In other words, we can make the case that for Jesus to say, *'Before Abraham was, I am'* was equivalent to claiming God's name for Himself. This is something the about which Jews would absolutely protest. Let's look at the arguments.

The first argument states that Jesus had upset the Jews so much by what He had been saying that when he finally made his statement in verse 58, it was the last straw, the Jews snapped, and then they tried to kill Him. But, they maintain, it wasn't because Jesus was claiming the divine title. They had just had enough.

What had Jesus been saying? These are some of the key state-ments Jesus had made in John 8 (NASB):

- *'I am the light of the world'* (v. 12).

- *'I am He who bears witness of Myself, and the Father who sent Me bears witness of me'* (v. 18).

- *'You know neither me nor my Father'* (v. 19).

- *'You are from below, I am from above'* (v. 23).

- *'...unless you believe that I am He, you shall die in your sins'* (v. 24).

- *'...the things which I heard from Him* [God the Father], *these I speak to the world'* (v. 26).

- *'I speak these things as the Father taught me'* (v. 28).

- *'I always do the things that are pleasing to Him'* (v. 29).

- *'I speak the things which I have seen with My Father...'* (v. 38).

- *'...you are seeking to kill Me, a man who has told you the truth, which I heard from God, this Abraham did not do'* (v. 40).

- *'...I proceeded forth and have come from God...'* (v. 42).

- *'Truly, truly, I say to you, if anyone keeps My word he shall never see death'* (v. 51).

- *'...it is my Father who glorifies Me...'* (v. 54).

- *'...before Abraham was, I am'* (v. 58).

This list includes many profound statements. It is perfectly understandable that the Jews would be upset. But, it was Jesus' statement in John 8:58 that triggered their murderous attempt. Was it because Jesus said, 'Before Abraham was, I have been' or *'Before Abraham was, I am.'* Which would be the phrase most likely to be the last straw for the Jews? It is quite possible that either statement would be sufficient. But, of course, any claim by Jesus to the divine name would be a stronger motivation for the Jews to kill Him.

The connection with John 10:30–33

Capital punishment was only for serious sins: blasphemy, adultery, etc. From what I can see in the Bible, making a statement asserting you had a preexistence isn't blasphemy. However, claiming to be one with God is quite different. In John 10:30–33 Jesus said,

> ' *"I and the Father are one." The Jews took up stones **again** to stone him. Jesus answered them, "I showed you many good works from the Father; for which of them are you stoning me?" The Jews answered Him, "For a good work we do not stone You, but for blasphemy; and because You, being a man, make Yourself out to be God."* '   (NASB)

Between John 8:59, where the Jews picked up stones to kill Jesus, and John 10:30–33, where they **again** picked up stones to kill him, there is no mention of stoning whatsoever. John 10:31 is refering back to John 8:59 when it says, *'The Jews took up stones **again** to stone Him.'* Note that they again wanted to kill Him and this time the reason why is given. They said it was because Jesus was claiming to be God. Now, where would they have got that idea? Could it have been when He said, *'Before Abraham was, I am?'* Could it be when He said, *'I and the Father are one'* (John 10:30). Since on both occasions they wanted to kill Him, it would seem that Jesus had been making some very serious claims. Or was it simply that the Pharisees misunderstood Jesus and that He never did claim to be God?

But, if Jesus was **not** claiming to be God in John 8:58 and 10:30, then what was it that He said that warranted such a violent response from the Jews in both cases? What statement from Jesus did the Jews react to and what 'misunderstanding' did they have that led them to claim that He was making Himself out to be God?

In my opinion, the best explanation for the Jews wanting to kill Jesus is because Jesus was claiming equality with God, which they considered blasphemy. After all, the Jews, like so many cult groups today, denied that Jesus was God.

If Jesus is not God, then explain...

1. How was it possible for Jesus to know all things (John 21:17)?
2. How can Jesus know all men (John 16:30)?
3. How can Jesus be everywhere (Matthew 28:20)?
4. How can Jesus, the Christ, dwell in you (Colossians 1:27)?
5. How can Jesus be the exact representation of the nature of God (Hebrews 1:3)?
6. How can Jesus be eternal (Micah 5:1–2)?
7. How can Jesus be the one who gives eternal life (John 10:27–28)?
8. How can He be our only Lord and Master (Jude 4)?
9. How can Jesus be called the Mighty God (Isaiah 9:6) if there is only one God in existence (Isaiah 44:6–8; 45:5)?
10. How was Jesus able to raise Himself from the dead (John 2:19–21)?
11. How can Jesus create all things (Colossians 1:16–17), yet it is God the Father who created all things by Himself (Isaiah 44:24)?
12. How can Jesus search the hearts and minds of the people (Revelation 2:23)?
13. Why was Jesus worshiped (Matthew 2:2, 11; 14:33; 28:9; John 9:35–38; Hebrews 1:6) when He says to worship God only (Matthew 4:10)? (The same Greek word for worship is used in each place.)
14. In the Old Testament God was seen (Exodus 6:2–3; 24:9–11; Numbers 12:6–9; cf. Acts 7:2), yet no man can see God (Exodus 33:20; John 1:18). It was not the Father that was seen in the Old Testament (John 6:46). Who, then, were they seeing? (*See* John 8:58.)
15. Then why did Jesus claim the divine name, 'I AM,' for Himself in John 8:58? (*See* Exodus 3:14.)
16. Then why did Jesus say you must honor Him even as you honor the Father (John 5:23)?
17. Then why is it that both the Father and the Son give life (John 5:21)?
18. Then why did Jesus bear witness of Himself (John 8:18; 14:6)?

Jehovah's Witnesses, Christ's resurrection, and His shed blood

The Witnesses maintain that the physical resurrection of Christ did not occur. They say, 'Having given up his flesh for the life of the world, Christ could never take it again and become a man once more.'[26] They will quote verses like 1 Peter 3:18 to support their view:

> *'For Christ also died for sins once for all, the just for the unjust, in order that He might bring us to God. He was put to death in the flesh but made alive in the spirit.'*   (1 Peter 3:18 NASB)

But they don't read the next verse that says, *'in which also He went and made proclamation to the spirits now in prison...'* This verse is talking about Jesus **before** His resurrection. There are different theories concerning what Jesus did between His death and resurrection, but one very plausible explanation is that He went to the spirits that were imprisoned from long ago and proclaimed to them the truth. It was after this that He was raised in His physical body.

The JWs state that if Jesus' body was raised then the sacrifice didn't remain; it was 'taken back.' The problem with that is that they fail to understand the nature of the sacrifice. Jesus' atoning sacrifice was His blood, not simply His body. Consider the following scriptures as support:

1. *'For the life of a creature is in the blood, and I have given it to you to make atonement for yourselves on the altar; it is the blood that makes atonement for one's life.'*   (Leviticus 17:11)

   ▶ The blood is what makes the atonement real, not the body.

2. *'In fact, the law requires that nearly everything be cleansed with blood, and without the shedding of blood there is no forgiveness.'*
   (Hebrews 9:22)

   ▶ The shedding of blood is what makes forgiveness real.

3. *'Since we have now been justified by His blood, how much more shall we be saved from God's wrath through Him!'*   (Romans 5:9)

   ▶ We are justified by Christ's shed blood.

4. *'This is my blood of the covenant, which is poured out for many for the forgiveness of sins.'*   (Matthew 26:28)

    ▶ Jesus' blood was poured out for the forgiveness of sins.

Even in the Jehovah's Witness book *Reasoning from the Scriptures* it says that 'His shed blood has value to provide deliverance for others' (p. 306). At least they understand that the shedding of blood is important. However, they err by saying that the sacrifice is not valid if the body of Christ is resurrected. The scripture says, *'flesh and blood cannot inherit the kingdom of God'* (1 Corinthians 15:50). Flesh and blood are references to the natural state (Genesis 29:14; 2 Samuel 5:1; Ephesians 6:12). But, after His resurrection Jesus said,

> *'... touch me and see, for a spirit does not have flesh and bones as you see that I have.'*   (Luke 24:39 NASB)

Every word in the Bible is inspired. Jesus said, *'... flesh and bones ...'* I believe this is because His resurrected body had no blood in it. It had been poured out (Matthew 26:28).

Therefore, His body has been raised and the sacrifice of His blood is maintained. He was raised to show that the sacrifice was acceptable to the Father and that death's power had been broken. His blood was poured out and the result is that we have forgiveness of sins. His body **was** raised, His blood wasn't.

False prophecies of the Jehovah's Witnesses

The Witnesses make many claims in their attempts to convert people to their faith. They profess to have the only true Christian Church, to be the only true representatives of God, to have the only correct biblical teaching, and to be the only true announcers of Jehovah's coming kingdom.

If they are the only true Church and are the only true voice of God's word, then what they say should prove to be true, especially in prophecy. When it comes to predicting the future, the Watchtower organization has failed miserably. Below are some of the false predictions made over the years by the Watchtower organization. If you present these to a JW, he or she will probably say something like, 'Those are taken out of context,' or 'They didn't claim to be the prophet of God,' or 'The light is getting brighter and we are understanding Bible prophecy better now,' etc. Make a copy of the false prophecies found in the appendix and give it to them to check. They are taken directly from the Witnesses' literature.

Remember,

> *'If what a prophet proclaims in the name of the* LORD *does not take place or come true, that is a message the* LORD *has not spoken. That prophet has spoken presumptuously. Do not be afraid of him.'*
> (Deuteronomy 18:22)

If someone makes a false prophecy, claiming to be a prophet of God, then he or she is a false prophet and is not to be listened to.

Do the Witnesses claim to be the prophet of God? Yes, they do.

1972: Identifying the 'Prophet'

> 'So does Jehovah have a prophet to help them, to warn them of dangers and to declare things to come? These questions can be answered in the affirmative. Who is this prophet? ... This "prophet" was not one man, but was a body of men and women. It was the small group of footstep followers of Jesus Christ, known at that time as International Bible Students. Today they are known as Jehovah's Christian Witnesses ... Of course, it is easy to say that this group acts as a "prophet" of God. It is another thing to prove it.'
> (*Watchtower*, 1 April 1972.
> *See* Deuteronomy 18:21.)

1899

> '...the "battle of the great day of God Almighty" (Revelation 16:14), which will end in AD 1914 with the complete over-throw of earth's present rulership, is already commenced.'
> (*The Time Is at Hand*, 1908 edition, p. 101)

1897

> 'Our Lord, the appointed King, is now present, since October 1874.'   (*Studies in the Scriptures*, vol. 4, p. 621)

1916

'The Bible chronology herein presented shows that the six great 10000 year days beginning with Adam are ended, and that the great 7th Day, the 1000 years of Christ's Reign, began in 1873.'   (*The Time Is at Hand*, page ii, forward)

1918

'Therefore we may confidently expect that 1925 will mark the return of Abraham, Isaac, Jacob and the faithful prophets of old, particularly those named by the Apostle in Hebrews 11, to the condition of human perfection.'

(*Millions Now Living Will Never Die*, p. 89)

1922

'The date 1925 is even more distinctly indicated by the Scriptures than 1914.' (*Watchtower*, 1 September 1922, p. 262)

1923

'Our thought is, that 1925 is definitely settled by the Scriptures. As to Noah, the Christian now has much more upon which to base his faith than Noah had upon which to base his faith in a coming deluge.'   (*Watchtower*, 1 April 1923, p. 106)

1925

'The year 1925 is here. With great expectation Christians have looked forward to this year. Many have confidently expected that all members of the body of Christ will be changed to heavenly glory during this year. This may be accomplished. It may not be. In his own due time God will accomplish his purposes concerning his people. Christians should not be so deeply concerned about what may transpire this year.'

(*Watchtower*, 1 January 1925, p. 3)

1925

'It is to be expected that Satan will try to inject into the minds of the consecrated, the thought that 1925 should see an end to the work.'   (*Watchtower*, September 1925, p. 262)

1926

'Some anticipated that the work would end in 1925, but the Lord did not state so. The difficulty was that the friends inflated their imaginations beyond reason; and that when their imaginations burst asunder, they were inclined to throw away everything.'   (*Watchtower*, issue, p. 232)

1931

'There was a measure of disappointment on the part of Jehovah's faithful ones on earth concerning the years 1917, 1918, and 1925, which disappointment lasted for a time ... and they also learned to quit fixing dates.'

(*Vindication*, p. 338)

1941

'Receiving the gift, the marching children clasped it to them, not a toy or plaything for idle pleasure, but the Lord's provided instrument for most effective work in the remaining months before Armageddon.'

(*Watchtower*, 15 September 1941, p. 288)

1968

'True, there have been those in times past who predicted an "end to the world", even announcing a specific date. Yet nothing happened. The "end" did not come. They were guilty of false prophesying. Why? What was missing? Missing from such people were God's truths and evidence that he was using and guiding them.'   (*Awake*, 8 October 1968)

1968

'Why are you looking forward to 1975?'

(*Watchtower*, 15 August 1968, p. 494).

A JW might say that the organization is still learning. If that is so, then how can they trust what they are now being taught by the *Watchtower*? Will what they are being taught now change also?

A true prophet of God won't err in prophesying. Only a false prophet does. The Jehovah's Witness organization, which claims to be a prophet of God, is really a false prophet. Jesus warned us by saying,

> *'For false Christs and false prophets will appear and perform great signs and miracles to deceive even the elect – if that were possible.'*
> (Matthew 24:24)

Interesting quotes from Watchtower literature

It is important to understand the position the Watchtower organization has in the lives of Jehovah's Witnesses. It is the guide, the teacher, the expounder of correct doctrine. JWs attend several meetings each week where they are repeatedly indoctrinated to believe Watchtower doctrines. All JWs think alike and have the same pat answers because they read from the same sources and are conditioned into thinking in one way: the Watchtower way. So, if you've witnessed to one JW, you've witnessed to them all.

In the Bible, Jesus is the mediator between God and human beings (1 Timothy 2:5). He alone is the one who reveals truth (John 1:17), not the Watchtower organization. As you will read in these quotes, the Watchtower organization subtly takes the place of Jesus. Though they claim to bear witness to Him and point to Him, they really don't.

> 'It should be expected that the Lord would have a means of communication to his people on the earth, and he has clearly shown that the magazine called *The Watchtower* is used for that purpose.'   (*1939 Yearbook of Jehovah's Witnesses*, p. 85)

> 'We all need help to understand the Bible, and we cannot find the Scriptural guidance we need outside the "faithful and discreet slave" organization.'
> (*Watchtower*, 15 February 1981)

> '... people cannot see the Divine Plan in studying the Bible by itself ... if he then lays them [Scripture Studies] aside and ignores them and goes to the Bible alone, though he has understood his Bible for ten years, our experience shows that

within two years he goes into darkness. On the other hand, if he had merely read the Scripture Studies with their references, and had not read a page of the Bible, as such, he would be in the light at the end of the two years, because he would have the light of the Scriptures.'

(*Watchtower*, 15 September 1910, p. 298)

'From time to time, there have arisen from among the ranks of Jehovah's people those, who, like the original Satan, have adopted an independent, faultfinding attitude ... They say that it is sufficient to read the Bible exclusively, either alone or in small groups at home. But, strangely, through such "Bible reading," they have reverted right back to the apostate doctrines that commentaries by Christendom's clergy were teaching 100 years ago ... '   (*Watchtower*, 15 August 1981)

'Thus the Bible is an organizational book and belongs to the Christian congregation as an organization, not to individuals, regardless of how sincerely they may believe that they can interpret the Bible.'   (*Watchtower*, 1 October 1967, p. 587)

'Make haste to identify the visible theocratic organization of God that represents his king, Jesus Christ. It is essential for life. Doing so, be complete in accepting its every aspect.'

(*Watchtower*, 1 October 1967, p. 591)

'If we are to walk in the light of truth we must recognize not only Jehovah God as our Father but his organization as our mother.'   (*Watchtower*, 1 May 1957, p. 274)

'We cannot claim to love God, yet deny his word and channel of communication.'   (*Watchtower*, 1 October 1967, p. 591)

'We should eat and digest and assimilate what is set before us, without shying away from parts of the food because it may not suit the fancy of our mental taste ... We should meekly go along with the Lord's theocratic organization and wait for further clarification, rather than balk at the first mention of a thought unpalatable to us and proceed to quibble and mouth our criticisms and opinions as though they were worth more than the slave's provision of spiritual food. Theocratic ones will appreciate the Lord's visible organization and not be so foolish as to put against Jehovah's channel their own human reasoning and sentiment and personal feelings.'

(*Watchtower*, 1 February 1952, pp. 79–80)

'After being nourished to our present spiritual strength and maturity, do we suddenly become smarter than our former provider and forsake the enlightening guidance of the organization that mothers us? "Forsake not the law of thy mother" (Prov. 6:20–23).'

(*Watchtower*, 1 February 1952, p. 80)

'Never was there a more deceptive doctrine advanced than that of the trinity. It could have originated only in one mind, and that the mind of Satan the Devil.'

(*Reconciliation*, 1928, p. 101)

'The doctrine, in brief, is that there are three gods in one: "God the Father, God the Son, and God the Holy Ghost; all three equal in power, substance and eternity.'

(*Let God be True*, 1952, p. 100. Here they misrepresent the doctrine of the Trinity.)

'Ask the student, "How many Jehovah's are there?" Let him answer. The answer is obvious that there is only one Jehovah ... If he is one Jehovah, then could he be three gods, God the Father, God the Son and God the Holy Ghost, as the Trinitarians teach?'

(*Watchtower*, 1 April 1970. p. 210. Again, the *Watchtower* misrepresents the doctrine of the Trinity.)

'The fact that our Lord received worship is claimed by some to be an evidence that while on earth he was God the Father disguised in a body of flesh and not really a man. Was he *really* worshiped, or is the translation faulty? Yes we believe our Lord Jesus while on earth was really worshiped, and properly so. While he was not *the* God, Jehovah, he was *a* God. The word 'God' signifies a "mighty one," and our Lord was indeed a mighty one. So it is stated in the first two verses of the gospel of John. It was proper for our Lord to receive worship in view of his having been the only begotten of the Father...'

(*Watchtower*, 15 July 1898, p. 216)

There are four requirements for salvation as taught by the Watchtower magazine of 15 February 1983, p. 12. One of them deals with the Watchtower organization.

1. Jesus Christ identified a first requirement when he said in prayer to his Father: 'This means everlasting life, their taking in knowledge of you, the only true God, and of the one whom you sent forth, Jesus Christ.' (John 17:3) Knowledge of God and of Jesus Christ includes knowledge of God's purposes regarding the earth and of Christ's role as earth's new King. Will you take in such knowledge by studying the Bible?

2. Many have found the second requirement more difficult. It is to obey God's laws, yes, to conform one's life to the moral requirements set out in the Bible. This includes refraining from a debauched, immoral way of life. – 1 Corinthians 6:9, 10; 1 Peter 4:3, 4.

3. A third requirement is that we be associated with God's channel, his organization. God has always used an organization. For example, only those in the ark in Noah's day survived the Flood, and only those associated with the Christian congregation in the first century had God's favor. (Acts 4:12) Similarly, Jehovah is using only one organization today to accomplish his will. To receive everlasting life in the earthly Paradise we must identify that organization and serve God as part of it.

4. The fourth requirement is connected with loyalty. God requires that prospective subjects of his Kingdom support his government by loyally advocating his Kingdom rule to others. Jesus Christ explained: 'This good news of the kingdom will be preached in all the inhabited earth.' (Matthew 24:14) Will you meet this requirement by telling others about God's Kingdom?

More interesting quotes from Watchtower literature

'Consider, too, the fact that Jehovah's organization alone, in all the earth, is directed by God's holy spirit or active force (Zech. 4:6). Only this organization functions for Jehovah's purpose and to his praise. To it alone God's Sacred Word, the Bible, is not a sealed book ... How very much true Christians appreciate associating with the only organization on earth that understands the "deep things of God"! ... Furthermore, this organization alone is supplied with "gifts in men," such as evangelizers, shepherd and teachers...'

(Watchtower, 1 July 1973)

'And the period of falling also corresponds; for the time our Lord said, "Your house is left unto you desolate," A.D. 33, to A.D. 70 was $36\frac{1}{2}$ years; and so from A.D. 1878 to the end of A.D. 1914 is $36\frac{1}{2}$ years. And with the end of A.D. 1914, what God calls Babylon, and what men call Christendom, will have passed away, as already shown from prophecy.'

(Thy Kingdom Come, 1891 edn, p. 153)

'The date of the close of that "battle" is definitely marked in Scripture as October, 1914. It is already in progress, its beginning dating from October, 1874.'

(Watchtower, 15 January 1892, pp. 21–23)

'For instance, as we look back and note that the Scriptures marked 1873 as the end of six thousand years from Adam to the beginning of the seventh thousand, and the fall of 1874 as the beginning of the forty-year harvest of the Gospel age and day of wrath for the overthrow of all the institutions of "this present evil world [or order of affairs]," we can see that facts have well borne out those predictions of Scripture.'

(View from the Tower, Allegheny, PA, 15 July 1894, vol. 15, no. 14 [1675])

'Be not surprised, then, when in subsequent chapters we present proofs that the setting up of the Kingdom of God is already begun, that it is pointed out in prophecy as due to begin the exercise of power in A.D. 1878, and that the "battle of the great day of God Almighty" (Rev. 16:14), which will end in A.D. 1914 with the complete overthrow of earth's present rulership, is already commenced.'

(*The Time is at Hand*, 1911 edn, p. 101)

'The Scriptural proof is that the second presence of the Lord Jesus Christ began in 1874 A.D.'   (*Prophecy*, 1929, p. 65)

It is obvious that the Watchtower Organization was wrong in its interpretation of prophetic events. It claims to be the only channel of God's truth yet it has missed the mark from the very beginning. Can it be trusted? No.

'The man Adam is not included in those ransomed. Why not? Because he was a willful sinner, was justly sentenced to death, and died deservedly, and God would not reverse his just judgment and give Adam life. He had a perfect life, and this he deliberately forfeited.'   (*Let God be True*, p. 119)

'Accepting the message of salvation and devoting ourselves to God through Christ and being baptized in water is only the beginning of our exercise of faith. It is only the beginning of our obedience to God. It sets us on the way to everlasting life, but it does not mean our final salvation.'

(*This Means Everlasting Life*, p. 181)

'Thus it is seen that the serpent (the Devil) is the one that originated the doctrine of the inherent immortality of human souls. This doctrine is the main one that the Devil has used down through the ages to deceive the people and hold them in bondage. In fact, it is the foundation doctrine of false religion.'   (*Let God be True*, pp. 74–75)

Questions to ask the Jehovah's Witnesses

1. The Watchtower organization has claimed to be the prophet of
    God (*Watchtower*, 1 April 1972, p. 197), yet it has made
    numerous false prophecies. In excuse for their false prophecies
    they have quoted Proverbs 4:18 which says,

    > '*But the path of the righteous ones is like the bright light that is
    > getting lighter and lighter until the day is firmly established.*'

    It would perhaps be more appropriate for Jehovah's Witnesses
    to judge their prophecies by the following verses in the New
    World Translation:

    > 'However, the prophet who presumes to speak in my name a
    > word that I have not commanded him to speak or who
    > speaks in the name of other gods, that prophet must die.
    > And in case you should say in your heart: "How shall we
    > know the word that Jehovah has not spoken?" when the
    > prophet speaks in the name of Jehovah and the word does
    > not occur or come true, that is the word that Jehovah did
    > not speak . . . '   (Deuteronomy 18:20–22)

    If the New World Translation condemns false prophecy and
    states that it is proof that God is not speaking through that
    prophet, then doesn't this prove that the Watchtower Bible
    and Tract Society is not speaking for God?

2. Why does the New World Translation insert the word Jehovah
    in the New Testament when there are absolutely no Greek
    manuscripts that have it in there? Isn't this playing with the
    text?

3. In the book *Salvation* by J.F. Rutherford (Watchtower Publica-
    tion, 1939, p. 311) it says,

    > 'At San Diego, California, there is a small piece of land, on
    > which, in the year 1929, there was built a house, which is
    > called and known as Beth-Sarim . . . that there might be some
    > tangible proof that there are those on earth today who fully
    > believe God and Christ Jesus and in His kingdom, and
    > who believe that the faithful men of old will soon be resur-
    > rected by the Lord, be back on earth, and take charge of the

visible affairs of earth. The title to Beth-Sarim is vested in the Watchtower Bible & Tract Society in trust, to be used by the president of the Society and his assistants for the present, and thereafter to be forever at the disposal of the afore-mentioned princes on earth ... while the unbelievers have mocked concerning it and spoken contemptuously of it, yet it stands there as a testimony to Jehovah's name; and if and when the princes do return and some of them occupy the property, such will be a confirmation of the faith and hope that induced the building of Beth-Sarim.'

This place was sold in 1942 after Rutherford's death. There-fore, it appears that the faithful were misled since the house was to 'be forever at the disposal of the aforementioned princes.' Is this really a testimony to Jehovah's name as it said? How can it be if they sold the house?

4. The Watchtower organization maintains that Jesus died on a stake, not a cross. The typical Watchtower representation of this is with Jesus on a single vertical stake, hands over his head with a single nail in his wrists. If Jesus were crucified on a cross, then two nails would be necessary, one in each hand. How then does the Watchtower organization handle the verse in the Bible that states that Jesus had nails (plural) in his hands?

    'Consequently the other disciples would say to him: "We have seen the Lord!" But he said to them: "Unless I see in his hands the print of the nails and stick my finger into the print of the nails and stick my hand into his side, I will certainly not believe."'   (John 20:25 NWT)

    Jesus had one nail in each hand. This is made clear by the use of the word 'nails' not 'nail.' Jesus must have been crucified on a cross, and not a stake as the Watchtower organization teaches. Why is it, then, that the Watchtower teaches some-thing that is so clearly unbiblical?

5. The Watchtower organization states that through good works and sincere effort only 144,000 elite JWs will go to heaven. The 144,000 are mentioned in two chapters in the Bible: Revelation 7 and 14. By looking at the verses it is obvious that the 144,000 are literal Jews of the ancient tribes with no Gentiles among

them (7:4–8). They are all males (14:4) and virgins (14:4). If JWs state that the reference to Jewish male virgins is figurative, what gives them, then, the right to say that number of 144,000 is literal?

History of Christian Science

Christian Science was founded by a woman named Mary Baker Eddy. She was born Mary Ann Morse Baker in New Hampshire in 1821 and was the daughter of a New Hampshire Congregationalist church member. As a child, she was frequently ill and was highly emotional. She is said to have been 'domineering, quarrelsome, and extremely self centered.'[27] At age twenty-two, she married George Glover, who died seven months later. She then married Dr Daniel Patterson, but that marriage failed in divorce. In 1862, while suffering from an illness, she visited a man named Phineas Quimby who believed that the mind had the power to heal the body and taught a system of healing dealing with the mind. He exerted a significant influence on her thinking regarding spiritual matters.

In 1866, she was seriously injured during a fall and was not expected to recover. She apparently read Matthew 9:2 (*'And, behold, they brought to him a man sick of the palsy, lying on a bed: and Jesus seeing their faith said unto the sick of the palsy; Son, be of good cheer; thy sins be forgiven thee'*) and experienced a miraculous cure. It was this experience that convinced her of the truth of Christian Science.

She first published *Science and Health with Key to the Scriptures* in 1875, when she was fifty-four. She claimed it was the final revelation of God to humankind and asserted that her work was inspired by God. The word 'Key' in the title of her book is a reference to the fact that she considered herself to be the woman of Revelation 12 with the ability to unlock the Bible which she called a dark book. She claimed the Bible had many mistakes and that her writings provided the 'key' spoken of in Revelation 3:7.

She married Asa Eddy in 1877.

In 1879, four years after the first publication of *Science and Health*, Mary Baker Eddy and some of her students established the Church of Christ (Scientist) in Boston Massachusetts. Of course, like all cults, it claimed to be the restoration of the original New Testament Church. In 1881 she opened a metaphysical college, charging $300 for twelve healing lessons. The Church was reorganized in 1892, and the Church Manual was first issued in 1895 which provided the structure for church government and missions.

She died in 1910, a millionaire.

Christian Science doctrine

Christian Science rejects the use of medicine, vitamins, nutrition, immunization, drugs, etc. This is because pain and sickness are all illusions of the mind. To correct the illusions, you must understand and practice Christian Science principles.

The book *Science and Health with Key to the Scriptures*, by Mary Baker Eddy, is considered a companion to the Bible.

1. God is infinite ... and there is no other power or source (*Science and Health*, 471:18).
2. God is Universal Principle (*Science and Health*, 331:18–19).
3. God cannot indwell a person (*Science and Health*, 336:19–20).
4. God did not create matter (*Science and Health*, 335:7–15).
5. The Trinity is Life, Truth, and Love (*Science and Health*, 331:26).
6. Belief in the traditional doctrine of the Trinity is polytheism (*Science and Health*, 256:9–11).
7. God is the Father–Mother (*Science and Health*, 331:30; 332:4).
8. Christ is the spiritual idea of son (*Science and Health*, 331:30–31).
9. Jesus was not the Christ (*Science and Health*, 333:3–15; 334:3).
10. 'Jesus Christ is not God, as Jesus himself declared ... ' (*Science and Health*, 361:12–13).
11. Jesus did not reflect the fullness of God (*Science and Health*, 336:20–21).
12. Jesus did not die (*Science and Health*, 45:32–46:3).
13. The Holy Spirit is divine science (*Science and Health*, 331:31).
14. God is the only intelligence in the universe, including human beings (*Science and Health*, 330:11–12).
15. God is Mind (*Science and Health*, 330:20–21).
16. There is no devil (*Science and Health*, 469:13–17).
17. There is no sin (*Science and Health*, 447:24).
18. Evil and good are not real (*Science and Health*, 330:25–27; 470:9–14).
19. Matter, disease, sin, and sickness are not real, but only illusions (*Science and Health*, 335:7–15; 447:27–28).
20. Life is not material or organic (*Science and Health*, 83:21).
21. The sacrifice of Jesus was not sufficient to cleanse from sin (*Science and Health*, 25:6).

22. True healings are the result of true belief (*Science and Health*, 194:6).

What is a Christian Science practitioner?

This is a Christian Scientist who devotes himself or herself full time to the ministry of Christian healing. To be a practitioner requires study, consecrated prayer, and a demonstrated ability to apply spiritual understanding to the overcoming of human ills and discords. Preparation includes a course of study with an authorized teacher of Christian Science and a record of successful healing of others.

Basic outline of Christian Science

Christian Science denies:

1. The Trinity, salvation by grace, the physical resurrection of Jesus.
2. The existence of hell and heaven as literal places.
   ▶ They are reflections of the human mind only.
3. The existence of sin, sickness, and judgement.
   ▶ They say this is an improper understanding of Divine Mind.
   ▶ Therefore they will not resist taking medicine, immunizations, etc.
4. The practice of baptism and taking communion.
   ▶ Baptism is submergence into spirit.
5. The existence of matter.

Christian Science affirms that:

1. God is all good.
2. Matter is only an interpretation of the reality of Divine Mind.
   ▶ Matter does not exist in reality.
3. All is God.
   ▶ We are part of God and divine.

Healings

1. Christian Science claims many healings.

    ▶ But this is not a guarantee of a true religion (Matthew 7:21–23).

2. Practitioners are those who practice the principles of Christian Science upon a person so as to bring healing.

God

1. God is 'All-in-all' (*Science and Health*, 113:16).
2. God is the Father–Mother (*Science and Health*, 331:30; 332:4).
3. God is Universal Principle (*Science and Health*, 331:18–19).
4. God is infinite ... and there is no other power or source (*Science and Health*, 471:18).
5. 'God is incorporeal, divine, supreme, infinite, Mind. Spirit Soul, Principle, Life, Truth, Love' (*Science and Health*, 465:9).
6. God is not a personal God (*Science and Health*, 336:19–20).

Jesus

1. Jesus is the human and Christ is the divine idea (*Science and Health*, 473:15–16)
2. 'The material blood of Jesus was no more efficacious to cleanse from sin when it was shed upon 'the accursed tree,' than when it was flowing in his veins as he went daily about his Father's business' (*Science and Health*, 25:6–9).
3. 'If there had never existed such a person as the Galilean Prophet, it would make no difference to me' (*Miscellany*, 318:31–319:2).
4. Jesus is 'The highest human corporeal concept of the divine idea, rebuking and destroying error and bringing to light man's immortality' (*Science and Health*, 589).
5. Jesus is not the Christ, but only a manifestation of the Christ consciousness that is in all of us.

Miscellaneous

1. *Death* – 'An illusion, the lie of life in matter.'
2. *Matter* – 'has no life, hence it has no real existence.'
3. *Devil* – 'Evil, a lie, error.' He is not an entity, not a person, has no existence. 'A belief in sin, sickness, and death.'
4. *Flesh* – 'An error of physical belief; a supposition that life, substance, and intelligence are in matter; an illusion.'
5. *Gods* – 'A belief that life, substance, and intelligence are both mental and material; a supposition of sentient physicality.'
6. *Heaven* – 'Harmony; the reign of Spirit; government of divine Principle.'
7. *Hell* – 'Mortal belief, error; lust; hatred, sin; sickness; effects of sin.'
8. *Knowledge* – 'Evidence obtained from the five corporeal senses; mortality; beliefs and opinions ... The opposite of spiritual Truth and understanding' (*Science and Health*, 590).
9. *Mortal Mind* – 'Nothing claiming to be something, for Mind is immortal; error creating other errors.'
10. *Mother* – 'God; divine and eternal Principle; Life, Truth, and Love.'
11. *Resurrection* – 'Spiritualization of thought; a new and higher idea of immortality, or spiritual existence; material belief yielding to spiritual understanding.'
12. *Salvation* – 'Life, Truth, and Love understood and demon-strated as supreme over all; sin, sickness, and death destroyed.'
13. *Spirit* – 'Divine substance; Mind; divine Principle; all that is good.'

Is Christian Science Christian?

Of all the biblically-based cults in America today, Christian Science is one of the most interesting. Not only does it deny the essential doctrines of Christianity, but it has completely reinterpreted the Bible. It drastically redefines the Bible's culture and terminology and rips thousands of scriptures out of their historical and biblical contexts. The result is a non-Christian mixture of metaphysical and philosophical thoughts. Christian Science is so foreign to the Bible that, if it didn't use words like Jesus, Trinity, love, grace, sin, etc., you'd never suspect it had anything to do with the Bible at all. Additionally, the book *Science and Health with Key to the Scriptures*, which is the Christian Scientist's mainstay of spiritual knowledge, reads with a rhythm of pseudo-logical statements that has the tendency to dull the senses when read long enough. Is Christian Science Christian? Definitely not.

Science and Health with Key to the Scriptures is the primary interpretive source of the Bible and source guide of Christian Science. It interprets the Bible in a radically different way. It is so different, in fact, that it absolutely rejects the substitutionary atonement of Jesus and states that it had no efficacious value (*Science and Health*, 25:6). It denies that Jesus is God, second person of the Trinity (*Science and Health*, 361:12–13). It says that sin is a false interpretation of Divine Mind and is nonexistent (*Science and Health*, 335:7–15). And it teaches that the Holy Spirit is Divine Science which is best represented by Christian Science (*Science and Health*, 331:31). The list can go on and, unfortunately, it does.

To the Christian Scientist, God (the Father–Mother) is a Principle known as the Divine Mind. It has no personhood and no personality. A catchphrase used in their literature is that God is 'All in All.' In other words, God is all that exists and what we perceive as matter is an interpretation of Divine Mind. Since God is love, it means that sin and sickness are only errors of interpreting the Divine Mind and have no true reality (*Science and Health*, 330:25–274; 470:9–14).

To the Christian Scientist, Jesus is a Way-shower. He is someone who epitomized the true principle of the Christ Consciousness which indwells us all. Therefore, Jesus did not really die on the cross. He was not God in flesh. He made no atonement in shedding His blood (*Science and Health*, 25:6).

Christian Science teaches that human beings do not have a sinful nature but are reflections of Divine Mind. To achieve 'salvation,' they need only to find the true reality of understanding, as revealed in Christian Science teachings. Unfortunately, these teachings are from Mary Baker Eddy, the woman who founded the religion in the 1870s, and not from God.

The Christian Scientists consider their philosophy to be consistent with the original teachings of Jesus. They consider truth a matter of higher understanding and learning. But the reality is that Christian Science has only produced unbiblical and false doctrines. Eternal destruction is the only thing that will result from its false teaching. The fires of hell will be a bitter reality for those who have been taught that they don't exist.

Interesting quotes from the writings of Mary Baker Eddy

The founder of Christian Science, Mary Baker Eddy, had some interesting things to say.

'One sacrifice, however great, is insufficient to pay the debt of sin. The atonement requires constant self-immolation on the sinner's part. That God's wrath should be vented upon His beloved Son, is divinely unnatural. Such a theory is man-made.'   (*Science and Health*, 23:3–7)

'The material blood of Jesus was no more efficacious to cleanse from sin when it was shed upon "the accursed tree," than when it was flowing in his veins as he went daily about his Father's business.'   (*Science and Health*, 25:6–8)

'His disciples believed Jesus to be dead while he was hidden in the sepulcher, whereas he was alive...'
(*Science and Health*, 44:28–29)

'...his body was not changed until he himself ascended, – or, in other words, rose even higher in the understand of Spirit, God ... and this exaltation explained his ascension, and revealed unmistakably a probationary and progressive state beyond the grave.'   (*Science and Health*, 46:15–17, 20–24)

'His students then received the Holy Ghost. By this is meant, that by all they had witnessed and suffered, they were roused to an enlarged understanding of divine Science.'
(*Science and Health*, 46:30–32)

'A scientific mental method is more sanitary than the use of drugs, and such a mental method produces permanent health.' (*Science and Health*, 79:7–9)

'It is contrary to Christian Science to suppose that life is either material or organically spiritual.'
(*Science and Health*, 83:21–22)

'The admission to one's self that man is God's own likeness sets man free to master the infinite idea.'
(*Science and Health*, 90:24–25)

'The theory of three person in one God (that is, a personal Trinity or Tri-unity) suggests polytheism...'
(*Science and Health*, 256:9–11)

'Father–Mother is the name for Deity, which indicates His tender relationship to His spiritual creation.'
(*Science and Health*, 332:4–5)

'The word *Christ* is not properly a synonym for Jesus, though it is commonly so used.' (*Science and Health*, 333:3–4)

'Mind is the I AM, or infinity. Mind never enters the finite ... but infinite Mind can never be in man ... a portion of God could not enter man.'
(*Science and Health*, 336:1–2, 13, 19–20)

'...and recognize that Jesus Christ is not God, as Jesus himself declared, but is the Son of God.'
(*Science and Health*, p. 361:11–13)

Speaking of Genesis 2:7, '*And the* LORD *God formed man from the dust of the ground, and breathed into his nostrils the breath of life; and man became a living being,*' Eddy says,

'Is this addition to His creation real or unreal? Is it the truth, or is it a lie concerning man and God? It must be a lie, for God presently curses the ground...'
(*Science and Health*, 524:13–27)

In describing what the Devil is, she writes,

> 'Evil; a lie; error; neither corporeality nor mind; the opposite of Truth; a belief in sin, sickness, and death; animal magnetism or hypnotism; the lust of the flesh, which saith: "I am life and intelligence in matter. There is more than one mind, for I am mind, – a wicked mind, self-made or created by a tribal god and put into the opposite of mind, termed matter, thence to reproduce a mortal universe, including man, not after the image and likeness of Spirit, but after its own image." '
>
> *(Science and Health,* 584:17–25)

> 'If there had never existed such a person as the Galilean Prophet, it would make no difference to me.'
>
> *(The First Church of Christ Scientist and Miscellany,* pp. 318, 319)

Definitions of Christian Science terms

Angels are God's thoughts passing to human beings, an inspiration of goodness and purity that counters evil and material reality.

Atonement is not the shedding of Christ's blood, but 'At-one-ment,' 'lifting the whole man into Christ Consciousness.' The biblical account is metaphorical, not real.

Baptism means the daily, ongoing purification of thought and deed. Eucharist is spiritual communion with God, celebrated with silent prayer and Christian living. It is a 'submergence in Spirit.'

Blasphemy of the Holy Spirit is the belief that God created disharmony in the world.

Body is 'the form of expression of both spirit and soul' (*Metaphysical Bible Dictionary*, p. 628). It is the apparent materialization of the limits of soul as influenced by a person's conscious development in Christian Science Principles.

Christ is the divine ideal man. Jesus was not the Christ but a perfect representation of the Christ consciousness that is the true and higher self of every person. Christ is the manifestation of all that is good and true, the realization of divine principle. A Christian Scientist can say, 'I am Christ.'

Creation is the product of Divine Mind. There is only one reality which emanates and is part of the Divine Mind. Anything that is not in harmony with the Divine Mind is not a reality, but a lack of understanding of the principles of Divine Mind brought about by people.

Death – 'An illusion, the lie of life in matter.'

Devil – 'Evil, a lie, error.' He is not an entity, not a person, has no existence. 'A belief in sin, sickness, and death.'

Flesh – 'An error of physical belief; a supposition that life, substance, and intelligence are in matter; an illusion.'

Gods – 'A belief that life, substance, and intelligence are both mental and material; a supposition of sentient physicality.'

God is Spirit who is ever-present, all-knowing, all-powerful, and good. God is the Father–Mother God. Other names for God are Divine Mind, Soul, Principle, Life, Truth, Love. To the Christian Scientist God is the governing Principle of the universe to which a person must harmonize his or her belief system.

Healing (*Science and Healing*, 194:6)

Heaven is not a literal place of eternal bliss, but a harmonious condition of understanding where a person's consciousness is in harmony with Divine Mind. 'Harmony; the reign of Spirit; government of divine Principle.'

Hell is a state of mind which can include the effects of their improper understanding of Divine Mind and Christian Science Principles. Hell is not a literal place of damnation and eternal torment. Hell exists when a person's thoughts are out of harmony with the reality of Divine Mind. 'Mortal belief, error; lust; hatred, sin; sickness; effects of sin.'

Holy Spirit, the, is Divine Science. It is the spirit of God and is only discernible and knowable by a person through his or spiritual awareness. It is an emanation, a presence, 'a law of God in action.'

Jesus' stripes are simply his rejection of error, not the beating he received in the flesh (*Science and Health*, 20:15).

Knowledge – 'Evidence obtained from the five corporeal senses; mortality; beliefs and opinions. The opposite of spiritual Truth and understanding' (*Science and Health*, 590).

Material reality is really non-existent. It is only an interpretation of Divine Mind. Even though someone might feel pain or sickness, in reality it does not exist.

Mortal Mind – 'Nothing claiming to be something, for Mind is immortal; error creating other errors.'

Pastor really means the combined books of the Bible and *Science and Health with Key to the Scriptures*.

Personhood is an aspect and reflection of Divine Mind.

Prayer is contemplation and internalization of divine truths. 'The taking hold of God's willingness.' It is an affirmation of God's being in relation to humankind.

Resurrection is 'Spiritualization of thought; a new and higher idea of immortality, or spiritual existence; material belief yielding to spiritual understanding.'

Salvation is 'Life, Truth, and Love understood and demonstrated as supreme over all; sin, sickness, and death destroyed.'

Sickness is the false understanding given the appearance of reality by the unfaithful and ignorant of Divine Principle and Mind.

Sin is not understanding and behaving according to the Divine Law of God and the law of our being.

Soul is 'man's consciousness – that which he has apprehended or developed out of Spirit ... Soul is both conscious and subconscious' (*Metaphysical Bible Dictionary*, p. 628).

Spirit is another name for God. Divine substance; Mind; divine Principle; 'all that is good'; Christ.

Wrath is really the working out of the law of God's being upon a person. It is not God's judgement upon a sinner.

Questions to ask Christian Scientists

1. If God is all in all, then where did evil come from?

2. If everything is an interpretation of Divine Mind, then why do people have different understandings of God?

3. If sickness is an illusion, why do you have practitioners who go out to Christian Scientists in attempts to heal them?

4. If sin is not real, then why does the Bible say that all have sinned and fallen short of the glory of God (Romans 3:23)?

5. If sin is not real, then why does the Bible say, *'If we claim to be without sin we deceive ourselves and the truth is not in us'* (1 John 1:8)?

6. In *Science and Health with Key to the Scriptures*, Mary Baker Eddy said, 'The material blood of Jesus was no more efficacious to cleanse from sin when it was shed upon "the accursed tree," than when it was flowing in his veins as he went daily about his Father's business.' Why would she contradict so plainly the teaching of Scripture that says, *'But if we walk in the light, as he is in the light, we have fellowship with one another, and the blood of Jesus, his Son, purifies us from all sin'* (1 John 1:7)?

7. Why would Mary Baker Eddy directly contradict Jesus' own claim about Himself? She said, 'Jesus is not God, as Jesus himself declared, but the Son of God' (*Science and Health*, 361:12–13). Is she calling Jesus a liar?

8. If 'Man is incapable of sin, sickness, and death, as Eddy said in *Science and Health*, 475:28, then why do people die? Why does the Bible say that the wages of sin is death (Romans 6:23)?

9. Why would Mrs Eddy say Jesus did not die (*Science and Health*, 45:32–46:3) when the Bible clearly teaches that He did (Romans 8:34; 1 Thessalonians 4:14; 1 Corinthians 8:11; 1 Peter 3:18; 1 John 1:7)?

10. If our physical senses do not tell us the truth about the material world then how can we trust them when we read the book *Science and Health with Key to the Scriptures* or hear its message with our ears?

History of Christadelphianism

Christadelphianism is a religious movement begun by Dr John Thomas, who was born in London, England, on 12 April 1805. In 1832, having decided to emigrate to the United States, his ship bound for New York encountered several terrible storms which threatened shipwreck and death. Dr Thomas promised God that if he were delivered, he would devote his life to the study of religion. He made it to America and kept his promise.

Upon arrival, he joined the Campbellite group also known as the Disciples. He was baptized and immersed himself in study, but soon found himself at odds with the Campbellites and left, taking with him many from the Campbellite group. This was the beginning of the Christadelphian movement, though it wasn't yet called that.

In 1834 Dr Thomas started a magazine called *The Apostolic Advocate*, through which he really began to disseminate his teachings. He was greatly interested in prophecy and devoted much effort to understanding biblical eschatology. In 1839 Thomas moved to Illinois and in 1842 he became editor of a magazine called *The Investigator*. Five years later, now living in Virginia, he started another magazine called *The Herald of the Future Age*.

In 1848, around the time Christadelphianism was founded in America, Thomas returned to England to speak on his brand of religion and found the soil there fertile. To this day, England has the largest number of Christadelphians. While in his native country, he wrote the book called *Elpis Israel*, meaning 'Hope of Israel,' which is a thorough work of his beliefs discussing creation, God's Law, sin, death, immortality, religion, the coming kingdom, and a host of other subjects. He then returned to America.

Since the Christadelphians do not believe in participating in war, when the Civil War broke out, they refused to enlist. In order to be recognized as a religious group with conscientious objections to fighting, they needed a name. Dr Thomas gave them the name 'Christadelphian' which in Greek means 'Brethren of Christ.'

In 1862, Thomas made another visit to England and found that his book *Elpis Israel* had helped to bring about congregations that followed his theology. He lectured extensively and helped to anchor Christadelphianism in England, before returning to America once again.

Thomas visited England one more time in 1869 after writing the book *Eureka*. On 5 March 1871 Dr Thomas died in New York and was buried in Brooklyn.

Thomas was a tireless worker who sought to study and discover God's true meaning and doctrine of the Bible. Unfortunately, despising the counsel and wisdom of those more learned than himself, he sought to singlehandedly 'rediscover' the true gospel which, in his opinion, had been lost from the earth. Like so many others in the nineteenth century, he began a religious movement that really is a development of his personal beliefs. Therefore, the Christadelphian religion, like Mormonism, Jehovah's Witnesses, and Christian Science, is merely another erring religious system begun by a single person who claimed to know more than anyone else about the Bible. It is a non-Christian cult.

Christadelphian doctrine

1. They believe the Bible is the infallible and inerrant Word of God (*The Christadelphians: What They Believe and Preach*, p. 82). [28]

2. They believe there is only one God (Isaiah 43–45).

3. They believe that Jesus had a sin nature (*What They Believe*, p. 74).

4. They believe that Jesus needed to save Himself, before He could save us (*Christadelphian Answers*, p. 24).

5. They believe that Jesus will return and set up His kingdom on earth (*What They Believe*, p. 268).

6. They believe that there has been an apostasy and that Christianity is a false religious system (a tract entitled 'Christendom Astray Since the Apostolic Age,' Detroit Christadelphian Book Supply).

7. They deny the immortality of the soul (*What They Believe*, pp. 17–18).

8. They believe in the annihilation of the wicked (*What They Believe*, p. 187).

9. They believe that baptism is necessary for salvation (*What They Believe*, pp. 71, 72, 207–210).

10. They believe that it is possible to lose one's salvation (*What They Believe*, p. 212).

11. They deny the doctrine of the Trinity (*What They Believe*, pp. 84–87).

12. They deny that Jesus is God in flesh (*Answers*, p. 22).

13. They deny that Jesus existed prior to his incarnation – John 3:13 (*What They Believe*, pp. 85, 86).

14. They deny the personhood and deity of the Holy Spirit (*What They Believe*, p. 115).

15. They deny the substitutionary atonement of Christ (*Answers*, p. 25; *What They Believe*, p. 71).

16. They deny salvation by grace through faith. (Instead, it is through baptism, *What They Believe*, p. 204.)

17. They deny immortality of the soul (*What They Believe*, p. 17).

18. They deny that a person exists after death (*What They Believe*, p. 17).

19. They deny the existence of hell and eternal punishment (*What They Believe*, pp. 188–189).

20. They deny the existence of the devil (*Answers*, p. 100).

As can be seen, the Christadelphians deny many commonly held doctrines of Christianity. More importantly, they deny two of the essential doctrines of Christianity, namely, the deity of Jesus and salvation by grace.

Is Christadelphianism Christian?

No, Christadelphianism is not Christian. Like all cults, Christadelphianism denies one or more of the essential doctrines of Christianity (see p. 000). In this case, it is the deity of Christ and salvation by grace through faith. Christadelphianism denies that Jesus is God in flesh and adds a requirement for salvation: baptism.

In regards to Jesus, Christadelphianism teaches that

- Jesus had a sinful nature (*What They Believe*, p. 74).
- Jesus needed salvation (*Answers*, p. 25).
- Jesus is not God in flesh (*Answers*, p. 22).

- Jesus' atonement was not substitutionary (*Answers*, p. 25; *What They Believe*, p. 71).

- baptism is necessary for salvation (*What They Believe*, pp. 71, 72, 207–210).

Of primary importance is what the Christadelphians say about Jesus. They deny He is God in flesh. Since we are justified by faith (Romans 5:1; Ephesians 2:8), it is crucial to believe in the truth and not a lie. All Satan has to do is to get people to believe in a false Jesus and they are lost (Matthew 24:24). A false Jesus cannot save and only the true Jesus reveals the true God (John 14:6; Luke 10:22; John 17:3). Since Jesus is actually God in flesh (John 1:1, 14; Colossians 2:9; Philippians 2:5–8; Hebrews 1:8), it follows that those who deny His divine nature – and ascribe a sinful one to Him – do not have the true Jesus and are, therefore, serving a false God. They are then damned.

Second, the Christadelphians deny the substitutionary atonement of Jesus. They say that He did not take our place on the cross and that He did not bear our sins. This is in direct contradiction to Scripture. In 1 Peter 2:24 we read:

'He himself bore our sins in his body on the tree, so that we might die to sins and live for righteousness; by his wounds you were healed.'

Instead, they teach a kind of representation that was not effective to remove sin and say, 'Christ did not die as our substitute, but as our representative' (*Answers*, p. 25).

Additionally, in *Answers* it says, 'But it is equally true that, being "made sin for us" (2 Cor. 5:21), he himself required a sin offering…' (p. 24). This is absolute heresy and needs to be labeled for what it is: demonic doctrine. Jesus was without sin (1 Peter 2:22), the exact representation of the nature of God (Hebrews 1:3). Since God is sinless and holy, so is Jesus.

Third, the Christadelphians add a work to salvation. They say that baptism is part of the saving process. But, baptism is not necessary for salvation. Instead, it is a representation of the inward reality of regeneration (1 Peter 3:21), a covenant sign of God's work upon the heart (Colossians 2:11–12). Galatians 5:1–12 speaks of the grave error of some people who thought that they needed to partake in some part of the Law (circumcision) to be saved. Paul quickly denounced them with very strong words (Galatians 5:12). Additionally, Romans 3:23 says we are saved not by the works of the Law, that is, not by anything we do. Since our righteous deeds are filthy rags before God (Isaiah 64:6), we must completely rely upon the grace of God for our salvation – which is by faith in Jesus who is God, the creator, in flesh.

The Christadelphian religion is a false religion. This is not to say that there are not decent people who intend to serve God honestly and truthfully. But sincerity does not bridge the gap between God and the human race. Only the blood of the real Jesus does that.

Interesting quotes from Christadelphianism

(Unless otherwise indicated all quotes on this page are from the book, *The Christadelphians: What They Believe and Preach* by Harry Tennant, published by The Christadelphian, 404 Shaftmoor Lane, Birmingham B28 8SZ, England, 1986.)

'It will surprise some readers to know that nowhere in Scripture are the words "immortal" and "soul" brought together. Immortality is God's own inherent nature, and His alone.'

(p. 17)

'The second secret of the cross is that it is the source of the forgiveness of sins. It is not a debt settled by due payment. It is not a substitutionary offering whereby someone is paid a price so that others might then go free.'   (p. 71)

'The Bible approach is much simpler and much more satisfying. Forgiveness comes to the man who believes the Gospel, repents, and is baptized in the name of Christ.'   (p. 71)

'The wondrous benefits from the saving work of Jesus flow to us and are effective for us when we come in faith, repentant, and join Jesus in his death by baptism into his name.' (p. 72)

'Therefore, we conclude that it is not only that Jesus was called a sinner at his trial by his enemies or that he was "numbered with the transgressors" when he was crucified between two thieves, but more particularly that he shared the very nature which had made a sinner out of every other man who had borne it.'   (p. 74)

'There is no hint in the Old Testament that the Son of God was already existent or in any way active at that time.'

(p. 85)

'Jesus Christ, the Son of God, was first promised, and came into being only when he was born of the virgin Mary.'

(p. 86)

'We ask the question: When was Jesus "in the form of God"? Christadelphians believe that Jesus was in the form of God by his birth through begettal by the Father, by speaking the words of God and doing His works.'   (p. 87)

'Jesus worships God: God worships no one.'   (p. 88)

'The Spirit is not a "separate" or "other" person. It is God's own radiant power, ever out flowing from Him, by which His "everywhereness" is achieved. The Spirit is personal in that it is of God Himself: it is not personal in the sense of being some other person within the Godhead.'   (p. 115)

'A believing, repentant person receives forgiveness of sins by being baptized.'   (pp. 207–8)

'True baptism removes past sins.'   (p. 208)

'Therefore the wonderful work of baptism is essential to salvation.'   (p. 210)

'*Salvation is not a one-for-all, irreversible happening.*'   (p. 212)

'There is, of course, no doubt that the Lord Jesus Christ will come back, personally, bodily, in glory and with the holy angels.'   (p. 268)

'He [Jesus] saved himself in order to save us.'

(*Christadelphian Answers*,
compiled by Frank G. Jannaway, p. 24)

'And it was for that very reason – being a member of a sinful race – that the Lord Jesus himself needed salvation.'

(*Answers*, p. 24)

'The terms Satan and Devil are simply expressive of "sin in the flesh" in individual, social, and political manifestations.'

(*Answers*, p. 100)

' "God is spirit," but this does not mean that He is unsubstantial; rather, that He is of spirit-substance. The teaching of Paul that all things are "out of Him", the One Source, means that they are not made out of nothing ... It supports the conclusion that He Himself is substantial, and denies the teaching of immanent philosophy that the person of God is distributed through all created matter.'

(*The Testimony: The distinctive beliefs of the Christadelphians,*
p. 224, col. A, second para.)

'Christ is "the image of the invisible God", "the express image of His person" (Col. 1:15; Heb. 1:2, 3). For this to be true the Father must have body and form ... '

(*The Testimony*, p. 224, col. A, third para.)

'Passages such as the first five above [1 Timothy 6:16; Psalm 104:2; 1 Kings 8:30; Matt. 6:9; Mark 16:19] are negated by ideas of immateriality or of the distribution of personality and intelligence throughout the universe. These ideas tend not to recognize the separation between God and man caused by Adam's sin. They are encouraged by a false belief in the immateriality (as well as immortality) of man's soul as part of God's nature.'   (*The Testimony*, p. 224, col. A, last para.)

The New Age Movement

What is the New Age Movement?

1. The New Age Movement (NAM) has many subdivisions, but it is generally a collection of Eastern-influenced metaphysical thought systems, a conglomeration of theologies, hopes, and expectations held together with an eclectic teaching of salvation, of 'correct thinking,' and 'correct knowledge.'

    Human beings are central to the NAM. Human beings are viewed as divine, as co-creators, as the hope for future peace and harmony. A representative quote might be: 'I am affected only by my thoughts. It needs but this to let salvation come to all the world. For in this single thought is everyone released at last from fear.'[29] Unfortunately for the NAM that fear might very well be the fear of damnation, of conviction of sin, and it is even, sometimes, fear of Christianity and Christians. Though the NAM is tolerant of almost any theological position, it is opposed to the 'narrow-mindedness' of Christianity.

2. The NAM is difficult to define because 'there is no hierarchy, dogma, doctrine, collection plate or membership.' It is a collection, an assortment, of different theologies with the common threads of toleration and divergence weaving through its tapestry of 'universal truth.'

3. The term 'New Age' refers to the 'Aquarian Age' which, according to New Age followers, is dawning. It is supposed to bring in peace and enlightenment and reunite the human race with God. Human beings are presently considered separated from God not because of sin (Isaiah 59:2), but because of lack of understanding and knowledge concerning the true nature of themselves, God, and reality.

The New Age Movement is a religious system with two basic beliefs: Evolutionary Godhood and Global Unity

1. What is Evolutionary Godhood?
    (a) It is the next step in evolution. It will not be physical, but spiritual.

For the most part, the NAM espouses evolution, both of body and spirit. The human race is developing and will soon leap forward into new spiritual horizons. Many New Age practices are designed to push people ahead into that horizon. Some of them are astral projection which is training your soul to leave your body and travel around; contacting spirits so they may speak through you or guide you; using crystals to purify your body's and mind's energy systems; visualization where you use mental imagery to imagine yourself as an animal, in the presence of a divine being, or being healed of sickness, etc.

(b) Evolutionary Godhood also means that humankind will soon see itself as god, as the 'Christ principle.'

(i) The NAM teaches that basic human nature is good and divine. This opposes God's Word which says that:

▶ we are sinners:

> *'Therefore, just as sin entered the world through one man, and death through sin, and in this way death came to all men, because all sinned.'*
> (Romans 5:12)

▶ our nature is corrupt:

> *'All of us also lived among them at one time, gratifying the cravings of our sinful nature and following its desires and thoughts. Like the rest, we were by nature objects of wrath.'*   (Ephesians 2:3)

(ii) As God, human beings can then create their own reality.

▶ This is an important part of NAM thinking. Because average New Agers believe themselves to be divine, they can then create their own reality. If, for example, they believe that reincarnation is true, that's fine. If someone they know doesn't believe in it, that is all right too. This is because their realities are different. They can each have created a reality for themselves that 'follows a different path.'

▶ God alone is the creator (Isaiah 44:24).

(c) Reincarnation

    (i) Though not all New Agers adhere to reincarnation, most do.

    (ii) This opposes the Word of God which says that it is appointed for human beings to die once, and after this comes judgement (Hebrews 9:27).

2. The second major element of the New Age Movement is Global Unity with three major divisions:

(a) **Human with human**

    (i) We will all learn our proper divine relationship with one another and achieve harmony and mutual love and acceptance.

       Within this hoped harmony is economic unity. The average New Ager is looking for a single world leader who, with New Age principles, will guide the world into a single harmonious economic whole.

       It is also hoped that this leader will unite the world into a spiritual unity as well; that is, a one-world religion.

    (ii) The New Age hope is reminiscent of the scriptures that speak of the coming Antichrist – 2 Thessalonians 2:3–4:

> *'Don't let anyone deceive you in any way, for that day will not come until the rebellion occurs and the man of lawlessness is revealed, the man doomed to destruction. He opposes and exalts himself over everything that is called God or is worshiped, and even sets himself up in God's temple, proclaiming himself to be God.'*

       (*See also* Revelation 13:17; 14:9, 11; 16:2; 19:20)

(b) **Human beings with nature**

    (i) Since God is all, and all is God, then nature is also part of God. Human beings must then get in tune with nature and learn to nurture it and be nurtured by it. In this, all people can unite.

    (ii) American Indian philosophies are popular among New Agers because they focus on the earth, on nature, and the human race's relationship to them.

(iii) New Age philosophy generally seeks to merge with those philosophies that put human beings and nature on an equal level. We are no more or less important or different than our cousin the animal, bird, or fish. We must live in harmony with them, understand them, and learn from them.

This is opposed to the Scriptural teaching of humankind's superiority over animals (Genesis 1:26–27; 2:19). The human race is given the responsibility of caring for and being stewards of God's creation (Genesis 2:15).

(iv) The earth, also known spiritually as Gaia, is likened to our mother. Gaia is to be revered and respected. Some New Agers even worship the earth and nature.

This opposes the scripture that says we are not to have any other gods before God (Exodus 20:3).

(c) **Human beings with God**

Since human beings are divine by nature, all people, once they see themselves as such, will be helped in their unity of purpose, love, and development. The goal is to realize fully our own goodness. It is obvious that this contradicts Scripture, cf:

> *'As it is written: "There is no-one righteous, not even one; there is no-one who understands, no-one who seeks God. All have turned away, they have together become worthless; there is no-one who does good, not even one.'*
> (Romans 3:10–12)

3. Additional beliefs are:

(a) God is impersonal, omnipresent, and benevolent.
  ▶ The New Age god is impersonal. An impersonal god will not reveal himself nor will he have specific requirements as to morality, belief, and behavior.
  ▶ It is because New Agers seek to have themselves elevated that they must lower the majesty and personhood of the true God.

(b) There are no moral absolutes. Therefore, they claim to have a spiritual tolerance for all 'truth systems.' They call this 'harmonization.'[30]

There is an obvious problem here. To say that there are no moral absolutes is an absolute in itself. Also, if morality is relative, then stealing may be right sometimes, along with lying, adultery, cheating, etc. Living in a world of moral relativism would not bring a promising future.

What the New Age Movement does

1. It is a sponge that attempts to absorb all religions, cultures, and governments.

2. It seeks to unify all systems and governments into one spiritual, socio-economic unity.

3. It uses various means to have mystical experiences with God, nature, and self. Some of the methods were described in *Omni Magazine* as *imagining*, where you imagine your own reality; *transcendence*, going beyond the limits of time; *sleep deprivation*, with the purpose of inducing a mystical experience; *focusing*, 'to experience all of reality as unified and not as a collection of disparate objects'; *avoidance*, where contact with the outside world is stopped in order to reinterpret the world without its influence on you; *identification*, 'To trade places mentally with a dog or a cat, canary, or animal in the zoo'; *reflection*, an exercise aimed at helping you view the coming year differently; and *star-gazing*, 'to induce a sense of objectivity about your life and a feeling of connectedness to the rest of cosmos.'[31]

4. It rejects Christianity but seeks to be identified with its moral truths.

What the New Age Movement does not do.

1. It does not teach that human beings are sinners (Romans 5:12; Ephesians 2:3).

2. It does not teach that human beings are dependent upon God for all things (Isaiah 43:7; James 1:17).

3. It does not teach that punishment is eternal (Revelation 14:11).

168 Right Answers for Wrong Beliefs

4. It does not teach that the wages of sin is eternal separation from God (Romans 6:23; Isaiah 59:2).

5. It does not teach that Jesus is the only way to God (Matthew 11:27; John 14:6).

6. It does not accept Christianity as the ultimate truth (2 Timothy 3:16).

New Age terminology

Human beings, the image bearers of God, are creatures of speech. In the New Age, they have developed their own terminology. A few of the common buzz words are: holistic, holographic, synergistic, unity, oneness, harmony, at-one-ment, transformation, personal growth, human potential, awakening, networking, energy, and consciousness. These words are prevalent in New Age conversations and writings.

The New Age interpretation of Christianity

1. God is not a personal heavenly Father but an impersonal force.

2. God is all and all is God. God is not the 'wholly other' creator of all, but part of nature.

3. There is nothing that is not God. (This is pantheism.)

4. There is no sin, only incorrect understanding of truth. Knowledge is what saves, not Jesus.

5. Hell is not a place but an experience here on earth; it is a state of mind.

6. Jesus was just one of many way-showers of divine truth. He exemplified the Christ consciousness probably better than anyone else.

7. Christ is a consciousness, a form of the higher self. It is possessed by all because everyone is divine. 'It is not Christ that can be crucified.' [32]

8. 'A miracle is a correction ... It merely looks on devastation, and reminds the mind that what it sees is false. It undoes error.' [33] A miracle to a New Ager is not God's intervention into this world to perform His will.

The New Age view of the human race

1. Since all is God, and human beings are part of all, then human beings are God. This is **pantheism**.

   ▶ This is an eastern mystical belief system that has crept into mainstream America.

   ▶ Human beings are not God, they are a creation (Genesis 1:26).

2. Therefore, human beings are good by nature.

   ▶ Human beings are not good by nature (Ephesians 2:3; Romans 3:10–12).

3. Human beings have infinite potential.

   ▶ This arrogant conclusion based upon false concepts of grandiose self-worth, is a deceptive, self-satisfying indulgence into pride. As Satan wanted to be like God (Isaiah 14:12–17) and encouraged Adam and Eve to be like God also (Genesis 3:1–5), the New Ager listens to the echo of that Edenic lie and yields to it willingly.

4. The human race is one with the universe.

   ▶ Again the difference between the human race and creation is blurred. Human beings are made in the image of God (Genesis 1:26). The universe is not. Human beings are different to creation.

The New Age view of salvation

1. Salvation in the NAM means to be in tune with the divine consciousness.

   ▶ In tune means to be in harmony with reality and whatever is perceived to be true.

2. Since the NAM doesn't acknowledge sin or sinfulness, there is no need for a redeemer like Jesus. Salvation, to them, is simply the realization of our divine nature. 'I am not a body. I am free. For I am still as God created me. Salvation of the world depends on me.'[34] Such arrogance of self-worth is mind-boggling.

3. Salvation, then, is a form of knowledge, of achieving correct thought. Therefore we need to be saved from ignorance, not sin. It is self-achieved through understanding your natural godlikeness and goodness, combined with proper knowledge.

Witnessing to New Agers

1. Ask questions:
    (a) If we are all God, then why do we act so badly?
        (i) They might say it is because we have not all come to a full realization of our true divine potentials. It is ignorance that leads to bad deeds.
        (ii) Then ask them how, if we are divine, our mere ignorant self could so easily override our divine goodness.
    (b) Why do our 'realities' contradict each other?
        (i) They might say that they don't contradict each other. They are simply different shades of light on the same picture (or something vague like that).
        (ii) Then ask if truth contradicts itself. It does not. The logic is that if we are all in different forms of truth, then these different truths can't ultimately contradict each other – or they wouldn't be true. However,
            ▶ the NAM says that Jesus is only one of many ways to God. But Jesus said He was the only way to God (John 14:6). They can't both be right; therefore, the NAM teaching that we can create our own truths can't be true.

2. Don't let them take Christian words and use them out of the context of biblical meaning.

    ▶ New Agers recognize the tremendous influence and spotless reputation of Jesus. They want Him to be associated with their beliefs. As a result, you might find yourself facing a New Ager who uses Christian words – but with non-Christian definitions. Listen carefully, and don't let them steal what is Christian and transplant it into their system.

3. Listen for internal contradictions.

    ▶ As mentioned above, truth does not contradict itself. You must listen to what they are saying and ask questions. Sooner or later you catch on to inconsistencies.

4. Tell them that God is personal, that He loves them, and that Jesus died for sin.

    ▶ The Word of God will not come back empty without accomplishing what God wishes it to (Isaiah 55:11). Focus on Jesus, tell them the truth about sin and salvation, and use Scripture. Then, at least, they will have heard the truth. Praise be to Jesus the Christ.

Biblical responses to the New Age Movement

1. God is personal. If God were impersonal, then the following qualities could not be His.
    (a) God speaks and has a self-given name: 'I AM' (Exodus 3:14; John 8:58).
    (b) God is long-suffering (Psalm 86:15; 2 Peter 3:15).
    (c) God is forgiving (Daniel 9:9; Ephesians 1:7; Psalm 86:5).
    (d) God hates sin (Psalm 5:5, 6; Habakkuk 1:13).

2. Human beings are not divine, but sinners (Romans 3:23).
    (a) They are deceitful and desperately sick (Jeremiah 17:9).
    (b) They are full of evil (Mark 7:21–23).
    (c) They love darkness rather than light (John 3:19).
    (d) They are unrighteous, do not understand, do not seek for God (Romans 3:10–12).
    (e) Salvation is God's deliverance from damnation (Ephesians 2:8–9; Romans 1:18; 2:5; 5:9).
    (f) This salvation is found in no one but Jesus alone (Acts 4:12).
    (g) He is dead in his trespasses and sins (Ephesians 2:1).
    (h) He is by nature a child of wrath (Ephesians 2:3).
    (i) He cannot understand spiritual things (1 Corinthians 2:14).

3. Salvation is not correct thought, but deliverance from the consequences of our sin (Romans 6:23; Ephesians 2:8, 9).

4. Miracles are from God not from the mind of human beings (Matthew 8:1–4; Mark 6:30–44; Luke 17:12–19; John 2:1–11).

    Miracles imply an action by someone who is greater than ourselves. If God is impersonal, miracles cannot occur. But they do occur today as well as in Bible times and are not simply proper thoughts or understanding.

5. Christ means 'anointed.' Jesus was the Christ, the 'anointed one.' It does not mean a consciousness or quality of person. Jesus was the Christ, the Messiah, the Deliverer from sin.

    (a) Jesus is the Christ (Matthew 16:16, 20; Luke 9:20).
    (b) *'Did not the Christ have to suffer these things and then enter his glory?'* (Luke 24:26).
    (c) *'This is what is written: The Christ will suffer and rise again from the dead on the third day'* (Luke 24:46).
    (d) *'We have found the Messiah (that is, the Christ)'* (John 1:41).
    (e) *'Seeing what was ahead, he* [David] *spoke of the resurrection of the Christ...'* (Acts 2:31).
    (f) *'...God has made this Jesus, whom you crucified, both Lord and Christ'* (Acts 2:36).
    (g) *'...at just the right time, when we were still powerless, Christ died for the ungodly'* (Romans 5:6).
    (h) *'We were therefore buried with Him through baptism into death in order that, just as Christ was raised from the dead through the glory of the Father, we too may live a new life'* (Romans 6:4).
    (i) Christ is crucified (1 Corinthians 1:23).
    (j) We sin against Christ (1 Corinthians 8:12).
    (k) The blood of Christ (1 Corinthians 10:16).

6. Only the Bible has the message of grace. Grace is the unmerited favor of God upon His people. Grace is the undeserved kindness of God. Grace is getting the blessings we do not deserve. Because of the death of Christ we are blessed; we are given grace; we are given eternal life and forgiveness of sins. Only Christianity has the message of free forgiveness given. Every other religious system on earth has some form of salvation dependent totally or in part on what the adherents do. Not so with Christianity.

7. Humanity is not unlimited, but just the opposite: it is under bondage (Romans 5:12). Sin is its master and a deadly and deceitful one at that.

8. True morality is that which is revealed by God in the Bible (Exodus 20). Anything else is only an imitation, a set of ideas laid down by human beings and originating in the mind of sinful human beings.

9. The Bible opposes almost all the tenets of the New Age Movement. As Christians, we should be watchful to recognize what is false and teach what is true. We should be wary because the Edenic lie still rings strong in the hearts of the deceived – and they want us to believe as they do.

Interesting quotes from New Age sources

'Representatives of some of the nation's largest corporations, including IBM, AT&T, and General Motors, met in New Mexico in July [1986] to discuss how metaphysics, the occult and Hindu mysticism might help executives compete in the world marketplace.'
    (*The New York Times*, 'Spiritual Concepts Drawing a Different Breed of Adherent,' 29 September 1986, section Y, p. 8)

'At Stanford University's well-regarded Graduate School of Business, the syllabus for a seminar on "Creativity in Business" includes meditation, chanting, "dream work," the use of tarot cards and discussion of the "New Age Capitalist."''
    (*The New York Times*, 'Spiritual Concepts Drawing a Different Breed of Adherent,' 29 September 1986, section Y, p. 8)

'One concept commonly transmitted in these sessions [seminars and workshops on human potential] ... is that because man is a deity equal to God he can do no wrong; thus, there is no sin, no reason for guilt in life.'
    (*The New York Times*, 'Spiritual Concepts Drawing a Different Breed of Adherent,' 29 September 1986, section Y, p. 8)

'"I am an entity much like you, Barbara. I simply don't have a body at this time."

'It was Dr. Carstairs talking. Dr. Carstairs is an English physician from the 1860s. His spirit generally spends its time floating around the astral plane, I am told, but at this particular moment it had taken up residence in the Body of Bonney Meyer, a registered nurse from San Diego.'

(*The San Diego Union*, 'Their spirits are willing,'
12 November 1987, section C, p. 1)

'There are many entities about such as myself. Man is not the only living, thinking, breathing creature in the galaxy. Entities that come from other planets right now are about your planet waiting for the time to introduce themselves.'

(*The San Diego Union*, 'Their spirits are willing,'
12 November 1987, section C, p. 1)

'Jach Pursel, a former Florida insurance agent living in Los Angeles, squints his eyes and speaks with the voice of Lazaris, a spiritual entity of uncertain origins.

"How old are you?" he asked.

"In our reality, we have no time," says Lazaris.

"Why are you making your presence known to man?"

"Because you are ready now..."

"Is the world about to end?"

"No. In a word, no. This is not the ending. This is the beginning."'

(*Time*, 'New Age Harmonies,' 7 December 1987, p. 66)

'Jo Ann Karl is a tall blond who ... gets $15 a customer for channeling the archangel Gabriel and a spirit named Ashtar.'

(*Time*, 'New Age Harmonies,' 7 December 1987, p. 66)

'We are at any given moment living the totality of everything ... The vibrational oscillation of nature is quickening ...
Just remember that you are God, and act accordingly.'

(Shirley Maclaine)

'In Egypt, a few bemused camel drivers and tourist guides looked on as a lone young man in white shorts and a glittering shawl danced near the pyramids at Giza. "I am God, I am God," he shouted.'   (*The San Diego Union*,

'5,000 greet new age at Mt. Shasta,' article by Paul Nussbaum
and Rick Lyman published on 17 August 1987, A-2)

'War is not man's great and terrible disease; war is a symptom, a result. The real disease is the virus of national sovereignty.'
(*The Urantia Book* (publisher), 1491.1)

'The goal of eternity is ahead! The adventure of divinity attainment lies before you! The race for perfection is on! Whosoever will may enter, and certain victory will crown the efforts of every human being who will run the race of faith and trust, depending every step of the way on the leading of the indwelling Adjuster and on the guidance of the good spirit of the Universal Son, which so freely has been poured out upon all flesh.'
(*The Urantia Book*, 365.4)

'T.I.C.'s (The Inner Christ) purpose is to assist every individual to know themselves as a Christ, to clearly and safely channel guidance and prophecy for themselves from their own Inner Christ and to gain dominion over their life circumstances through prayer and self-revelation. T.I.C. makes the intellectual concept that we are God a reality.'
(From a tract produced by the Teaching of the Inner Christ, 'What is T.I.C.?')

'The Pleiadians are a collective of extraterrestrials from the star system the Pleiades. The Pleiadian culture is ancient and was "seeded" from another universe of love long before earth was created. They have formed a tremendous society which operates with love, with ideas and ideals with which we are yet unfamiliar. Although the Pleiadians exist in what we would call our future, they call themselves our ancient family because many of us came here from the Pleiades to participate in the experiment of earth. As they once promised us, the Pleiadians have returned to earth and are now here to help guide us during this time of planetary awakening as earth moves through her transition from the third to the fourth dimension and to assist each of us in our personal journeys of remembering, deepening awareness and knowing.'
(From a handout at the San Diego Convention Center, *The Pleiadians*, channeled by Barbara J. Marciniak)

'Awareness ... Building a Better World. In Seven Days of Self-Transformation, You Will: reclaim your infinite potential; Learn how to resolve any emotional issue which limits the quality of YOUR life, in any way; Discover what Higher Consciousness is all about; Re-establish an intimate, knowledgeable relationship with YOUR HIGHER SELF. Restore all the Peace, Love, & Joy YOUR LIFE DESERVES.'

(From a handout at a New Age Convention)

'Learn the Ancient secrets of Creating Perfect Health within Your Being. The Essenes were the writers of the Dead Sea Scrolls. Their ability as Natural Physicians and Healers, their Psychic expertise, their knowledge of Nature, and their Mastery of the Order of the Universe is legendary. Among their adepts are Pythagoras and Jesus. The Essenes knew the secrets of healing utilizing all the elements of nature; including sun, air, water, touch, breath and centeredness.'

(From a handout for a seminar by David Carmos,
Lecture 5/58/95, San Diego Convention Center)

'The ancient prophecies of Mesoamerica pinpoint the return of Quetzalcoatl, Lord of the Dawn to the time that correlates with August 16/17, 1987 in the Gregorian Calendar. Quetzalcoatl represents the force of cosmic intelligence, the spiraling, serpentine pattern that governs the movement of all things in this universe. Quetzalcoatl is the enlightened state, the kundalini energy soaring to the crown chakra. Quetzalcoatl lives as potentiality, a seed within each on of us. 144,000 Human Beings will emerge to be the sprouting of that seed on the day of Harmonic Convergence, and will grow to flower and seed again towards the awakening of all humanity in the years that follow.'

(Handout from the International Sacred Sites Festival,
15 March 1987)

The 'Key to Visualization Course' teaches:

- The most powerful and correct use of visualization
- The strongest and most effective visualization techniques
- How to apply the meditative technique easily
- How to remove blockages successfully
- How to stay focused without using mind control
- The process of falling apart/falling together
- How to release with confidence and feel light

- Relationships – blending of male/female energy systems
- The power exercise and being a transparency.
(Handout on Inner Vision Dynamics, 3419 Via Lido, Suite 346, Newport Beach, CA 92663)

The following is a guideline for interpreting the meaning of the colors in your energy field taken from a handout at a New Age Convention:

'**Red**: Red is the color for vitality and physical health. Red also can represent anger or the use of anger to create change.

Orange: Orange is a healing color. If you have a lot of orange in your energy field then you are a natural healer or you are doing some healing work on yourself.

Yellow: Yellow represents personal power and/or a highly developed intellect.

Green: Green represents high affinity between the body and soul. Or green could represent growth and/or changes ahead or in present time.

Blue: Blue in your energy field indicates high certainty or a lot of creativity. In most cases, this represents that the individual's creative channels are clear.

Violet: Very psychic, much spiritual information and/or in the process of spiritual transmutation.

White: This individual is a highly evolved being who has the ability to focus or concentrate his/her energy in or around the body.'

The following is the description for a New Age workshop. Fee $5.

'FULL MOON MEDITATION. – This Full Moon is called the Moon of Humanity, and the Festival of Goodwill. This time is a gateway to higher worlds, through acts of service. The Moon is in Sagittarius, a sign of higher mind, philosophy, the traveler, and teacher. The Sun is in the opposite sign of Gemini, a mental sign of communication and the exchange of ideas. This combination creates a time where the mind is stimulated and there is an understood duality, balance, change. Resolve opposition, and seek inspiration especially outdoors in nature. The symbol is the winged Caduceus the magic wand where positive and negative energies are beautifully balanced producing light.'

PART 4

Various Minor Cults and Groups

The Unification Church

Also known as The Moonies.

Founder
The Rev. Sun Myung Moon in 1954. Born 6 January 1920 in Korea.

Headquarters
Korea.

Membership
Approximately three million worldwide.

Origins
Moon was born to parents who adhered to Confucianism until
their conversion to Presbyterianism in 1930. Moon claims that in
1935 Jesus appeared to him on a mountain in Korea and told him
to finish the work of establishing God's kingdom on earth. By 1945
he had written down the precepts of his system in the book, *Divine
Principles*. He went to North Korea to preach and was imprisoned
first in 1946 and then, in April of 1948, for a longer five-year
sentence in Hungnam. In 1950 he was liberated from the prison by
the Americans involved in the Korean War. On 1 May 1954, in
Seoul, Moon founded the Holy Spirit Association for the Unification of World Christianity. In 1958 he sent missionaries to Japan
and in 1959 to America, where he himself moved in 1971. He has
been invited to the Whitehouse and has spoken to Congress.

Practices
In August of 1992 in Seoul Korea, Moon presided over a mass
wedding of 30,00 couples.

Teachings
Moon claims to be the messiah of the second coming and that his
wife is the Holy Spirit. He and his wife, called the True Parents –
with him the True Father and his wife the True Mother – are the
first couple to be able to produce children with no original sin. 'The
cross is the symbol of the defeat of Christianity.'[35] The Bible is
considered scripture alongside Moon's work *Divine Principles*. Sin

is genetically based; it is not a moral issue. The thieves on the cross represent political movements; the thief on the right side of Jesus represents democracy, the thief on the left communism. Adam and Eve fell because of sexual sin; Eve had sexual relations with Satan. Jesus is a 'true person' though not God in flesh. The Holy Spirit is 'the True Mother,' or 'the Second Eve.' The church denies the doctrine of the Trinity. Nature is dualistic: male and female, positive and negative, external and internal. The external aspect of God, the Universal Prime Energy, creates, develops, and sustains the cosmos. His internal aspect of has to do with personhood – motivation, purpose and identity. People determine their own future place in the spirit world after death through what they do here on earth.

Notes

The church has over 300 financial institutions all over the world including publishers, jewelers, and clothing stores. Moon has spent time in a US prison for tax evasion. Moon claims to receive revelations from God. He has been involved in seances and other occult practices like clairvoyance, trances, etc.

Publications

Divine Principles, a 536-page work by Moon which is considered divinely inspired scripture.

Comments

Moon uses an anti-communism stance, many legitimate businesses, and philanthropic endeavors all over the world to garner support and influence for his one-world religious system. Through his political social outreaches he has deceived a great many people into believing his self-exalting and self-serving theology. It is a dangerous group.

The Christian Identity Movement

Also known as Anglo-Israelism or Israel Identity.

Founder

Some think it to be Wesley Swift born in the 1800s. Others claim it can be traced back to the 1600s.

Headquarters

None.

Membership

Less than 50,000, solely in America.

Origins

This movement has its origins in nineteenth-century America where it grew up in the shadow of the developing and successful conquering of the American continent combined with racial prejudices. Many of the whites believed that North America was ordained by God and blessed by Him to be supreme in the world. All other racial groups were considered inferior. Early contributing movements to the Christian Identity Movement were the Nativist movement and Anglo-Israelism.

The philosophy of nativism held that those not born in America (excluding American Indians) and not Protestant, were harmful to the American System. In particular, it advocated a strong anti-Catholic disposition. Manifestations of this philosophy resulted in physical persecutions of many Catholics in New York.

Anglo-Israelism (also known as British Israelism) is the belief that the British and, therefore, the Americans and Canadians, are the true descendants of the ancient Israelites – the ten lost tribes. The present Jews in Israel are really a false group descended from Cain. Identity believers usually act out their faith through social, military, and political agendas.

An early proponent of this movement, Charles Carroll, who considered Negroes to be subhuman, wrote a book called *The Negro a Beast*. The Ku Klux Klan is usually associated with this group.

Doctrines

A theological system centered on racism, anti-Semitism and white supremacy. It seems to use religious arguments to justify political agendas.

Practices

- *Structure* – the movement does not have a centralized organizational structure.
- *Recruitment* – through extreme right-wing churches, survival groups, and word of mouth.
- *Adherents* – generally are members of the Ku Klux Klan, Aryan Nation, Nazi Party, White Separatist groups, etc.

Texts

Old and New Testaments of the Bible, some think sections of the US Constitution were divinely inspired.

Comments

True Christianity is Christ centered and focuses on love, forgiveness, and patience and is opposed to racism, all of which are lacking in the Christian Identity Movement which advocates racism and anti-Semitism. It is a dangerous group.

Eckankar

Founder

Paul Twitchell in 1965. He died in 1971.

Headquarters

Chanhassen, Minnesota.

Membership

Estimated at 50,000.

Origins

Paul Twitchell, who was involved in the occult, formed the first Eckankar group in 1965. Its origins go back to Hinduistic philosophy. The present leader is Sri Harold Kemp, who is known as Mahanta.

Practices

Spiritual exercises are built upon the foundation of the 'Holy Spirit' which is the Light and Sound of God, known as SUGMAD. These exercises are intended to bring the person's mental and spiritual state into a proper awareness of past lives, in order to facilitate the contact and aid of present ECK masters who are on different spiritual planes in the astral realm. By following their teachings, the subjects can remove bad karma and advance in their spiritual progression through various reincarnations. Usually, these exercises consist of meditation on a repeated word or phrase. After these exercises the meditators say, 'I now put my inner experiences into your hands, Mahanta. Take me wherever is best for my own unfoldment at this particular time.' Mahanta is the highest state of God consciousness on earth, the 'inner, or spiritual form of the living ECK Master.' The Mahanta is given great respect, but is not worshiped. Group chanting sessions sometimes involve repeating the name of God 'Hu' (pronounced as hue) which is considered a love song to God. Interpretation of dreams is a very important part of Eckankar practice. Eckankar encourages Astral Projection, in which a person seeks to leave his body and have his soul travel to different places and meet different spiritual beings. Eckankar claims that a soul can achieve omniscience through astral projection.

186 Right Answers for Wrong Beliefs

Teachings

ECK is the Divine Spirit, or 'Current' of life that flows through all living things. Eckankar is a system of belief that seeks to unify the person's soul with Light and Sound which are twin aspects of the Holy Spirit, or the Divine Spirit. The human soul is eternal and is on a spiritual journey of reincarnation to discover and improve the true self thereby realizing his or her own true inner divinity. This process can include incarnations as animal forms. Through ECK teachings, people can learn from their past lives and understand their karma. Journeys in soul and in dreams are aided by the Spiritual Eye, a part of one's inner self that helps individuals see God and their divine self. ECK masters are agents of God, vehicles of the Divine Spirit that guide people through spiritual learning, past life regressions, dreams, soul travel, and meditations. Past ECK masters are said to include Socrates, Plato, Jesus, Moses, Martin Luther, Michelangelo, Mozart, Einstein, etc., who all allegedly made astral journeys for their discoveries. There are eleven different levels of the astral plane. Christ is a state of consciousness.

Publications

The Key to Secret Worlds, Stranger by the River, both by Paul Twitchell. *The Wind of Change, Soul Travelers of the Far Country*, both by Sri Harold Klemp. The *Shariyat-Ki-Sugmad*.

Comments

This New Age philosophy is nothing more than Hinduism in another package. It focuses on God, the self, and love to a great extent, but its real purpose is the exaltation of the self. Be careful of the deception: it appears calm and loving on the outside, but it houses occultic doctrines and practices.

Resources

www.eckankar.org
Bob Larson, *Larson's Book of Cults* (Tyndale House Pub., 1982).

The Farm

Founder

Stephen Gaskin, born 16 February 1935 in Denver, Colorado. He served in the Marines from 1952–1955 and taught creative writing at San Francisco State College during the 1960s. He used drugs and was involved in the hippy movement. He served a one- to three-year prison term in the Tennessee State Penitentiary.

Headquarters

Summertown, Tennessee, located in an isolated area on a three-square-mile campus.

Membership

Several hundred in the USA.

Doctrines

'Ex-members accuse him [Stephen Gaskin] of openly declaring to be a messenger from God.' Mystical religious experiences are encouraged, along with a mixture of beliefs ranging from *tantra* (ritualistic sex), *karma*, and *mantras*, to *bodhisattvas* (incarnations of God in Budhism)'. [36] They are pacifists and claim to be a non-denominational church that freely discusses all religious options. Marijuana is considered a sacrament that can improve your relationship with God and your family, help you in communication, and aid your love life.

Origins

In the 1960s, disillusioned with the Vietnam war, full of energy, rebellious against the 'establishment,' many hippies moved to the west coast where drugs and sexual freedom were abundant. Gaskin taught a writing class where open discussion became a draw for up to 1500 students. In 1970 a caravan of sixty school buses embarked on a 1500-mile journey across the United States, settling about sixty miles north of Nashville, Tennessee. There were initial setbacks including illnesses, persecutions, and a famine.

Nevertheless, by 1980 the Farm had grown to about 1200, which exceeded the capacity of the land so they purchased more acreage and changed their governmental system to accommodate their growth. They are basically a small town with a hospital, school, radio station, etc. More recently the group has decreased in size to several hundred.

Practices

Most are vegetarians. They live in a communal system and are self-supporting. Some work outside the commune in various industries. They are very active in what are called 'green' communities, which are 'earth friendly' groups seeking 'to lay the foundation for a major shift in Western consumer lifestyles across the broader culture.' Philanthropic outreaches to communities and other countries include rebuilding homes, improving sanitation conditions, laying water pipes, etc.

Publications

Voices from the Farm, Native American Music Directory, Spiritual Midwifery, Home Pest Control, and many others.

Comments

This is not a particularly dangerous group as far as size is concerned. It isn't Christian, encourages drug use – not only of marijuana – and is basically no different from any other belief system that hides a person from salvation in Jesus.

Resources

www.thefarm.org
Bob Larson, *Larson's Book of Cults* (Tyndale House Pub., 1982).

The International Church of Christ

Also known as: The Boston Church of Christ, The Crossroads Movement, Multiplying Ministries, The Discipling Movement, The International Church of Christ, The London Church of Christ, The San Diego Church of Christ, etc.

Doctrines

1. They believe in the Bible as the inerrant and infallible Word of God.
2. They are Trinitarian, and believe in the resurrection of Jesus and the sacrificial atonement.

False teachings

1. The Boston Church of Christ is the only true church.
2. Baptismal regeneration.
    *   Baptism is necessary for salvation.
    *   Baptism into their church with a proper understanding that baptism saves.
3. Heavy discipleship.
4. Unquestioned submission to authority.

History

1. Its distant origins go back to a man called Charles Lucas in Gainesville, Florida.
    *   In 1967 Lucas started a program called the Multiplying Ministries Program which was very successful.
2. The movement we are concerned with here originated in the Crossroads Church of Christ in Florida in 1985.
    *   Kip McKean had been trained in the Discipling methodology pioneered by Lucas. From Charleston, Ill., McKean moved to Massachusetts and, using the methods he had learned under Lucas, started a church which began to grow.
3. In the first year, 103 people were baptized into their church; the second year 200; the third year 256; the fourth year 368; the fifth 457; the sixth 679, the seventh 735; the eighth

947; the ninth 1424; and in the tenth year, 1621: *a total of 6790 people* (as quoted in Jerry Jones, *What Does The Boston Movement Teach?* (publisher vol. 1, p. 125).

> 'From its modest beginnings, the church has grown into 103 congregations all over the world with total Sunday attendance of 50,000.'   (*Time*, 18 May 1992, p. 62)

4. In 1982 the Boston Movement began planting their pillar churches.
   - These are churches in key cities throughout the world. The first two were established in Chicago and London.
   - In 1986, a program called 'reconstruction' was undertaken, a process whereby ministers in established Church of Christ churches were replaced with Boston Church of Christ trained ministers (Jones, *What Does The Boston Movement Teach*, pp. 126–127).
   - This caused problems among the organization, but it helped to solidify this group.

Church structure

Kip McKean is the director and unquestioned leader.

- Under McKean are Elders.

- Under the Elders are Evangelists.

- Then Zone Leaders.

- Then House Church Leaders (obsolete in most congregations).

- Then Assistant Bible Talk Leaders.

- 'McKean says these leaders govern by consensus but adds, "I'm the one who gives them direction."'

- Al Baird, an important Boston Church of Christ elder, said, 'It's not a dictatorship. It's a theocracy, with God on top' (*Time*, 18 May 1992, p. 62).

- Baird also said, 'In questions of spiritual leaders abusing their authority, it is not an option to rebel against their authority' (Jones, *What Does The Boston Movement Teach?* p. 7).

2. It is highly authoritarian.

Authority and submission

(Power corrupts and absolute power corrupts absolutely)

1. In a discussion on submission, Al Baird said,

    'Let us begin our discussion of submission by talking about what it is not. (1) Submission is not agreeing. When one agrees with the decision that he is called to submit to, he does not really have to submit in any way. By definition, submission is doing something one has been asked to do that he would not do if he had his own way. (2) Submission is not just outward obedience. It includes that, but also involves obedience from the heart. It is a wholehearted giving-up of one's own desires. (3) Submission is not conditional. We submit to authority, not because the one in authority deserves it, but because the authority comes from God; therefore, we are in reality submitting to God.'

    (Authority and Submission,
    Parts III, V and VII as quoted in Jones,
    What Does The Boston Movement Teach?, pp. 59–63)

2. Later in this same series, Baird states,

    'When we are under authority, we are to submit and obey our leaders even when they are not very Christ-like. However, God has standards for His leaders, and they will be accountable to God for ignoring those standards.'

    (*ibid.*)

3. Baird has said that if the leader commands a member to do something, even if it is not 'Christ-like,' that person must submit! (*ibid.*, p. 104).

4. Many who have left the Boston Church 'complain that the advice, which members are expected to obey, may include such details as where to live, whom and when to date, what courses to take in school, even how often to have sex with a spouse' (*Time*, 18 May 1992, p. 62).

5. Those who think for themselves and question the authority system are labeled.
    *   'Bad heart,' 'struggling' and 'not really a disciple' are terms used when someone disagrees with a leader.
    *   The group, then, instantly accepts these labels upon a person.

Discipleship

1. Step one: invitation to a Bible talk.

   (a) The environment and topics are non-threatening.
       - The basics of Christianity are covered, with easy to understand discussions.
   (b) The potential converts are befriended, and given invitations to further talks.
   (c) They are then urged to join with a discipler to study the Bible and learn how to be more like Jesus.
   (d) From then on the practices and studies become stricter and more emotionally involving.

2. *'Hooking'* is a technique employed to try to discover the potential converts' interests, hobbies, and other personal information for the purpose of flattering them. This is done to attract them to the group, rather than out of sincere interest.

3. *'Love bombing'* attempts to inundate visitors with flattery and friendliness in order to produce the feeling that the group will fulfill many of their needs and desires.

4. Once potential members are assigned a discipler, they are led through a series of Bible studies.

   (a) The first study is called **'First Principles'** and covers the simple basics of the Bible.
   (b) The second is **'The Sins of Galatians'** study. It aims to get individuals to repent, to confess their sins, etc.
       - After reading Galatians 5:19–21 the disciples are told to make a list of their sins, before being guided to other scriptures that have the similar effect of making them feel guilty and full of sin. More sin lists follow.
       - Sometimes a list is kept of the disciples' sins and they are brought up in various situations – ultimately, to keep control over them.
       - This can be used to break people down emotionally
   (c) The third study covers **'The Cross'**.
       - The disciple listens to the discipler read the crucifixion account and is asked to say, 'I am Judas – I am Peter.'
       - The more unpleasant details of the crucifixion are described and the discipler reads from the disciple's sin list.

> ▶ Often, sentences are spoken such as, 'You punched Him in the face', 'You taunted Him', 'You whipped Him.'
> ▶ The disciple is supposed to be 'broken' in this process, and often is ... emotionally.

Baptism

1. 'The Boston Church of Christ teaches that when one initially receives Jesus Christ, one's response must include faith, repentance, confession, and water baptism. It teaches that apart from water baptism, one's sins are not forgiven.'

(E. Bourland, P. Owen and P. Reid,
The Issue of Water Baptism and the Boston Church of Christ,
publisher, p. 1).

2. Not only must one be baptized, but one must also be baptized in the Boston Church of Christ. Anyone who has been a member of another church before joining the Boston Church, must be rebaptized because the original baptism was done in a false church without a proper understanding of baptism.

   • Also, a person must be baptized by someone in authority in the Boston Church of Christ, i.e., International Church of Christ Movement.

3. Therefore, salvation is gained by believing in Jesus' death on the cross and on being baptized.

Miscellaneous information

So many people have been injured by the Church's authoritarian and intrusive structure that some schools, including the Boston University, Marquette University, University of Southern California, Northeastern University, and Vanderbilt University, have banned the Boston Church of Christ (*Miami Herald*, 25 March 1992, p. 1A, 15A).

Swedenborgianism

Also known as The New Church, the Church of New Jerusalem.

Founder
Emanuel Swedenborg (1688–1722), born in Stockholm, Sweden.

Headquarters
Philadelphia, England.

Membership
150,000 worldwide.

Doctrines
Denies the atonement, the Trinity, the deity of Christ and the Holy Spirit, and teaches that all religions lead to God. One of its goals is to bring the world together under a new religious understanding. It teaches a need for Christianity to undergo a rebirth – according to Swedenborgian interpretations.

There is no devil. The Scriptures can only be properly interpreted through Swedenborgianism. It is possible to sin in heaven. They reject everything in the New Testament apart from the four Gospels and Revelation. Salvation is earned by good works. There is no physical resurrection. After death, a person becomes an angel or an evil spirit. Angels are not supernatural creations of God.

At death, a person's mind falls asleep for three days in a place called the world of the spirits. At the end of this period, he awakens spirits who have died before to help him adjust. He then forms his own spiritual body in which to reside.

There is marriage in heaven.

Origins
Emanuel Swedenborg was born in Stockholm on 29 January 1688, the son of a Lutheran minister. He was very bright and had an inquisitive mind. He was particularly interested in science and religion and was recognized as an expert in geology. In 1744 he was stricken with a severe delirium which seems to have affected his mind for the rest of his life.

In 1745 Swedenborg had a vision in which loathsome creatures seemed to be crawling on the walls of his room. Then a man appeared who claimed to be God and told him that he was to be the one who would communicate the teachings of the unseen realm to the people of the world. He would be the means by which God would further reveal Himself to the world.

He organized his first church in London in 1787. James Glen introduced this cult to the USA in 1784.

Practices

Astral projection, automatic handwriting. *Publications*

Arcana Coelestia: The Earths in the Universe, the thirty-five volumes of writings by Swedenborg.

Comments

This is a dangerous mystical cult with a blend of New Age and Mind Science theologies.

Resources

www.ntro.org, www.newchurch.org

Theosophy

Founders

Madame Helena Blavatsky (1831–1891), born in Russia, and Henry Steel Olcott, a New York lawyer. Theosophy was founded in New York City in 1875.

Headquarters

International headquarters – Adyar, India; America – Wheaton, Illinois.

Membership

Approximately 120 study centers in the USA.

Origins

Mme Blavatsky was born in Russia into an affluent and capable family. She traveled extensively around the world in search of spiritual understanding of the purpose of human existence and spent some time in India. Eventually, she brought the principles she learned to America.

Olcott was a civil war veteran who became the first president of the Theosophical Society and extended its influence greatly.

Teachings

It has no official doctrinal statement other than three major objectives:

1. To form a nucleus of the universal brotherhood of humanity, without distinction of race, creed, sex, caste, or color.
2. To encourage the comparative study of religion, philosophy, and science.
3. To investigate unexplained laws of nature and the powers latent in humanity.

Theosophy teaches that the universe is one interrelated whole. Everything in the universe, people included, participates in the same life-creating reality. Matter and Spirit are the two main elements of the universe and everything is evolving into a higher plane of spiritual awareness and interconnectedness. Through reincarnation, people become more aware of their unity with the

Divine One. After a long cycle of reincarnations, they attain enlightenment when they are unified with all other parts of the universe.

Both the Earth and the human race are going through stages. The earth is in its fourth stage and the human race is in its fifth. 'The human body is comprised of seven qualities: divine, monadic, spiritual, intuitional, mental, astral and physical.' [37]

Theosophy accepts the miraculous as true and attempts to understand it using philosophy and science. Theosophy claims to be a scientific way of understanding religious systems. The name 'Theosophy' is derived from the Greek *theos* (God) and *sophia* (wisdom): hence, Theosophia, or Theosophy.

Blavatsky believed that there is an ancient society of Masters or Adepts who have complete understanding of the Divine Wisdom. Mdm Blavatsky claimed to have been taught by these Masters with whom she was in contact. Jesus is considered to be the reincarnation of Krishna.

Theosophy claims an influence upon much of society, particularly in some of the poets, writers, and artists of the past one hundred years. A key phrase of Theosophy is, 'There is no religion higher than truth.'

Texts

The Secret Doctrine, Isis Unveiled, The Key to Theosophy, and *The Voice of the Silence*, which are all written by Mme Blavatsky and are considered divinely inspired.

Comments

Theosophy is nothing more than a variation of the ancient Gnosticism which was addressed in 1 John. It is heavily influenced by the Hinduism Mme Blavatsky learned in the East. It teaches inner divinity, and adopts a pantheon of gods. It is not Christian in any sense and is dangerous to the soul. It separates the Christ from Jesus, as many New Age type cults do, thus reducing His true nature.

Unity School of Christianity

Founders

Charles and Myrtle Fillmore.

Headquarters

Lee's Summit, Missouri.

Membership

Over one million.

Origins

Unity began in Kansas City in 1889. Both Charles (a spiritist with no Christian background) and Myrtle (raised a Methodist; d. 1931) were involved with Christian Science and claimed that Christian Science principles led to healings in their lives. However, since they disagreed with the Christian Science doctrine that matter is not real, they broke away, taught the reality of matter and added, among other doctrines, the belief in reincarnation. Charles even believed he was the reincarnation of Paul the apostle. The Fillmores studied Hinduism and wove many of its other principles into their philosophy as their new religion grew. Unity is a mind science cult.

Doctrines

Unity School of Christianity denies the Trinity, the deity of Jesus, the necessity of the atonement of Jesus for our sins, heaven, hell, sin, and the existence of the devil. It teaches reincarnation. 'The second birth is that in which we "put on Christ." It is a process of mental adjustment and body transmutation that takes place right here on earth.' They are largely vegetarians. Unity teaches that experience, for those who are 'in tune' with God, is more accurate and reliable than the Bible. God is a divine universal consciousness. Human beings are a part of that divine consciousness and are divine.

Unity separates Jesus from Christ saying that Jesus was a man, but that we all possess the Christ consciousness within us. Christ is the one complete idea of perfect man and Divine Mind. Atonement is the reconciliation of our minds with the Divine Mind. It says that the Holy Spirit is a latent power within every one of us. Problems disappear when people think correctly; that is, when they think according to the principles of Divine Mind as revealed in Unity. God is within us all as well as creation. 'God slumbers in the rocks. God stirs in the flowers. God awakens in Man.' All are children of God and Jesus was simply here to show us what we, as children of God, can do. It denies that Jesus is God in flesh and that He is to be worshiped. 'But because He remained in a high state of spiritual consciousness, He became the ethical Messiah of the world.'

The following quotes are from Charles Fillmore's book *Christian Healing* (Unity School of Christianity, Unity Village, MO). They are at the end of each chapter and are meant as summaries and points for meditation:

> 'God is the name of the everywhere Principle, in whom I live, move, and have my being.'   (p. 17)

> 'I am the son of God, and the Spirit of the Most High dwells in me.'   (p. 29)

> 'I am the only begotten son, dwelling in the bosom of the Father.'   (p. 29)

> 'I am the Christ of God.'   (p. 29)

> 'I and my Father are one.'   (p. 29)

> 'I am one with Almightiness.'   (p. 29)

> 'God is good, and God is all, therefore I refuse to believe in the reality of evil in any of its forms.'   (p. 60)

Publications

Wee Wisdom, for children; *Good Business*, for business people; *Weekly Unity*, their devotional magazine. They use mail order extensively. There are many other writings, including *Mysteries of Genesis* and *Christian Healing* both by Charles Fillmore.

Comments

To uphold its doctrinal position, like most cults, the true Christian position is misrepresented in order to justify this cult's 'more correct' view. For example, because Christianity teaches that God made men and women in His image, Unity claims that it views

God as a man. This is an erring assumption on their part as well as a misrepresentation. Unity uses the Bible and Jesus when it suits its needs but is not faithful to the biblical revelation of who and what God is, what Jesus has done, and the nature of the Trinity and salvation. It is a dangerous non-Christian cult and should be avoided.

The Way International

Founder
Victor Paul Wierwille, born 1917.

Headquarters
Just outside New Knoxville in Ohio.

Membership
Over 100,000 all over the world.

Doctrines
Like many cult groups, the Way claims the Bible is the Word of God, yet it denies the doctrine of the Trinity, the deity of Christ, the personhood and deity of the Holy Spirit, and salvation by grace. In regards to the Holy Spirit, Wierwille draws a distinction between the Holy Spirit and the holy spirit. While the first is the same as God the Father, the second is an emanation or power from God. Jesus was not born of a virgin. The dead are 'unconscious' after death; that is, they don't exist until they are brought back to life at the judgement. The Way also denies the efficacious nature of the atonement.

The Way teaches that Jesus was raised on Saturday and that there were four people crucified with Him, not two. Only true believers who lived after Pentecost will be saved. Speaking in tongues is taught as a mandatory practice and part of salvation to be cultivated by the members daily.

In addition, the Way teaches that once people are saved, they cannot sin in their spirit. Their body and soul can sin, but not their spirit – this can lead to sinful practices that are said not to affect the spirit of a person.

Origins
According to Wierwille, in 1942 God audibly spoke to him and told him that he would interpret the Bible in a new way and would teach it according to the principles of the early Church. But it wasn't until 1957 that Wierwille resigned his pastorate in the United Church of Christ.

He developed a radio program and began to preach his new doctrines fervently. Many began to follow. Presently, they run a college in Kansas called The Way College of Emporia, where naturally Wierwille's aberrant theology is taught.

Practices

The Way International uses a teaching series called 'The Way of Abundance and Power.'

The organization is arranged using the metaphor of a tree. Home fellowships are called Twigs with each member being a leaf. Twigs are arranged into Limbs (city groups), Limbs are arranged into Branches (state groups) and Branches are arranged into Trunks (countries), which are all under the Root (Wierwille) at New Knoxville, Ohio. The members practice a 15 per cent 'tithe.' The group has missionaries, ordain women, and have WOW disciples.[38] Presently, there are several thousand WOW disciples. The Way International has an annual convention called Rock of Ages.

Publications

Jesus Christ is not God by V.P. Wierwille.

Comments

The Way International uses many of the same arguments as the Jehovah's Witnesses in regard to the Trinity and the deity of Jesus. The Way teaches that God cannot die, therefore Jesus was not God in flesh. They fail to understand that the Word which was God and with God had always existed (John 1:1) and became flesh (John 1:14). This incarnation of the Word is Jesus. Jesus had two natures. He was both God and man. As a man, He could die, yet as God, He lived on.

The people in The Way International need to be prayed for and given the same consideration and politeness as anyone lost in deception.

PART 5

*Principles of
Effective Evangelism
and Witnessing to Cults*

An easy and powerful way to witness to the cults

The following method of witnessing to cultists is non-offensive and powerful. It focuses on Jesus, the gospel, and uses Scripture. This is important for three reasons:

1. Jesus draws all people to Himself (John 12:32).

2. The gospel is powerful for salvation (Romans 1:16).

3. God's Word accomplishes what God wants it to (Isaiah 55:11).

Faith in the Jesus of Mormonism, of Jehovah's Witnesses, or of any other cult, is useless. The validity of faith does not rest in itself, but in its object. The greatest faith in someone false is the same as no faith at all. That is the case with the Mormons and the Jehovah's Witnesses. Each group believes in a Jesus, but not in the Jesus of the Bible, and because they each have a false Jesus (2 Corinthians 11:4), they each preach a false gospel (Galatians 1:8–9). They may be sincere, but they are sincerely wrong – dead wrong.

The official theologies of the Mormons and Jehovah's Witnesses do not permit prayer to or the worship of Jesus. They also deny that He can be called their God. But the Bible permits, even encourages, the true believer to do these things. The true Jesus, the Jesus of the Bible, is prayed to, worshiped, and called God. And, this is where we must begin.

If you can prove a cultist wrong in a minor point of theology, he is still a cultist. But, if you show him that the Jesus he believes in is not the same one found in the Bible, then you have undermined his entire theology.

In brief, you should introduce the cultist to the real Jesus: the One of the Bible who is prayed to (Acts 7:59; 1 Corinthians 1:1–2), worshiped (Matthew 2:2, 11; 14:33; 28:9; John 9:35–38; Hebrews 1:6), and called God (John 20:28; Hebrews 1:8; Titus 2:13). The hope is that once the cultist sees that he is without the Jesus of the Bible, he will realize he doesn't have the true God. Then, hopefully, he will accept Christ and leave his cult. If not, at least the seeds of truth will have been planted and he will have been exposed to the true Jesus.

The 'approach' is simple.

1. Establish a common ground: the need to know the Father.

2. Establish that the only way to the Father is through Jesus: the Jesus of the Bible.

3. Demonstrate the need for having the correct Jesus, the One of historical (and biblical) Christianity.

4. Establish that the Jesus of the Bible is prayed to, worshiped, and called God.

5. Ask the cultist if he prays to, worships, and calls Jesus God.

6. Ask the cultist why he is right and you are wrong if you do what the Scriptures teach and he doesn't.

7. Present the gospel.

Remember, a false Jesus cannot save. Sincerity and false messiahs do not bridge the gap of sin between God and human beings, only the Jesus of the Bible does that.

Here is a sample dialogue between a Christian and a cultist.

[*Christian*]: Would you agree with me that we both want to know the Father and do what He wants us to do?

[*Cultist*]:   Yes.

[*Christian*]: How, then, do we get to know the Father?

[*Cultist*]:   Through prayer and reading the Bible.

[*Christian*]: Well, that's not a bad answer. But Jesus said that He was the One who revealed the Father to us (Matthew 11:27 [39] and Luke 10:22). So, to know the true Father we must first know the true Jesus, right?

[*Cultist*]:   Yes, that seems reasonable.

(You are not attacking his doctrine, you are appealing to his desires which, on the surface, are identical to yours: to serve and love God. You can catch more bees with honey than with a hammer.)

[*Christian*]: Well, let me ask you another question. Will a false Jesus reveal the true God?

[*Cultist*]:   No. I suppose not.

[*Christian*]: That's right. The real issue, then, isn't that we are going to church or are nice people. It's whether or not we know the true Jesus so that He can reveal to us the true God. Right?

[*Cultist*]:   Right.

[*Christian*]: The question is, 'How do we find the true Jesus?' The only way I can think of is if we go to the Bible. That is where the true Jesus is, right?

[*Cultist*]: Right. But you could also pray and ask God to reveal Him to you.

[*Christian*]: I see what you mean. But how could you pray to God if the only way to get to Him is through Jesus, and you don't have the right Jesus? Wouldn't prayer, then, be useless?

[*Cultist*]: Not if you're sincere.

[*Christian*]: But then you are saying that if you are sincere, you don't need Jesus. Do you see the problem with that? Sincerity doesn't make access to God possible. Only Jesus does that. Remember, Jesus said that no one comes to the Father, except by Him (John 14:6).

[*Cultist*]: But doesn't James 1:5 say if you lack wisdom to ask God and He will give it to you? So couldn't you ask God for wisdom about what is true?

[*Christian*]: James was written to those who were already believers; they already had the true Jesus and, therefore, the true Father. Also, wisdom is the proper use of knowledge. It isn't the gaining of knowledge, nor is it gaining access to God. Do you see that you still have to have the true Jesus. Because if you were to pray to God for wisdom, and you served a false Jesus, then who is going to answer your prayers? It wouldn't be God, would it?

[*Cultist*]: I see your point.

[*Christian*]: Good. Now let me ask you a couple of questions to get things started. If you were to say, 'Father receive my spirit,' whom would you be praying to?

[*Cultist*]: I would be praying to the Father.

[*Christian*]: Right. If you were to say, 'Jesus, receive my spirit,' whom would you be praying to?

[*Cultist*]: I wouldn't pray to Jesus. I would only pray to the Father. That is what He said to do in Matthew 6. He said to pray, 'Our Father, who art in heaven...'

[*Christian*]: Yes, that's true. But if you believe it, do you do it? Do you pray that way all the time?

[*Cultist*]: Of course I do.

[*Christian*]: No, what I mean is. Do you pray that prayer? If you believe that is what you are to pray, then you could only pray that particular prayer. You would have to repeat it every time you prayed. But that isn't what Jesus intended. It was a model prayer. It is what we are to follow. May we continue? You'll see what I'm getting at in a moment.

[*Cultist*]:   Sure. Go ahead.

[*Christian*]: Just for the sake of argument, if you were to say, 'Jesus, receive my spirit,' whom would you be praying to?

[*Cultist*]:   I would be praying to Jesus.

[*Christian*]: Right. Now, in Acts 7:55–60, Stephen, while full of the Holy Spirit, prayed to Jesus. It says, *'While they were stoning him Stephen prayed, "Lord Jesus, receive my spirit."'* (*See also* Acts 9:13; Romans 10:13.) Stephen prayed **to** Jesus, not just through Him. If it was acceptable for him, then it should be all right for you. The Jesus of the Bible is prayed to. I pray to Jesus. Do you? If yes, good. If not, why not?
(If you are talking to a Mormon, you may want to mention that in the Book of Mormon, in 3 Nephi 19:18, Jesus is prayed to – not just through!)

[*Cultist*]:   Jesus said to pray to the Father. So, I do.

[*Christian*]: Yes, I agree. I do too. But I also pray to Jesus as Stephen did. If the church is only to pray to the Father, then why did Stephen, under the inspiration of the Holy Spirit, address Jesus in his prayer? Was he wrong?

[*Cultist*]:   I don't have an answer.

[*Christian*]: Also, what does it mean to call upon the name of the Lord?

[*Cultist*]:   I don't know. What does it mean?

[*Christian*]: It means to seek God, even to pray to God. For example, in Psalm 116:4 it says, *'Then I called on the name of the* LORD: *"O* LORD, *save me!"'* In 1 Corinthians 1:1–2 the church calls upon the name of the Lord Jesus. That is, they prayed to Jesus. Now, if Stephen, full of the Holy Spirit, could pray to Jesus, and the church in 1 Corinthians 1:1–2 could too, then shouldn't you be able to do the same thing?

[*Cultist*]:   Well, I'm not sure. I've never really considered this before.

[*Christian*]: Glad to see you're honest. Let's continue. Jesus was also worshiped. We see that in the verses: *'Then those who were in the boat worshiped him, saying, "Truly, you are the Son of God!"'* (Matthew 14:33). *'Suddenly, Jesus met them. "Greetings," he said. They came to him, clasped his feet and worshiped him'* (Matthew 28:9). (*See also* Matthew 2:2, 11; John 9:35–39; Hebrews 1:6.) Do you do what His disciples did? Do you worship Jesus?

(Mormon theology does not allow worship of Jesus. However, some Mormons do anyway – they just don't know that their Church teaches against doing so. If the person says he worships Jesus, ask him how he can do that without praying to Him. If, on the other hand, the Mormon has said he does pray **to** Jesus and that he does worship Jesus, then encourage him to continue and remind him that it is Jesus who has the authority (Matthew 28:18) to forgive sins (Luke 5:20–24; 7:48–49); He judges (John 5:22, 27); He gives eternal life (John 10:28; 5:40), etc. See '100 Truths About Jesus.' The whole point is to try to get him to ask the true Jesus to forgive him his sins and reveal the Father to him.)

(All Jehovah's Witnesses say no to worshiping Jesus. In their own Bible they have mistranslated the word 'worship,' wherever it refers to Jesus, to the words 'do obeisance' which means to show respect or honor to someone. Because of this, using the verse about worship will not carry much weight. In that case, you will want to substitute this . . .)

[*Christian*]: Do you honor Him as much as you do the Father, as Jesus said to do in John 5:23?

[*Cultist*]:   Not equally. The Father is greater than Jesus.

[*Christian*]: The Father was greater in position. Remember, Jesus was made for a little while lower than the angels (Hebrews 2:9). It was in this humbled state that He said the Father was greater than He. He didn't say different or better, only greater. You must understand that Jesus was fully man as well as fully God and as a man was in a lesser position. Scripture still requires that you honor

Him as much as you do the Father, as Jesus said. If you don't, then why not?

[*Cultist*]:   I don't have an answer.

[*Christian*]: All right. There is just one more issue to address. Do you call Jesus your Lord and your God?

[*Cultist*]:   No, I don't.

[*Christian*]: After Jesus' resurrection He showed Himself to many people. One of them was Thomas. John 20:28 says, *'Thomas said to him* [Jesus], *"My Lord and my God!" Then Jesus told him, "Because you have seen me, you have believed..."'*

In addition, God calls Jesus God in Hebrews 1:8, *'But about the Son he* [the Father] *says, "Your throne, O God, will last for ever and ever..."*[40] The Father calls Jesus God. Thomas called Him his Lord and God. Do you call Jesus your Lord and your God?

[*Cultist*]:   No. I don't call Jesus my Lord and God.

(Jehovah's Witnesses will say that Thomas was swearing. Ask them why Jesus didn't rebuke Thomas for swearing? Besides, in the Greek, Thomas literally said, *'The Lord of me and the God of me.'*)

(With a Mormon, you can again mention the reference in the Book of Mormon, 3 Nephi 19:18, where Jesus is also called Lord and God.)[41]

[*Christian*]: My question to you is this. If I have the wrong Jesus, and therefore I serve the wrong God, then why do I pray to Jesus, worship Him, and call Him my Lord and God as the Scriptures teach? But, if you have the true Jesus, why is it you don't do those things?

[*Cultist*]:   (Silence!)

[*Christian*]: It seems clear that if you want your sins forgiven, then you need to go to Jesus and ask Him to forgive you. Remember, the true Jesus, the Jesus of the Bible, is prayed to, worshiped, and called God. That is the same Jesus I serve. Which one do you serve?

[*Christian*]: Since Jesus is the one who forgives sins, then I go to Him. You can too. All you have to do is pray to Him and ask Him to forgive you your sins. You already know you are a sinner. So simply go to Him, the real Jesus, and receive the forgiveness of sins through faith in Him.

This brief approach is powerful because it brings the cultist face to face with the Jesus of the Bible. Though the cultist won't respond by dropping to his knees, at least you will have exposed him to the real Jesus. Also, remember that the Word of God will accomplish what God wishes it to:

> *'so is my word that goes out from my mouth: It will not return to me empty but will accomplish what I desire . . . '*   (Isaiah 55:11)

The do's and don'ts of witnessing

Witnessing is and isn't easy to do. If you are one of those people who are easily intimidated at the prospect of witnessing, don't fret. You're normal. People are intimidated for different reasons: some because they lack knowledge, others because they lack the confidence, and still others because they lack both. This notebook can help you with all three. If you have studied the material up to this point, then you are truly equipped for witnessing. All you need to do ... is witness. It's a bit like swimming: to learn it you have to do it.

However, there are things you need to do to prepare yourself. First, pray that God will use you, that He will provide opportunities for you to be able to share God's Word, and that He will speak through you. Yield yourself to Him as an instrument of His righteousness. Don't be afraid to trust God. Remember, to trust God is to trust His love. He will never leave you or forsake you (Hebrews 13:5) even while you are witnessing. And, if you haven't already experienced it, when you witness, the Holy Spirit helps you to remember scriptures to use and thoughts to say that are, well, sometimes surprising. It's wonderful to be used by God.

Here is a brief list of some basic do's and don'ts of witnessing. Simply think about them and what they mean and ask the Lord to help you focus on those areas that are important for you. He will bless you mightily.

Do's

- pray
- read your Bible
- speak to please God
- start with a positive witness for Christ
- keep things simple
- share with them your salvation experience, how Jesus changed your life
- know what you believe
- have a genuine love for them
- be simple and define your terms
- memorize appropriate scriptures

- be patient and gentle
- be attentive
- listen attentively
- answer their questions
- ask questions
- let them save face
- bring them, if possible, to a decision about Jesus
- encourage them to study the Bible by itself
- use scripture in context
- remember that greater is He that is in you than he that is in the world (1 John 4:4)

Don'ts

- attack directly or make fun of them
- jump from subject to subject
- expect too much from them
- have a spiritual chip on your shoulder
- lose patience
- come on too strong
- debate peripheral issues or doctrines
- get sidetracked defending your denomination
- be uptight
- assume
- argue
- speak too fast or unclearly
- worry
- forget to pray afterwards
- forget to give God the glory

It is the Lord who saves. But that doesn't mean you can't be His effective tool. So, pray, study, ask God for the opportunity, and when it arises, witness. You'll do fine.

Three important verses in witnessing

If you only study one page in this section on evangelism, make it this one. Why? Because you will learn three of the most important verses for evangelism: Isaiah 55:11, Romans 1:16; and John 12:32.

Isaiah 55:11

> *'So shall My word be which goes forth from My mouth; it shall not return to Me empty, without accomplishing what I desire, and without succeeding in the matter for which I sent it.'*   (NASB)

God's work is unique. It was by His word (speech) that God created, *'God said, "Let there be light"; and there was light'* (Genesis 1:3). *'By faith we understand that the worlds were prepared by the word of God...'* (Hebrews 11:3 NASB). Jesus is called the Word:

> *'In the beginning was the Word, and the Word was with God, and the Word was God ... and the Word became flesh and lived for a while among us...'*   (John 1:1, 14)

When Jesus was on the earth, He taught. He taught with words and His words had a very strong effect on people. They angered some and broke others. But when Jesus spoke, things happened. Jesus forgave sins by speaking, *'When Jesus saw their faith, He said, "Friend, your sins are forgiven"'* (Luke 5:20). He raised the dead by speaking, *'Lazarus, come out'* (John 11:43). He calmed the wind and sea with words, *'Then he got up, and rebuked the winds and the sea; and it was completely calm'* (Matthew 8:26). He cast out demons by speech, *'And he said to them, "Go!" So they came out...'* (Matthew 8:32). He healed by speech, *'Jesus reached out his hand and touched the man. "I am willing," he said. "Be clean." Immediately he was cured of his leprosy'* (Matthew 8:3). God's words are powerful.

Romans 1:16

> *'I am not ashamed of the gospel, because it is the power of God for salvation of everyone who believes, first for the Jew, then for the Gentile.'*

What is the gospel? In 1 Corinthians 15:1–4 Paul says it is the sacrificial death and physical resurrection of Jesus for sins. It is the powerful message of salvation to sinners. If you know that the

Word of God will accomplish what God wants it to and if you know that the gospel has power to save, then it should ease your mind to know that in witnessing you are using two very powerful weapons: God's Word and God's gospel. The Word of God is the Bible. The gospel of God is His revelation or redemption.

John 12:32

'And I, if I be lifted up from the earth, will draw all men to Myself.'
(NASB)

Here Jesus speaks specifically about His crucifixion. It is He who draws to Himself all who are to be saved. When you present the gospel (1 Corinthians 15:1–4), the sacrificial death and resurrection of Jesus for sins, Jesus draws the sinner to Himself. He does the work, not you.

As a Christian, you are to witness with truth, honesty, and integrity. As the Lord provides the opportunity, you should respond in a humble and gentle spirit (2 Timothy 2:24–26). And in doing that, you should point people to Jesus. It is He alone who saves.

If you know that God's Word will accomplish what God desires, that the gospel is powerful to save, and that it is Jesus who draws all people to Himself, then you should realize that the responsibility for salvation does not rest on you, but on God. You are the teacher, the deliverer of good news.

'...how can they believe in the one of whom they have not heard?'
(Romans 10:14)

You help them hear!

These three verses should help you to gain confidence. You witness; God saves. You plant the seeds; God waters. He uses you. It is His Word that accomplishes salvation. It is His gospel that is powerful. It is His Son Jesus who draws. You witness in power when you witness with the Word of God.

How to memorize Scripture

There are four easy steps to Scripture memorization. Let's use 1 Peter 2:24 as an example:

> '... and He Himself bore our sins in His body on the cross, that we might die to sin and live to righteousness; for by His wounds you were healed.'   (NASB)

Step 1: Location

The first step is to memorize the location, not the verse. The reason for this is if you forget the verse, but you've memorized the location, you can always look it up.

First, memorize the location: '1 Peter 2:24.' Say '1 Peter 2:24' over and over again. Don't worry about what it says at first, just memorize the location. Make sure that when you say '1 Peter 2:24' it flows smoothly off your lips. Emphasize different syllables. Say '1 **Peter** 2:24,' or '1 Peter **2**:24' or '1 Peter 2:**24**' or even '**1** Peter 2:24.' But say '1 Peter 2:24' enough times that it becomes as natural as breathing.

Step 2: Gist

The second step is to learn the gist of what the verse says. In this case it is very simple, *'Jesus bore our sins in His body on the cross.'* Say, *'Jesus bore our sins in His body on the cross,'* emphasizing different words: *'**Jesus** bore our sins in His body on the cross,'* or *'Jesus bore our **sins** in His body on the cross,'* and *'Jesus bore our sins in His **body** on the cross,'* etc. But repeat *'Jesus bore our sins in His body on the cross'* enough times that it becomes as natural as saying '1 Peter 2:24.' (Kind of repetitive, isn't it?)

Step 3: Association

The third part is more fun. This is where you associate the two together. Say, '1 Peter 2:24 is *Jesus bore our sins in His body on the cross. Jesus bore our sins in His body on the cross* is 1 Peter 2:24. 1 Peter 2:24 is *Jesus bore our sins in His body on the cross* ... ' Say this over and over again, about ten times. In no time, if you do this, you will have it memorized.

This association part is important because it helps you to think of one part whenever you think of the other. For example, if someone asked you, 'Where does it say that Jesus bore our sin in His body?', you'd immediately reply '1 Peter 2:24.' It works.

Step 4: A piece of paper

The fourth and final part is to take a piece of lined paper and draw a vertical line about one inch from the left-hand side.

Write the verse location in the left-hand column on your paper and on the right side simply write the verse. Do this with each verse you want to remember. Fold it up, put it in your pocket or purse, and carry it with you everywhere you go. When you forget a verse or its location simply pull out the paper and refresh your memory. In no time at all, you'll have over one hundred verses committed to memory.

Memorization is like exercise. The more you do it, the easier it gets; the less you do the harder it gets. So do it. If you follow this procedure your mind will become like a sponge: you'll end up memorizing all sorts of stuff with the greatest of ease, like how many socks are in your drawer, everything that is in your refrigerator, and even where your car keys are.

And one more thing. You will be amazed at how the Lord uses what you've memorized.

The Four Spiritual Laws

If you've had a good discussion with someone and you want to present the gospel message in a simple and systematic way, the well-known 'Four Spiritual Laws' can be of help. They are simple, to the point, and use Scripture to convict, convince, and convert. They are:

1. **God loves you.**

   'For God so loved the world, that he gave his one and only Son, that whoever believes in him shall not perish, but have eternal life.' (John 3:16)

2. **Human beings are sinful and separated from God.**

   '...for all have sinned and fall short of the glory of God...' (Romans 3:23)

   'For the wages of sin is death...' (Romans 6:23)

   'But your iniquities have separated you from your God...' (Isaiah 59:2)

3. **Jesus Christ is God's only provision for human beings' sin. Through Him we may reach God.**

   'I am the way and the truth and the life. No-one comes to the Father, except through me.' (John 14:6)

   'But God demonstrates his own love for us in this: While we were still sinners, Christ died for us.' (Romans 5:8)

4. **We must individually receive Jesus as Savior and Lord.**

   'Yet to all who received him, to those who believed in his name, he gave the right to become children of God.' (John 1:12)

   '...if you confess with your mouth, "Jesus is Lord," and believe in your heart that God raised him from the dead, you will be saved.' (Romans 10:9)

   'For it is by grace you have been saved, through faith – and this not from yourselves, it is the gift of God...' (Ephesians 2:8)

The Roman Road

Another list of verses which can be used in the same way as the Four Spiritual Laws is the 'Roman Road.' The advantage of these seven verses is that they are all in the book of Romans. This can sometimes be helpful when you don't want to flip through a lot of pages.

1. *'As it is written, "There is no-one righteous, not even one..."'*
   (Romans 3:10)

2. *'...for all have sinned and fall short of the glory of God.'*
   (Romans 3:23)

3. *'Therefore, just as sin entered the world through one man, and death through sin, and in this way death came to all men, because all sinned.'* (Romans 5:12)

4. *'For the wages of sin is death, but the gift of God is eternal life in Christ Jesus our Lord.'* (Romans 6:23)

5. *'But God demonstrates his own love for us in this: While we were still sinners, Christ died for us.'* (Romans 5:8)

6. *'if you confess with your mouth, "Jesus is Lord," and believe in your heart that God raised him from the dead, you will be saved. For it is with your heart that you believe and are justified, and it is with your mouth that you confess and are saved.'* (Romans 10:9–10)

7. *'...for, "Everyone who calls on the name of the Lord will be saved."'* (Romans 10:13)

I recommend you put the Roman Road in your Bible. Go to Romans 3:10 underline it and write Romans 3:28 next to it. Then go to Romans 3:28, underline it and write Romans 5:12 next to it, and so on. That way all you need to do is memorize where you start: Romans 3:10.

Christian CPR

Almost everyone has heard of CPR, cardiopulmonary resuscitation. It has saved many lives. I would like to introduce you to Christian CPR. It can save your spiritual life. It's simple: Confess, Pray, and Read.

Confess

The first of the three letters represents Confession: our human need. Each person who witnesses should have his or her own life right with God. That doesn't mean being perfect, but it does mean actively seeking to walk in accord with God's will. It means regularly confessing your sins to God and forsaking them. This is done in prayer.

Sin is not something to be taken lightly. It is so bad, so evil, so wicked, that it cost Jesus His life. The greatness of the sacrifice of Christ only reflects the greatness of the depth of sin. It took something as incredible as God on the cross to undo sin. Sin can hinder your effectiveness so you need to make sure you confess any sin of which you have not repented to God. He will forgive you and your fellowship with Him is then restored. In that proper relationship, He will guide you and empower you to speak boldly for Him.

The Bible says,

> *'If we confess our sins, he is faithful and just and will forgive us our sins and purify us from all unrighteousness.'* (1 John 1:9)

Confession is good for the soul they say – and it is true. It is good to bow before the Lord in humility and seek His forgiveness:

> *'Humble yourselves before the Lord and He will lift you up.'*
> (James 4:10)

Be ready to confess and forsake your sins. That is what God asks.

Pray

The second letter represents Prayer: your special privilege. Through prayer you are in fellowship with the Holy Creator of the universe. You can actually speak to Him. You can worship, love, and spend time with Him. Because of what Jesus has done for you on the cross, God hears your prayers.

When you desire to pray, is it your flesh that seeks Him? No. Since your natural self does not seek God and since you are still in sinful flesh, when the inclination to pray comes over you, it is God calling you to spend time with Him. He wants you to fellowship with Him. In 1 Corinthians 1:9 it says:

> *'God is faithful, through whom you were called into fellowship with His Son, Jesus Christ our Lord.'*   (NASB)

He wants you to be in His presence and be dependent upon Him. Those who are in the presence of the Lord cannot but have their hearts filled by Him. They cannot but speak of Him:

> *'Out of the abundance of the heart, the mouth speaks.'*
> (Matthew 12:34 NKJV)

When Moses was in the presence of God, his face shone (2 Corinthians 3:7). When you are in the presence of God your heart will shine. Prayer is the practice of the presence of God. To be effective, you need to be in fellowship with God. To be in fellowship, you need to be praying, constantly.

Read

The third letter represents Reading: your daily bread. It is in reading the Bible that God speaks to you. The Bible is, of course, the Word of God. It is,

> *'...God-breathed and is useful for teaching, for rebuking, for correcting, and training in righteousness; so that the man of God may be thoroughly equipped for every good work.'*
> (2 Timothy 3:16–17)

One of the ways God has made Himself known to you is through His Word. It is light for your soul, food for your thoughts, and the guide to shape your life. By reading the Bible and memorizing Scripture, you are a much greater threat to Satan. When Jesus was tempted by Satan what did He use to rebuke Him? A miracle? A powerful sweep of His hand? No. He quoted Scripture (Matthew 4).

Follow Jesus' example. Learn Scripture. Use it. Let it dwell in your heart and mind. Rebuke the enemy with it. Learn from it. It will nourish you.

A final word on witnessing

When witnessing we need to teach. Teaching is giving people knowledge and understanding that they don't have. One of the major points of Christianity is the relationship between the Law and the gospel (*See* 'Law and Gospel', pp. 00–00.) Understanding this enables us to teach a person what God's grace really is. Of course, this can be done in a number of theological ways, but why delve unnecessarily into deep waters with someone you're witnessing to? It is important that **you** understand what grace is in relationship to the Law and it's important that the one you are witnessing to understands it also. However, teaching this subject can be a bit tricky, especially if you want to do it well and quickly. So, an illustration can be very helpful. In fact, the following two illustrations, if used properly, can really help someone understand what the free gift of salvation is all about. Study them, understand them, use them, adapt them, and make them 'your own.'

Justice, mercy, and grace

- Justice is getting what we deserve.

- Mercy is not getting what we deserve.

- Grace is getting what we don't deserve.

The first scenario is this: Let's suppose you have a bicycle and I want it. So, one night I sneak over to your house and steal it. You catch me and I go to jail. (Jail would be where I 'pay' for my crime of breaking the law.) The penalty is met and that is justice. I get what I deserve.

In the next scenario, I sneak over to your house and steal your bike. You catch me. You don't send me to jail. Instead, you tell me to forget about it. The penalty (jail) is not met. That is mercy. I did not get what I deserved.

Finally, I sneak over to your house and steal your bike. You catch me. You don't send me to jail. In fact, you give me the bike plus one hundred dollars. That is grace. The penalty is met (by you paying the 'damages') **and** I was given what I did not deserve (the bike and money).

Justice demands payment so it does not meet the requirement of mercy. Mercy seeks forgiveness so it does not meet the requirement of justice. But, in the case of God, grace meets both because mercy is given to the one forgiven and justice is required of the one forgiving. It is just that we be punished for our sin against God. But God's justice fell upon Himself (Jesus), and we receive mercy (forgiveness of sins). Additionally, we receive eternal life, fellowship with God, a resurrected body at the return of Christ, etc. (grace).

The lamp analogy [42]

Let's say I am over at your house or apartment with my wife. We are discussing theology and in my zeal I accidentally knock over one of your lamps. Now, this lamp is special to you. A dear friend gave it to you and it has great sentimental value, and besides you need a light in your room. After a moment or two you realize that the damage is done and decide to forgive. You say to me, 'That's all right, Matt. I forgive you for breaking the lamp, but give me ten dollars.'

Is asking for ten dollars after you've just forgiven me true forgiveness? I don't see how it could be. When God forgives our sins, He says He will remember them no more (Jeremiah 31:34). Forgive and forget are similar in spelling and similar in meaning. If you forgive me, can you demand payment? No, because a forgiven debt does not exist.

Let's say that, instead of asking me for ten dollars, you turn to my wife and say, 'Matt broke my lamp. You give me ten dollars for it.'

I ask you again. Is that true forgiveness? No. You are simply transferring the debt to someone who was not involved in the original offense, who is, in fact, innocent. But, we still have a problem: the lamp needs to be replaced. In true forgiveness, then, who pays for its replacement? (Think about this a bit before you go on to read the answer.) Who pays? You do! You're the only one left. Remember, if you've forgiven me the debt, how can you demand payment?

Now, whom was my offense against? You. Who forgave? You did. Who paid? You did.

When we sin, whom do we sin against? God. Who forgives? God. Who pays? God! Did you get that? God pays! How does He do that? Simple. Two thousand years ago on a hill outside the city of Jerusalem He bore our sins in His body and died on the cross (1 Peter 2:24). He took our punishment:

> *'Surely he took up our infirmities, and carried our sorrows ... But he was pierced for our transgressions, He was crushed for our iniquities and by his wounds we are healed.'*   (Isaiah 53:4, 5)

God is just. God is merciful. God is gracious. In the justice of God, He took our place. In the mercy of God we don't get punished. In the grace of God, He gives us eternal life.

Even though we are unworthy of salvation, even though we are unworthy of God's love, even though we are unworthy of mercy, God saved us. He did so not because of who we are, but because of who He is, not because of what we do, but because of what **He** did. God is love (1 John 4:16). God is holy (1 Peter 1:16). God is good (Psalm 34:8). We could never fathom the depths of His purity and kindness (Romans 11:33). We could never, on our own efforts, attain Him. There is only one thing left for us. We worship Him. We love Him and we serve Him. He is worthy. Blessed be the name of the Lord.

One additional note. One of the reasons cults are wrong is because they have a false Jesus. In this lamp analogy, the one who is offended is the one who pays. In the cults, Jesus is not the one offended. In the Trinitarian God, Jesus **is** the one offended; after all, He is God in flesh. In the cults, they are transferring the debt to someone else, someone (like my wife in the analogy) who is not involved in the issue. Because, to them, Jesus is a creation separate from God, He is not the one offended. He is simply a bystander who is required to pay for the sins of another. That isn't true forgiveness, is it?

Forty tough questions and objections with responses

'But sanctify Christ as lord in your hearts, always being ready to make a defense to everyone who asks you to give an account for the hope that is in you, yet with gentleness and reverence.'

(1 Peter 3:15 NASB)

Answering questions and objections about Christianity can play a large part in your Christian life. Some questions are easy; others can be quite difficult. If you aren't prepared, you might miss a vital witnessing opportunity. That is why it is good to think ahead, to study difficult issues, and try to formulate your response.

With the answers provided below to some difficult questions and objections to the Christian faith, you should be able to feel more confident about witnessing. If you have information (like that provided in this notebook), you can use it, combine it in different ways and, with just a little practice, feel confident enough to answer any objection that comes your way. You will find that the more you know, the more the Holy Spirit will use you and teach you new things from what you have already learned.

I've listed forty questions and objections and then given possible answers arranged as '(a)', '(b)', '(c)', etc. Remember, they are not 'the' right answers, only possible answers that can help you get started. Perhaps yours will be better.

When you need to answer a question from an unbeliever, take a moment to pray and let the Holy Spirit work in your heart and mind, trusting Him to give you the wisdom when you need it. You will be amazed at how well and how often He will do just that. Trust God and go!

1. **I am not a sinner!**
   (a) Maybe you don't realize that you are saying you are perfect. If you are, then you're the first perfect person I've ever met.
   (b) Are you saying you've never broken the Law of God? Have you ever lied, cheated, or stolen? If you have, then you are a sinner whether you think so or not. The laws of God have punishments (a law without a punishment is only a

slogan). As a sinner, you are separated from God (Isaiah 59:2). However, God loves you enough not to want you to be separated from Him. He sent Jesus (1 John 4:10) to pay for sins on the cross. So, the only way to have your sins forgiven is to put your trust in Jesus and the sacrifice He made.

(c) The Bible says that everyone has sinned (Romans 5:12). That means you, too.

2. **What is sin?**

(a) Sin is doing what is wrong as well as not doing what is right. It is breaking the Law of God (1 John 3:4). In other words, it is doing what is against God's will. If He says, 'Do not lie' and you lie, then you have sinned. If He says, 'Do not steal' and you steal then you have sinned. And, according to God, sin separates you from Him (Isaiah 59:2). *See* 'Sin' and 'Law and Gospel.'

(b) Sin is an offense to God's character. Because God cannot lie, it is wrong for you to lie. Because God cannot steal, it is wrong for you to steal. Right and wrong, then, is a manifestation of the character of God. God is holy; He cannot sin. Sin offends Him personally because it is His laws of right and wrong you are breaking. If you have offended Him then you must find a way to 'unoffend' Him. The problem is that you can't, but He can and has, by offering His Son, Jesus Christ, on the cross as a sacrifice for sin.

3. **I am too big a sinner.**

(a) Nobody is too big a sinner. The love of God and the sacrifice of Jesus is capable of cleansing the worst of all sin. Even Hitler could have been saved if he had turned to Christ. You have sinned the same as anyone else. It is just that your sins are yours. They aren't too big for God to wipe away. Sin has no power over God, only over you.

(b) Let me ask you something. Do you think murder and adultery are serious sins? Yes? Well, David, a man in the Bible whom God called a man after His own heart (Acts 13:22), was a murderer and an adulterer. He even tried to hide his sin from everyone. But God knew his sins and exposed them. David repented and threw himself on the mercy of the Lord. God forgave him and loved him. God loves you and He will forgive you if you put your trust in Jesus and ask Him to forgive you for your sins (Romans 10:9–10).

4. **What is salvation?**

   (a) Salvation is the forgiveness of sins. It is only accomplished through faith in Jesus as Savior. He died on the cross for sins. If you want salvation, you need to trust in what Jesus did on the cross. Only then can you have eternal life and be with God. *See* 'Salvation', p. 17.

   (b) Salvation is rescuing a person from damnation. Damnation is the judgement sinners receive. This judgement consists of God condemning the sinner to eternal punishment in hell. This is the destination of all who reject God's provision for the forgiveness of sins. If you want salvation, then you need to recognize that you are a sinner and ask Jesus to forgive you. He will.

5. **What do I do to be saved?**

   (a) Salvation is a free gift from God (Romans 6:23). Jesus bore sin in His body (1 Peter 2:24) and paid the penalty for breaking the Law of God, which is spiritual death (eternal separation from God). If you want salvation, you need to admit that you are a sinner and that you want Jesus to forgive you for your sins. You must acknowledge that there is nothing you can do to earn forgiveness. Pray and ask Him to forgive you. You need to trust in Jesus. Seek Him; He will save you.

   (b) Repentance is part of salvation. Once saved, you should stop doing those things that are displeasing to God. He will live in you and give you the ability and desire to resist sin (1 Corinthians 10:13). When you are saved, expect to change – for the better.

6. **Is baptism necessary for salvation?**

   (a) No. Faith in Jesus is sufficient for salvation. You don't have to do anything because Christ has done it all on the cross. However, baptism is very important and all believers should be baptized. If you refuse baptism after salvation, I would doubt your conversion.

(b) There are Christian denominations that believe baptism is necessary for salvation. The arguments used, on the surface, seem to be powerful, but upon examination, baptism is found to occur after conversion and is not in any way a cause or part of it. Take, for example, Acts 10:44–47:

> 'While Peter was still speaking, the Holy Spirit came on all those who heard the message ... they heard them speaking in tongues and praising God. Then Peter said, "Can anyone keep these people from being baptised with water? They have received the Holy Spirit just as we have.'

▶ This passage shows that baptism happens after salvation. How do we know they were saved? They were speaking in tongues – which is a gift from God (1 Corinthians 14) to believers and they were praising God. Non-believers do not praise God. Also, Peter said they had received the Holy Spirit. Only Christians receive the Holy Spirit, and on this occasion they had this experience before baptism.

▶ Another verse relevant to this issue is 1 Corinthians 1:17. Paul says, 'For Christ did not send me to baptise, but to preach the gospel ... ' The gospel is what saves and it is explained in 1 Corinthians 15:1–4. Baptism is not part of the gospel; it is something that the believer does after salvation.

(c) Baptism is only a symbol of that which saves and symbols don't save.

(d) Baptism is a covenant sign. It replaces Old Testament circumcision (Colossians 2:11–12).

7. **I am already good enough**

(a) How good do you have to be to get to heaven? God is holy and requires holiness. Holiness is purity. Even though you may think you are good enough, even one sin disqualifies you from being in the presence of God. You could never be good enough. That is why you need Jesus.

(b) The Bible says that there is none good enough. 'There is no-one who does good, not even one' (Romans 3:12). Goodness is measured by God's standard not yours.

   (c) To say that you are good enough means that Christ did not have to die. But He did die to save sinners. The Bible says if righteousness can come by good deeds then Christ didn't need to die (Galatians 3:21), but He did, so being good isn't enough.

8. **I am doing the best I can and I'm sincere.**

   (a) Even if you could do far better than you are doing now you still can't do well enough because you don't please God by being good (Galatians 2:21), but by accepting Jesus (John 1:12).

   (b) Sincerity is not the way to heaven. What if you are sincerely wrong? (Remember John 14:6?)

   (c) If you are relying on your sincerity, then are you saying that because you are sincere you are good enough on your own to be with God. Don't you see, to appeal to your sincerity is to appeal to pride, because you are appealing to something that is in **you** and not God for your reason to go to heaven. I am sorry, sincerity is not enough. You must have faith in Jesus and trust Him alone.

   (d) How long have you been doing your best? Has it worked so far? Has it given you eternal life?

9. **I am skeptical**

   (a) Are you honestly looking for answers? If you are, I would be very willing to talk more with you about Jesus, the Bible, or whatever else you have doubts about. Perhaps through discussion, your skepticism can be answered.

   (b) What are you skeptical about? Perhaps we can talk about some of the things that you feel keeps you from a saving knowledge of Jesus.

10. **I tried Christianity once**

   (a) The Bible says that once you are saved, you are never the same again, you are a new creature (2 Corinthians 5:17). If you have gone back to your old ways, then most probably you were never saved. If, however, you were saved, then God won't let you stay in rebellion for long. He will deal with you in whatever way is necessary to bring you back into fellowship with Him.

(b) Did you become a Christian by going to church or by asking Jesus to forgive you for your sins? The latter makes you a Christian, the former doesn't.

11. **I knew some Christians once and they wronged me.**

(a) Christians aren't perfect. They make mistakes like anyone else. I hope you can find it in your heart to forgive them. I think that is what they would do for you.

(b) Maybe they didn't know they wronged you. Was it something really bad or was it just a mistake? Have you gone to them and spoken to them about it? Maybe if you were to forgive them you would begin to understand the forgiveness God has for you. We all need to be forgiven, don't you agree?

12. **I'll take my chances.**

(a) With what, eternity? Eternity is a long time to be wrong. Why would you want to take a gamble on something as important as your eternal destiny. It takes only a moment to trust Christ for your salvation. There will be an eternity of pain and regret if you don't.

(b) You don't take chances with guns, do you? You don't take chances and run red lights do you? Why would you take a chance on something that is far more important than these? Don't take a chance on something eternal. It isn't worth it.

(c) Jesus said He was the only way to God. He forgave sins, walked on water, calmed a storm with a command, raised people from the dead, and rose from the dead Himself. No one else in history has done that. If He can do all that, don't you think you should listen to Him?

13. **I am not that bad a person.**

(a) Whether or not you feel you are bad or good is not the real issue. The Bible says that all have sinned (Romans 3:23). If all have sinned, then all will suffer the judgement of God. God does not require people to be pretty good; He requires them not to sin at all. But He knows that you cannot be sinless. That is why He gave His only begotten Son that whosoever would believe in Him would not perish but have everlasting life (John 3:16).

(b) The Bible says that our good works are filthy rags before God (Isaiah 64:6). It isn't saying that we might not try to be good, it is saying that whatever good we do, it is not good enough. It also says that there is no one who does good (Romans 3:12). The standard God seeks is perfection. We cannot please God on our own. That is why Jesus died on behalf of sinners. If you want to be good enough, then you must let God see you through the righteousness of Jesus Christ. That is the only goodness that counts to God.

(c) Maybe you are a great person who does a lot of really good works and is honest and trustworthy. But the Bible says that if righteousness could come by the Law, by what we do because we are good, then Jesus died needlessly (Galatians 2:21). But Jesus still went to the cross to die for sins. Being good isn't good enough.

14. **I am too old (or too young).**

(a) You are never too old to trust in Jesus as your Savior. As long as you are alive you can call on Him to forgive you for your sins. He is as close as the call of your heart.

(b) (Granted there may be some who are too young to understand the gospel message, but here we will address those who simply use that as an excuse.) Youth is a blessing from God. Don't use it as an excuse to stay away from Him. If you can understand what sin is and your need for deliverance from it, then you are not too young to receive Jesus as your Savior. He saves everyone, young and old.

15. **I can't believe in a God who would send people to hell.**

(a) Hell was originally created for Satan and his angels. In the future it will contain those who join Satan in rejecting God. If you reject God's provision for the forgiveness of your sins then you will join the devil who rejected God from the beginning. Is that what you want?

(b) Could you believe in a God who would become a human, suffer at the hands of humans, and be killed by them, all so that His death could be the payment for their sins? That is extremely loving. God is saving people who deserve to go to hell – and that is all of us. Remember that the same God that sends people to hell also died for them. If they reject what God has provided, then what is God left to do? He has to judge them.

(c) Whether you believe in something or not does not change the fact of its existence. Jesus spoke often about hell (Matthew 25:41–46; Mark 9:47–48; Luke 16:19–31) and warned us so we would not go there. Would you say Jesus didn't know what He was talking about?

(d) Are you implying that it is unjust for God to send people to hell? If so, then you are accusing Him of injustice. Sin is wrong and it must be punished. What would you have God do to those who oppose Him and do evil? Do you want Him to ignore wrongdoing? Do you want Him to turn His head and not be holy and righteous?

16. **I will worry about it in the next life.**

(a) That you may very well do, forever. Eternity is a long time to be wrong, especially about Jesus.

(b) Do you think that reincarnation is the truth? That is not what the Bible teaches. If reincarnation were true, why is it you could not attain your 'enlightenment' at your first incarnation since you had perfect karma?

(c) God has warned us in the Bible that it is appointed for human beings to die once, then judgement (Hebrews 9:27). After death you will be judged. Do you want to face eternity without the sacrifice of Jesus Christ accounted to you? God hates sin and you have sinned. God will punish sinners if they reject Jesus. However, He loves you. That is why He sent His Son to die for sins. If you want eternal life, then you need to worry about it now. Eternity is a long time to be wrong, especially about Jesus.

(d) There is no next life. The Bible says after death you face God for judgement (Hebrews 9:27).

17. **I don't want to give up what I like doing.**

(a) Are you saying that, if you become a Christian, you must stop doing what you're doing now. That means you know it is wrong. Let me ask you something. If you were to become a Christian and God were to live in your heart and you looked back upon your life now, would you say to yourself, 'I did a lot of things I wish I hadn't done?' Probably so.

   (b) The Bible speaks about just such a thing. In Romans 6:21 it says,

> '... *what benefit were you then deriving from the things of which you are now ashamed? For the outcome of those things is death.'* (NASB)

What you are saying is that God will require you to give up certain things that you like to do. Since God only wants what is good and right, and you say you don't want to give up what your are doing, then you are saying you want what is wrong.

   (c) Will you let your pleasures get in the way of salvation? Is your life of sin worth an eternity of pain? Jesus said,

> *'What good is it for a man if he gains the whole world, yet forfeit his soul?'* (Mark 8:36)

18. **Christianity is boring.**

   (a) Then you haven't experienced it. No one who is a Christian will ever say that it is boring.

   (b) How do you know? Have you tried it? There are millions of people who have a lot of fun being Christians. We just do it with a lot less sin, and, therefore, a lot less problems. Maybe it's only your problems that keep you from getting bored.

   (c) What do you think we do all day, sit around fireplaces and read Bibles? We ski, swim, play sports, read, have friends and problems like anybody else. Christianity is not boring. It is an adventure.

19. **I am an atheist. I don't believe in God.**

   (a) Some atheists say they **know** there is no God. But they cannot know that for sure, because they would have to know all things in order to know if there is or isn't a God. If they knew all things then they would be God.

   (b) Other atheists say they simply lack belief in God – they don't **not** believe. They neither believe nor not believe in God.

       ▶ Then ask if the person is open to examining the evidence.

(c) What do you believe in, evolution? If so, have you ever studied it or do you believe what they tell you on television? Evolution has a lot of problems with it. It seems to me that it takes a lot of faith to believe that you developed out of ocean slime, simply by chance. At least as a Christian I have the evidence of the resurrection of Christ from eyewitnesses as recorded by them in the Gospels. Evolution or not, Jesus rose from the dead, claimed to be God, and forgave sins. I'll put my faith in Him instead of evolution.

(d) If there is no God, then in the end I lose nothing. But if there is a God like I say, in the end you lose everything.

(e) Why don't you believe in God? Is their any intellectual reason for you to reject His existence? Or, do you simply desire not to believe in Him?

(f) The Bible doesn't attempt to prove that God exists. It simply speaks as though He does. Maybe I can't prove to you that there is a God, but I can introduce Him to you through His Son Jesus Christ and you can judge for yourself if the words of Christ in the Bible convince you of His existence.

20. **I am trying to be a Christian.**

(a) You become a Christian by simply putting your trust in Jesus and His sacrifice for you on the cross. There is no trying involved. If you trust Jesus, if you ask Him to forgive you for your sins and be your Savior, then you are a Christian. It is living like a Christian **after** you've become one that is difficult.

(b) If you believe that in order to become a Christian you must be good, then you misunderstand or don't have a good understanding of salvation. Becoming a Christian is the gift of God (Romans 6:23), not the result of human effort (Ephesians 2:8–9). There is nothing you can do to earn salvation or keep salvation. It is simply something God freely gives you. If you want it, confess your sins, repent, turn to God, and trust Jesus as your only Savior. Then, and only then, will you become a Christian.

21. **I am already religious.**

   (a) Who said God wants you to be religious? He wants a relationship with you. Religion is a human attempt to reach God. Christianity is God reaching men and women. In 1 Corinthians 1:9 it says that God wants you to have fellowship with Jesus. He is talking about a relationship, someone you can talk to. He doesn't want to weigh you down with a bunch of dos and don'ts. He wants to extend a loving hand to you and help you live a good clean life. But that cannot be done until the real problem in you is done away with, and that is sin. Sin separates you from God (Isaiah 59:2). If you want salvation instead of 'religion,' then go to Jesus. Seek Him. He will never let you down.

   (b) I see. Where do you attend church?

22. **I don't need God.**

   (a) If you say you don't need Him, then you believe He exists. If you do, why would you say you don't need Him? Isn't He the One who determines your destiny? Doesn't He have the authority and power to do as He pleases and to send you to heaven or hell? It is foolish to say you don't need the One who is your Creator, who loves you and has provided the way for forgiveness of sin. You need God because only He can cleanse you from your sins.

   (b) What do you need? Are you really doing that well without God? Are you happy with the way things are in your life? If you aren't, then you need Jesus. And even if you are happy, you still need Him, because you can't take what makes you happy with you when you die.

23. **I have things I need to do before I become a Christian.**

   (a) Like what? Why do you need to do these things before you come to God? Are they bad things or good? If they are bad, then you shouldn't do them. If they are good, why can't you become a Christian and then do them?

   (b) Nothing you can do could be more important than your relationship with God. To put Him off is unwise. What if you die before you become a Christian? Then you would be eternally without hope.

(c) Your statement implies you believe following God will mean you won't be able to do the things you want to do. If that is true, then that means the things you intend to do would displease God. Are you saying you prefer to do something God wouldn't want you to do? If that is so, you are willfully sinning against God and putting yourself in a dangerous situation. That is all the more reason why you need His forgiveness.

24. **I prefer to remain open-minded.**

(a) Good, for a minute there I thought you were going to reject Christianity completely.

(b) Open-mindedness means looking at everything honestly. Are you willing to do that with Christianity? Do you want to see what Jesus has said and learn about what He can offer?

(c) If you say you are going to remain open-minded and not accept Christianity, then in reality you are being very closed-minded. Maybe Christianity is true. Your open-mindedness could keep you from discovering it.

25. **I already believe in God.**

(a) Are you living your life as if that were true? Does your belief in God affect the way you live or do you still do entirely as you please?

(b) If you say you believe in God, then how do you know what He wants for you? Are you in contact with Him? Do you just trust that whatever you feel is right?

(c) The Bible says the devil believes in God (James 2:19) and he is lost. If all you do is simply believe that God exists, then you are no better off than he is. It is not intellectual acknowledgment of God's existence that God wants, but your accepting the sacrifice Jesus made on behalf of sinners that pleases God. Simply believing is not enough. You must choose to follow Him.

(d) It is not **that** you believe; it is **whom** you put your faith in. Who is this God you believe in? Is He the Christian one? Is he Allah? Is he from another planet? Is he whatever you feel is right? Is he loving? Believing in God is fine unless your god is false. The important thing is that you must believe in the true God, not a false one, and the true one is found in the Bible.

26. I'll choose God later.

(a) If you won't choose Him now, what makes you think you'll choose Him later? The longer you go without God, the harder it will be for you to come to Him. The longer you sin, the harder your heart will become and the further from God you will be (Hebrews 3:13). To wait is dangerous. God calls you to repent from sin now, not later. Which will you choose?

(b) If you say you will choose Him later, do you admit then that you need Him now? If so, then why do you wait? You might die soon and then it would be too late.

27. There are too many hypocrites in the church.

(a) Church is a good place for hypocrites, as well as liars and thieves. It is there where they will be exposed to the Word of God and learn that hypocrisy is wrong. For you to judge those in the church is to condemn yourself, because we are all hypocrites in one form or another. Your recognition and condemnation of it tells me you know it is wrong. Is it hypocrisy to point a finger at the church full of sinners when you yourself are one as well?

(b) It has been said that you must be smaller than the thing you hide behind. Are you hiding behind the hypocrisy of others to keep you out of church? You must realize that you are responsible for yourself and God won't ask others about you on Judgement Day. He will come to you and ask you to give an account for your life. The hypocrites in the church will also stand before God, with or without you there.

(c) People don't counterfeit pennies. Why do you think there are hypocrites? Because Christianity is valuable.

28. Why are we here? Or, why did God make us?

(a) God made us so we could glorify Him and have fellowship with Him (1 John 1:1–3). He made Adam and Eve and put them in the garden and then He walked in fellowship with them. He gave them the greatest thing they could have, His love and presence. After they sinned, God said, '*Adam, where are you?*' God looked for Adam. In Exodus 25:8 we read that God said to Moses while Israel was in the wilderness, *'Then have them make a sanctuary for Me, and I may dwell among them.'* In the New Testament in John 1:14 it says, *'And the Word became flesh and dwelt* [tabernacled] *among us...'* (NASB) [43] God seeks our presence. He wants to have fellowship with us. He made us so that He could give us His love and we could enjoy His presence. But human beings sinned and separated themselves from God. That is why Christ died for sins, so that our fellowship with God would be restored.

29. **What about those who have never heard the gospel?**

    (a) That is a good question. The Bible says that God is just. We know that whatever He does is right. When it comes to those who have never heard the gospel, He will do what is right, whatever that is. But as for you, you have heard the gospel and He will judge you according to how you respond. He is calling you to repentance, to turn from sin and come to Him.

    (b) In Romans 2:12–16 it speaks about those who have never heard the Law of God and explains they will be judged according to the law that is written in their hearts. The law written in their hearts is the knowledge of right and wrong. Perhaps God's judgement of those without a proper knowledge of Him is included there where it says that they will be judged according to their own consciences that *'*[bear] *witness, and their thoughts now accusing, now even defending them.'* All I know is that God will do what is right and the only way to have your sins forgiven is through Jesus.

30. **Jesus is only one of many great men of history**.
    (*See also* question 32.)

    (a) Granted, Jesus was a great man of history. That is a fact. But, He is different from all the other great men of history. How many great men of history rose from the dead, calmed a sea, walked on water, raised others from the dead, healed sickness, and forgave sins? There aren't any others that I know of. Do you know of any? These things make Him more than great. They make Him special and unique.

(b) You are right, Jesus was a great man. But let me ask you. If He were great, would He lie? Of course not. If He were great, would He be insane? No. You see, Jesus claimed to be God (John 8:58 with Exodus 3:14; John 5:18; 10:30–33). If He were lying, we shouldn't listen to Him and we couldn't call Him great. If He were insane, then we shouldn't listen to Him and again we couldn't call Him great. If He is great, then He must be telling the truth. And He was great, right?

31. **Why is there evil and suffering in the world?**

(a) The question implies that if a good God exists, then evil shouldn't, because God, being all powerful, should stop it.

(b) We need to ask and answer two questions. First, what is evil? It is that which is against God. It is anything morally bad or wrong. It is injurious, depraved, wicked. Some acceptable examples might be murder, rape, stealing, lying, and cheating. Second, if we want God to stop evil, do we want Him to stop all evil or just some of it? In other words, if just some of it then why? If He were to stop only part of the evil, then we would still be asking the question, 'Why is there evil in the world?'

(c) Let's suppose that someone was about to commit murder. God would have to stop him, maybe whisper in his ear, or, if that didn't work, do something a little more drastic like have something fall on him, or stop his heart, or make his hands suddenly fall off. Anyway, God would have to do something.

(d) What if somebody wanted to steal? God would have to stop her too, right? Undoubtedly, God's imagination would permit a more practical method than I have suggested, but the end results would be the same.

(e) What about lying? If someone were to tell a lie, then to be consistent wouldn't you want God right there to stop that person from lying? After all, He couldn't let any evil occur, could He?

(f) Let's take it a step further. Suppose someone thought something evil. Then, of course, God would have to step in and prevent her from thinking anything bad at all, right? The end result would be that God could not allow anyone to think freely. Since everyone thinks and no one thinks only pure thoughts, God would be pretty busy and we wouldn't be able to think. Anyway, at what point do we stop, at the murder level, stealing level, lying level, or thinking level? As your question implies, if you want God to stop evil, you would have to be consistent and want Him to do it everywhere all the time, not just pick and choose. It wouldn't work.

(g) Evil is in this world partly because we give it its place but ultimately because God, in His sovereignty, permits it (*see* (b)) and keeps it under His control.

(h) Then you might say, 'Couldn't He just make us perfect and that way we wouldn't sin?' He already did that. He made a perfect angel, Satan, but he sinned. He made a perfect man, Adam, but he sinned. He made a perfect woman, Eve, but she sinned. God knows what He is doing. He made us the way we are for a purpose. We don't fully understand that purpose, but He does.

(i) God is sovereign; He has the right to do as He wishes. He has the right to permit evil in order to accomplish His ultimate will. How can He do that? Simple, look at the cross. It was by evil means that men conspired to crucify Jesus. Yet God in His infinite wisdom used this evil for good. It was on the cross that Jesus bore our sins in His body (1 Peter 2:24) and it is because of the cross that we can have forgiveness of sins.

(j) Consider the biblical example of Joseph in the Old Testament. He was sold into slavery by his brothers. Though they meant it for evil, God meant it for good (Genesis 50:20). God is so great that nothing happens without His permission, and in that permission His ultimate plan unfolds. In His plan He is able to use for good what human beings intend for evil. God is in control.

32. **What makes Jesus so special?**

(a) Who He said He was. He said He was God. In John 8:58, Jesus said, *'I tell you the truth ... before Abraham was born, I AM.'* When He said, *'I AM,'* He was quoting from Exodus 3:14 in the Old Testament. That is where Moses asked God

His name. God answered and said, *'I AM.'* When Jesus said *'I AM,'* He was claiming the name of God for Himself and thereby claiming to be God. Other great men of history point to a philosophy and teach good ideas. Only Jesus pointed to Himself, claimed to be God, and spoke with authority that matched His claim.

(b) What He did. Jesus forgave sins (Luke 5:20), He rose from the dead (Luke 24), raised others from the dead (John 11:43–44), and He walked on water (John 6:19). No one on earth has ever done the things Jesus did. There is no way around it. Jesus is special; about that there can be no doubt.

33. **Why did Jesus have to die in order for me to go to heaven?**

(a) Because the wages of sin is death (Romans 6:23). Though Jesus never sinned (1 Peter 2:22), He bore our sins in His body on the cross (1 Peter 2:24) and died. He died in our place. Instead of God making us pay for our sins, He did it Himself by becoming one of us.

(b) Two things happen when we sin: one to God and one to ourselves. When we sin, God is offended. Why? Because it is His Law that we are breaking. Also, when we sin we are killed. We don't die right there on the spot, we will face a death that is far more severe. Sin kills us (Romans 8:13) by causing eternal separation from God (Isaiah 59:2). God hates sin (Habakkuk 1:13) and sin must be punished. Since we are unable to please God because we are all sinners, He made an offering that is pleasing to Him. That offering was the sacrifice of Jesus on the cross. There was no other way. If there were, God would have done it.

34. **What makes you think the Bible is the Word of God?**

(a) Prophecy. The Old Testament was written before Jesus was ever born. The New Testament was written by the men who knew Jesus, who walked with Him, ate with Him, and learned from Him. In the Old Testament there are prophecies concerning His birthplace (Micah 5:1–2), that He would be born of a virgin (Isaiah 7:14), that He would be rejected by His own people (Isaiah 53:3), that He would be betrayed by a close friend (Psalm 41:9), that He would die by having His hands and feet pierced (Psalms

22:16–18), and that He would rise from the dead (Psalms 16:10, 49:15). In the New Testament all these prophecies, and many more, are fulfilled by Jesus. Now, this is the question you must answer: 'If the Bible is not inspired from God, then why does it have so many fulfilled prophecies?' How is that possible if the Bible were not from God?

(b) Only God knows the future, has power over it, and can look into it to tell us exactly what will happen. In the Bible we have the fingerprints of God: fulfilled prophecy!

(c) Wisdom. The Bible is full of the greatest truths about human beings and God, sin, and salvation. The Sermon on the Mount (Matthew 5) is beautiful in its wisdom, humility, and love. The Psalms are incredible poetry of great depth and beauty. The New Testament epistles are great descriptions of love, forgiveness, long-suffering, kindness, etc. Even if you don't want to become a Christian, studying the truth God has revealed in the Bible will greatly help you in your life. (The aim is not merely to get the person to use the Bible as a guide to good living, but to encourage him to read it. This way, he will at least be reading the Word of God and be that much closer to conversion because God's Word will accomplish what He wants it to (Isaiah 55:11).)

35. **The New Testament was written to make it look as if Jesus fulfilled prophecy.**

(a) Then what you are saying is that the New Testament writers lied about Jesus. He really didn't rise from the dead and all those miracles about Him are really false, right?

(b) I could see your point, but there is just one problem. How do you account for the writers of the New Testament teaching about truth, love, honesty, giving, etc. all based on lies? Why would they suffer hardships like beatings, starvation, shipwreck, imprisonments, and finally execution for nothing but lies? What you are saying doesn't make any sense and raises more questions than it answers.

(c) The only logical explanation is that the fulfilled prophecies really did happen. Jesus actually rose from the dead; He performed miracles and He forgave sins. He forgave sins then and He can still do it now. My sins are forgiven, are yours?

36. **The Bible is full of contradictions.**

   (a) Really. Do you know of any? Could you quote me one or two?

   (b) (Just in case someone actually does quote what he thinks is a contradiction, it is up to you to give a competent answer (1 Peter 3:15). If you can't, don't worry. Simply tell him that you will research it and get back to him, and make sure you do.)

   (c) There **are** areas of Scripture that are difficult to understand. This does not mean the Bible is untrustworthy. A very good book to have is the *Encyclopedia of Bible Difficulties* by Gleason Archer (Grand Rapids, Michigan: Zondervan Publishing House).

37. **How do I know which religion is right?**

   (a) This is a difficult question to answer because it involves discussing some principles that the person you are witnessing to may or may not agree with. For example, does he or she agree with you that truth is knowable, that God would attempt to communicate with His people, or that only one religion may be right? Usually, I start by acknowledging the difficulty of coming to an easy answer. However, I tell the person that I do have an answer; I am sure it is the right one, because it is an answer based on evidence. What kind of evidence? Prophecy and its fulfillment (*see* question 34), Jesus and His miracles (*see* question 32), the resurrection of Christ, etc. Then I ask that person if he or she knows of these things happening in other religions. The answer is invariably, 'No.' Then I point out that they have only happened in Christianity. If any religion were true, Christianity fits the bill.

   ▶ Note: Be careful. Just because someone does not know if there have been any similar occurrences in other religions doesn't mean that there haven't been. You should point that out. However, no other religion in the world has ever made the claims that Christianity has, and lived up to them.

38. Religion is whatever you feel is right.

(a) How do you know what you feel is right? Haven't your feelings ever turned out to be wrong? Are you saying that what you feel determines truth? If so, then you are putting yourself in the place of God and looking to yourself for what you 'feel' is right.

(b) If religion is whatever you feel is right then that could lead to chaos. What if some people had a religion where they felt stealing was acceptable? And what about lying and cheating? Would you trust someone who believed in a religion that felt it was all right to steal, lie, and cheat?

(c) Hitler felt killing Jews was right. He was wrong. The Bible says that the heart is deceitful and untrustworthy (Jeremiah 17:9). If you could come to know truth by what you felt, then the Bible, which is the revelation of God, didn't need to be written. But it has been written and it has revealed that only God is the Source of truth, not your feelings.

(d) I've never known truth to contradict itself. What if someone felt that something was right and another person felt it was wrong. Would they both be right? If your statement is true and feelings determine truth, then how would it be possible to have a contradiction like that?

39. All religions are different paths to the same place.

(a) If all religions are different paths to the same place then why do the paths contradict each other? Does truth contradict itself? Let's review the teachings of just three religions:

(b) Buddhism is pantheistic and says there is no personal God and everyone can reach Godlikeness on his or her own. Islam says that Jesus was just a prophet and not the only way to God. Christianity says that there is a personal God and that the only way to Him is through Jesus (John 14:6). If these three religions are, as you say, different paths to the same place, then why do they contradict each other? Does truth contradict itself?

40. What about dinosaurs and evolution?

(a) Again, you could read a couple of books: *Evolution The Fossils Say No!* by Duane T. Gish (San Diego: Creation Life

Publishers), and *Man's Origin, Man's Destiny* by A.E. Wilder-Smith (Minneapolis, Minn.: Bethany House Publishers). Both books will help you greatly.

(b) Even if evolution were true (it isn't – but just for the sake of argument), does that mean there is no God? How do you know God didn't use it to get us here? (I am not teaching that evolution is true, nor that God used it, which is called theistic evolution, I am simply reasoning with the person asking the question.) If you believe in evolution does that mean you aren't a sinner? God won't accept the excuse that you believed in evolution and not Him.

(c) Have you examined evolution to see if it is true? Evolution is not all that you are led to believe. There are all kinds of problems in the fossil record. New theories are being raised all the time to account for why there aren't any un-disputed transitional forms found between any species of any kind, anywhere, anytime in all the fossil record. But, you wouldn't know these things because you haven't studied. You need to know the facts about evolution and you need to know the facts about Jesus.

Berkhof, L., *Systematic Theology* (Grand Rapids, Michigan: Wm B. Eerdmans Publishing Co., 1988).

Baker's Dictionary of Theology, edited by Everett F. Harrison, Geoffrey W. Bromiley, Carl F.H. Henry (Grand Rapids, Michigan: Baker Book House, 1960).

Bromiley, G.W. (ed.), *The International Standard Bible Encyclopedia*, Vol. 1 (Grand Rapids, Michigan: Eerdmans Publishing Co. 1979).

Guralnik, David B. (ed.), *Webster's New World Dictionary of the American Language*, second edn (New York: Simon and Schuster, 1984).

Harrison, Everett F. (ed.), *Baker's Dictionary of Theology* (Grand Rapids, Michigan: Baker Book House), 1960.

Milne, Bruce, *Know the Truth* (Downers Grove, Illinois: InterVarsity Press, 1982).

The Open Bible, 'Encyclopedic Index' (Lockman Foundation, La Habra, California: Thomas Nelson Publishers, 1979).

The Open Bible (Nashville: Thomas Nelson Publishers, 1979).

Thomas, Robert L. (ed.), *New American Standard Exhaustive Concordance of the Bible* (Nashville: Holman Bible Publishers, 1981).

Unger, Merrill F., *Unger's Bible Dictionary* (Chicago: Moody Press, 1966).

Notes

1. Three gods in the godhead would make a Triad. A Trinity is one God in three persons. A Triad and a Trinity are not the same thing.

2. The *New International Dictionary of the Christian Church*, ed. J.D. Douglas (Paternoster Press, 1978), p. 706.

3. Additionally, in ancient covenants, each party received a copy of the covenant document. When Moses returned from Mount Horeb he carried two tablets. Some scholars think these were the two copies of the covenant between God and the human race known as the Ten Commandments. Both copies were stored in the ark of the covenant (Deuteronomy 10:4) which was, of course, kept by Israel. The ark was housed in the tabernacle where God dwelt among His people (Exodus 25:8). Hence, both parties had copies of the covenant documents.

4. John 6:39: *And this is the will of him who sent me, that I shall lose none of all that he has given me, but raise them up at the last day.'*

5. Elect: the Bible refers to the 'elect' of God many times (Matthew 24:22, 24, 31; Romans 11:7; 1 Timothy 5:21; Titus 1:1; 1 Peter 1:1). Some believe it is a reference to those who are predestined to salvation (Romans 8:29–30; Ephesians 1:5–11) by God. They would be the chosen ones (Romans 8:33; 11:5; Ephesians 1:11).

6. *The Pearl of Great Price*, Section 2, verses 1–25.

7. This murderous act by the mob provided martyr status for Joseph Smith and helped fuel Mormonism's growth. However, Joseph didn't go like a lamb to the slaughter. Rather, with a gun that had been smuggled into him, he fired back into the crowd (*History of the Church (pub)* Vol. 6, p. 618). Typically, biblical martyrs go peaceably to their deaths praying for the salvation of their persecutors, not so with Joseph Smith.

8. A document written in Joseph Smith's own handwriting seems to support this claim. It was dated 17 January 1844.

9. 'Exalted' is a term used by the Mormons to signify a person becoming a god.

10. In actuality, 'Elohim' is the Hebrew word for God. It is not the name of God the Father as Mormons incorrectly use it. In addition, the word 'Jehovah' is used by them as the name for Jesus as He appeared in the Old Testament. In truth, the name of God is derived from the

four Hebrew letters YHWH from which the name 'Jehovah' is derived. Jehovah, then, is the name of Elohim. See 1 Kings 8:60 which says that Jehovah is Elohim.

11. The Mormon temple is a special place where many secret and occultic rituals take place.

12. What Paul said was, *'For even if there are so-called gods, whether in heaven or on earth as indeed there are many "gods" and many "lords" . . .'* (1 Corinthians 8:5). Joseph Smith took this verse out of context. It does not say that there are many gods, it says that there are 'so-called' gods. They are not gods by nature (Galatians 4:8), they are false gods.

13. Improvement Era, January 1968, p. 25; as cited in 'By His Own Hand Upon Papyrus' by Charles M. Larson (Grand Rapids, MI: Institute for Religious Research, 49505–4604, 1992).

14. Wesley P. Walters, *Joseph Smith Among the Egyptians*, 1973 (reprinted by Utah Lighthouse Ministry, Box 1884, Salt Lake City, Utah 84110).

15. Dr Klaus Baer, 'The Breathing Permit of Hor. A Translation of the Apparent Source of the Book of Abraham,' pp. 119–120 as cited in *Joseph Smith Among the Egyptians* by Wesley Walters.

16. Larson, 'By His Own Hand upon Papyrus', p. 62.

17. *ibid.*, p. 102.

18. *ibid.*, p. 104.

19. Walters, *Joseph Smith Among the Egyptians*, p. 29.

20. Gerald and Sandra Tanner, *Mormonism – Shadow or Reality?* (Utah Lighthouse Ministry, PO Box Salt Lake City, Utah 84110, 1982, p. 302). Richard A. Parker was from the Department of Egyptology at Brown University.

21. *Bible Knowledge Commentary* on 1 Corinthians 15:29 (Dallas Seminary Faculty).

22. Walter Martin, *Kingdom of the Cults* (Bethany House, 1982), p. 34.

23. Bob Larson, *Larson's Book of Cults* (Tyndale House Pub., 1982), p. 147.

24. 'LORD' is equivalent to YHWH, or Yahweh, or Jehovah, which is the name of God. In today's Bibles it is translated as 'LORD' because the true spelling and pronunciation of the name of God has been lost. In the JW Bible it is translated as Jehovah. So, when reading the Bible with a JW and you come across 'LORD,' you can say 'Jehovah.' It will make more sense for the JW.

25. The Pharisees denied the resurrection of the wicked, as is mentioned by Josephus in *Ant. XVIII.* 1, 3; *Wars* II. 8.14. Cited in Berkhoff's *Systematic Theology* (Wm B Eerdmans, 1988), p. 723.

26. Add details.

27. F.E. Meyer, *The Religious Bodies of America* (Saint Louis, Missouri: Concordia Publishing House, 1961), p. 532.

28. The Books used here are published by the Christadelphian Organization: Harry Tennant, *The Christadelphians: What They Believe and Preach* (The Christadelphian, 404 Shaftmoor Lane, Birmingham B28 8SZ, England, 1986); *Christadelphian Answers*, compiled by Frank G. Jannaway (a reproduction of an original edition by The Herald Press, 4011 Bolivia, Houston, Texas, 77092, 1920).

29. The Foundation for Inner Peace, *A Course in Miracles* (Huntington Station, NY), Lesson 228, p. 461.

30. Harmonization is simply a word given to describe the attempt or success of achieving 'oneness' with any of the universal principles.

31. *Omni Magazine*, 'How to Have a Mystical Experience', December 1988, pp. 137–145.

32. The Foundation for Inner Peace, *Miracles*, Lesson 303, p. 441.

33. *ibid.*, p. 463.

34. *ibid.*, Lesson 206, p. 380.

35. *Larson's Book of Cults*, p. 224.

36. *Larson's Book of Cults*.

37. *ibid.*, p. 328.

38. WOW stands for 'The Word over the World.'

39. *'All things have been committed to me by my Father. No-one knows the Son except the Father, and no-one knows the Father except the Son and those to whom the Son chooses to reveal him'* (Matthew 11:27).

40. In the JW Bible they have translated Hebrews 1:8 as 'God is your throne forever.' This cannot be correct because Hebrews 1:8 is a quote from Psalms 45:6 that says, *'Thy throne, O God, is forever and ever,'* which is the best translation from the Hebrew. Unfortunately, even in Psalm 45:6, the New World Translation has mistranslated it to agree with their rendering in Hebrews 1:8. The writer of Hebrews attributes the verse as an address to Jesus. In it, God the Father is calling Jesus

God. Since the JWs deny Jesus is God, they have changed the Bible to suit their own theological needs.

41. You might become confused by the apparent Christian references found in the Book of Mormon, i.e., Jesus being prayed to and called God, cf. 3 Nephi 19:18. This is because the strange theology of Mormonism didn't really start developing until after the *Book of Mormon* was written. With Christian words in print from earlier times, the Mormons were left with changing the meaning of those words to suit their theological needs (*see also* p. 000).

42. This analogy is adapted from a small booklet called *Forgiveness* (Downers Grove: Illinois InterVarsity Press).

43. John 1:1 says, *'In the beginning was the Word, and the Word was with God, and the Word was God.'* Verse 14 says, *'The Word became flesh…'* The Word is Jesus.

Index

If you have enjoyed this book and would like to help us to send a copy of it and many other titles to needy pastors in the **Third World**, please write for further information or send your gift to:

Sovereign World Trust
PO Box 777, Tonbridge
Kent TN11 0ZS
United Kingdom

or to the **'Sovereign World'** distributor in your country.

Visit our website at **www.sovereign-world.org**
for a full range of Sovereign World books.